Named 'The Skincare Innovator' by Net-a-Porter magazine, Carla Oates is the founder and 'chef' behind Australian beauty and wellness brand The Beauty Chef. A former newspaper beauty columnist, naturalist, gut-health advocate and author of the best selling book *Feeding Your Skin*, Carla is also the editor of *WellBeing Beauty Book*, is the natural beauty columnist for *Wellbeing Magazine*, is a Goodwill Ambassador for Australian Organic, and has been researching, writing and teaching about organic beauty and health for the past 15 years.

THEBEAUTYCHEF.COM

For my beautiful babies, Jeet and Otis, and my husband, Davor.

*And for my mum – who, through her own challenging health journey
over the last two years, has learned the power of food as medicine,
even though, no matter how many ways we have tried
to camouflage it, she still hates kale.*

The Beauty Chef

CARLA OATES

Hardie Grant

BOOKS

If you are using this recipe book in the United States, note that Australian tablespoons, used here, are 20 ml, not 15 ml, which is the US standard. This is especially important to note in the baking recipes.

Introduction

It's hard to believe it has been more than 12 years since I wrote my first book, *Feeding Your Skin*. Since then, in addition to raising two gorgeous children who are now teenagers, I have continued my research into finding organic solutions to creating radiant skin and good gut health. This led me to founding The Beauty Chef, a beauty and wellness company that makes skincare products and Certified Organic inner beauty powders and elixirs, based on bio-fermented nutrition, prebiotics and probiotics.

Looking after my own skin and health issues is where my inner beauty journey began and I have seen that what I put into my mouth has a profound effect on my health. It is serendipitous, then, that cooking is one of my favourite things to do. I love combining the joy of cooking with the science of nutrition. This, together with being asked by my customers what they should eat for radiant skin and robust health, is the inspiration for this cookbook.

I believe that beauty is an inside-out process. Glowing skin is basically a reflection of healthy cells and the solution to a clearer, more radiant complexion and general wellbeing occurs when you balance your gut and feed your body nutrient-dense food.

I know it doesn't sound very glamorous, but the gut is where the seeds for health and beauty are planted. Research in the fields of microbiology and the human microbiome has shown the connection between the state of our gut bacteria and pretty much every aspect of our health, including our skin. We are made up of cells and bacteria, so for them to be strong and healthy we need to feed them properly with nutrients: amino acids, vitamins, minerals, essential fatty acids, antioxidants and prebiotics and probiotics – all of which can be obtained from unprocessed and lacto-fermented foods.

What we eat can have a medicinal effect on our bodies. Not only because food literally feeds our cells, but also because when it comes to microbes, the species and numbers found in our gut are influenced by what we eat. In addition, our immune system is also influenced by the microbes contained in our food. So the food we eat provides the ecosystem that interacts with our immune system to maintain our health and skin and overall wellbeing!

There is not a one-size-fits-all diet solution for everyone, but irrespective of whether you eat a vegan, paleo, vegetarian, pescetarian or any other kind of diet, I have found that unprocessed, organic, free-range, low GI and low HI (human intervention), sustainable foods are best for our bodies, the food chain, the animals and the environment. It makes sense to nurture, support and respect not only the soil, water and air, but also the people who grow, raise and produce our food and care for the environment in which it is harvested.

The following pages contain more than 150 gluten-free, mostly dairy-free, skin- and gut-loving recipes that are nutritious, delicious, and will feed your cells and your gut microbes. I have also shared my tips and wisdom on how to prepare food and what I find brings health and pleasure.

I hope that no matter what your food philosophy is, you will find recipes in this book to enjoy, benefit from and share with your loved ones. I also hope this book will guide you to making choices that lead to a happy gut and a radiant complexion, because beauty really does begin in the belly.

Carla x

Throughout my teens I suffered from eczema and allergies. When doctors prescribed steroid cream as a treatment, my mother began intuitively looking into natural remedies as an alternative. She engaged a naturopath and through applying homeopathic ointments, cutting out dairy, eliminating certain foods and introducing others, my eczema improved dramatically.

Working as a writer and stylist for fashion magazines in the 1990s, I was offered a job as a beauty editor for a national newspaper and although I enjoyed writing and was passionate about health and skin health, I realised – ironically – that I was a beauty editor who didn't use commercial beauty products! I was uncomfortable with all the synthetic ingredients used in the products that crossed my desk and was instead forever scouring the shelves of health food stores, searching for unusual natural oils or creams instead of the expensive lotions I was sent.

This led me to write my first book, *Feeding Your Skin*, which is full of recipes that use fruits, vegetables and grains from your kitchen cupboard to make natural beauty products that are safe for your skin and are literally good enough to eat.

For the past 15 years, I've been researching, writing and teaching about organic beauty and gut health, have been the editor of the *WellBeing Beauty Book* and a regular columnist for *WellBeing Magazine*, in addition to writing the *DIY Beauty* column for eight years for the *Sunday Telegraph*. I also researched and formulated products for beauty and wellness brands before creating my own Certified Organic inner and outer skincare range, The Beauty Chef, six years ago.

HOW THE BEAUTY CHEF WAS BORN

Around 10 years ago, my daughter experienced some skin issues that led me to research what might be causing them. After investigating various studies that looked at what we eat and how food affects the gut and the connection between gut health and skin health, I put my family on a gut-healing protocol. Part of this protocol was the inclusion of lacto-fermented wholefoods. After I began including these foods regularly in the meals I cooked for my family (and they overcame the sulphuric smell of sauerkraut!), I noticed a profound difference in my and my daughter's skin, and improved wellbeing of the whole family.

Being a time-strapped mum, I needed a quick fermented-food fix that was easy to make and easy to eat, so I began dabbling in the fermentation process in my Bondi kitchen. When friends and family started asking me what I was putting on my skin, as it looked so 'glowy', I realised the power of the gut/skin connection. I began experimenting with lacto-fermenting 24 superfoods that had powerful skin benefits and that's how GLOW, my first Beauty Chef inner beauty product, was created.

At the time many people thought it was an unusual idea – the concept of creating a fermented powder that you eat to make your skin radiant – but since then, bio-fermented organic foods for gut and skin health have taken off. Eight years later, our GLOW powder has become an international bestseller and GLOW can now be found all over the world, from the shelves of Selfridges in London to stores in New York and all over the USA, to shops in South-East Asia and even online at Net-a-Porter. There has been a paradigm shift in the beauty industry – beauty is health and health is beauty – and it is so exciting to be a part of that beauty revolution.

WHY I'M SO PASSIONATE ABOUT FERMENTATION

Of course I didn't come up with the idea of fermenting foods! Fermented foods exist in many traditional cultures: in Korea, kimchi; in Japan, miso; Eastern Europe, sauerkraut and kefir; in Africa, soured grains; and so on. For me, eating fermented food is the key to good gut health – if your gut bacteria is not in balance, your skin won't be either. Fermented foods are a powerful way to encourage good gut health. Think of it like soil in a garden – it needs to have the right bacterial balance and nutrients for plants to be healthy and lustrous. Your skin is the same – your gut needs to be in harmonious equilibrium for it to look its best.

People often think of beer or wine when they hear the term 'fermentation' and hope that this is what I mean by consuming more fermented foods. To their great disappointment, however, that is alcohol fermentation. While a lovely glass of red wine is fine in moderation, I'm referring to lacto-fermentation, the 'lacto' referring to a specific species of bacteria, *Lactobacillus*, which increases the vitamin and enzyme levels of the food that has been fermented and aids digestion. *Lactobacillus* is a genus of bacteria with many beneficial species in its family. It's found in our digestive systems as well as on the surface of plants (which is why eating plants should not only be about replenishing nutrients but also about replenishing good bacteria). While you can lacto-ferment your veggies with a lactic acid–producing mother culture, it is optional as the bacteria on the surface of the plant will do it for you.

The genius of lacto-fermentation seems to be boundless – it also helps neutralise anti-nutrients in food that prevent us from absorbing vital nutrients. When we eat food normally, we may only digest between 12 and 25 per cent of what we consume, but, when it is fermented, we can digest up to 85 per cent. Lacto-fermentation also produces natural, broad-spectrum probiotics, which are vitally important for gut health. Fermented foods also act as a prebiotic in the gut – healthy lunch for your microbes. You'll see in this book that there are many lacto-fermented basics that I encourage you to include in your everyday diet – I hope you do, as the benefits are so worth it.

FOLLOW YOUR GUT INSTINCT

Our guts are a thriving invisible ecosystem: they contain around 100 trillion organisms. Just like our fingerprints, the composition of gut microbiota is unique to each person and the fact that our bodies are comprised of 10 times more bacteria than cells makes it unsurprising that bacteria – both good and bad – can powerfully affect our digestive health and overall health.

Our gut is where 70 per cent of our immune system lies, we make nutrients (that make collagen), anti-oxidants (that protect our skin), metabolise hormones, neutralise pathogens, make neurotransmitters and detoxifying enzymes, so it's little wonder that the state of the gut has a profound effect on our skin.

A recent study showed that SIBO (small intestine bacterial overgrowth) is 10 times more prevalent in people with rosacea, and dermatitis occurs in a quarter of people with celiac disease. Countless studies show a link between leaky gut and skin problems, while a lack of hydrochloric acid in the gut can contribute to both acne and rosacea. Studies also show that those with good digestion have a healthier fatty-acids profile in their skin, making their skin plumper, more hydrated and more moisturised.

Good bacteria is your best friend when it comes to beautiful skin, hair and nails and by boosting it with lactic-acid bacteria (found in lacto-fermented foods), you can increase levels of hydrochloric acid and probiotics and help ameliorate and heal your skin complaints. There are numerous clinical trials that link a specific strain of bacteria with a positive health or skin benefit, for example *Lactobacillus acidophilus* for acne, *Lactobacillus delbrueckii* for atopic dermatitis. The beauty of lacto-fermented foods is that you are consuming a broad-spectrum *Lactobacillus* probiotic, not just one or two strains as might be found in a commercial probiotic product.

The gut is so much more than just a place for digesting food – not only is it intricately linked to the state of our skin, but poor digestion can affect the health and functioning of every system in the body: the brain, nervous system, hormonal balance, reproductive system and even the liver's ability to properly detoxify. Unfortunately, if your gut isn't balanced, your body won't be able to properly digest and utilise the nutrients from your food. As the skin, hair and nails are the last places to get nutrients (they go to more important organs first), those areas can become starved of nutrition. Additionally, if your gut is out of balance, you won't be detoxifying optimally and the skin will suffer. Our gut is where our neurotransmitters and feel-good hormones such as serotonin are made. So, by looking after your gut health, not only will you be helping your skin age well, but you will feel better about your lines and wrinkles!

Studies show that consuming lacto-fermented foods can influence both mood and acne by reducing systemic inflammation, and probiotics (created through lacto-fermentation) can help eliminate disease-promoting pathogenic bacteria in the gut.

INFLAMMATION

Unfortunately, modern-day living is not good for gut health – poor soils, overconsumption of processed food and eating products from animals fed on unnatural feed, the over-prescription of medications, pollution and stress all lead to imbalanced gut flora and inflammation.

Inflammation is the main way our body protects itself from injury, infection, bacteria and pathogens – it's a response triggered when damage occurs to our tissues that allows the body to localise the damaged area and then heal itself (think a swollen sore throat or the swelling around an insect bite). The trouble is, if the body is unable to repair itself quickly and heal the damaged tissues, long-term chronic inflammation can occur, which sends the immune system into overdrive and can stress the digestive system.

Put into the context of your gut, if you eat foods that irritate your gut lining over and over again, you're injuring your gut three meals a day, 365 days a year. You may not see the inflammation in your gut, but it's there, compromising the gut lining, allowing indigestible matter and toxins to flood through into the bloodstream where at some point it may manifest in skin problems, *candida*, learning difficulties, allergies, lethargy or susceptibility to colds, flu and autoimmune problems. Where there is gut inflammation, there will be skin inflammation, and this means an accelerated decline of collagen and elastin as well as susceptibility to skin problems from acne to eczema.

Looking after your digestive system with gut-friendly foods and probiotics and filling your plate with unprocessed, organic, antioxidant-rich fruit and veggies, seeds, nuts, herbs and spices is a great way to keep inflammation and disease at bay. Antioxidants help to mop up free radicals, which cause oxidative stress and inflammation in the body.

When it comes to digesting food efficiently, the problem is not often about the food itself, but rather the way we grow it and prepare it and the ratios in which we eat it. Refrigeration, industrialisation and our busy, modern, time-strapped lives mean that we have lost much of the knowledge of how to grow and prepare food effectively. Grains, nuts and legumes can be difficult for many of us to digest, but by fermenting and soaking them, as some cultures have done for millennia, you help reduce and eliminate gut-compromising anti-nutrients and break down the hard-to-digest proteins.

Grain-raised meat contains inflammatory fats, whereas grass-fed meat contains anti-inflammatory fats. Animals are meant to eat grass, not grains; and they are not meant to be pumped with antibiotics and hormones. For those who find eating meat hard on their digestion and avoid it, slow-cooking it with spices in soups and stews will help to make it easier to digest. Eating lacto-fermented foods alongside meals, as has been practised by many cultures for centuries, also aids the digestion process.

Over-farming means that conventional veggies are grown in mineral-depleted soils, which is why choosing organic is so important – plus they are non-GMO, taste better and are richer in skin-boosting plant nutrients. They also come without gut-compromising pesticides and herbicides.

For good health, instead of a meal with a predominance of meat and simple carbs, I prefer 50 per cent veggies (non-tubers), 30 per cent protein and 20 per cent complex carbohydrates, such as sweet potato, on my plate. If I'm very hungry, I'll load up on vegetables and foods containing healthy fats such avocados, activated nuts and grass-fed meats instead of reaching for a crusty loaf.

GRAIN PAIN?

Even though wheat, rice, corn, oats, rye and barley are staples of the modern diet, many of us are unable to digest them unless they are prepared properly (soaked or fermented). While dairy and gluten are, for many, difficult to digest (and I rarely consume them), there is a movement against grains generally, including non-gluten grains or 'pseudo grains'. This is because many grains, nuts and legumes contain 'anti-nutrients' such as phytic acid which, when eaten, bind to essential minerals and proteins such as zinc and calcium, preventing absorption.

Grains also contain lectins, which can damage the lining of the gut and inhibit digestion. When the gut is out of whack, chances are everything else is, too, and eating unprepared grains will only worsen a gut problem. However, preparing these foods properly by soaking and fermenting them can help to reduce and sometimes even eliminate these anti-nutrients, so you get the good without the bad.

Properly prepared legumes, seeds and gluten-free pseudo-grains are a great source of soluble fibre which is very beneficial for our gut health as well as acting as prebiotics for our gut microbiota. How effectively we digest food varies depending on the status of our gut (sometimes you need to heal your gut before you can properly digest these foods – which can be done under the guidance of a health practitioner).

DAIRY

My childhood eczema and allergies were fuelled by certain foods that my body had difficulty digesting, one of which was the protein (casein) found in dairy foods. Milk in its pasteurised and homogenised form is, for many people, inflammatory, but what is interesting is that I can tolerate fermented dairy – kefir, yoghurt, sour cream and some cultured cheeses – as fermentation reduces casein and can remove lactose completely. Studies also show that unfermented dairy is associated with acne, but fermented dairy isn't.

FAT

I often get asked about whether eating fat is good for your skin and my reply is always a resounding yes! Our brain, body and skin need fats in order to function well, as do our cells, and they are super important for making healthy hormones – omega-3 fats found in oily fish, such as salmon, krill oil and sardines as well as flax seeds (linseeds), chia seeds and walnuts help protect against inflammation.

Where the problem with fats lies is that the ratio is out of balance. The Western diet favours too many omega-6-containing foods (oils from nuts and seeds – safflower, sunflower, soybean, peanut) and not enough omega-3s. Signs of a deficiency of omega-3 or too much omega-6 can be dry, itchy, flaky skin, rashes, eczema, psoriasis and brittle hair and nails.

Although saturated fats get a lot of bad press (meat, whole eggs, coconut oil and organic butter), they have many skin and health benefits. Saturated fats make cholesterol, which is needed to keep the skin healthy. Fat from grass-fed meats is richer in conjugated linoleic acid, which is anti-inflammatory, immune-boosting and, ironically, fat busting.

I tend to cook with small amounts of ghee, coconut oil or butter as they are much more stable at high temperatures, unlike their vegetable oil counterparts. Butter is dairy, but it is much lower in lactose and negligible in casein and, if you ferment it, lactose is eliminated. It is also an excellent source of vitamins A, D, E and lecithin (which is essential for cholesterol metabolism), lauric acid (which is anti-inflammatory), a good source of iodine and, if you opt for grass-fed butter, it's rich in vitamin K2.

When it comes to most omega-6 vegetable and nut oils, I like to eat nuts in their whole form (except for macadamia nut oil, which is relatively stable at high temperatures) and use olive oil, which is rich in skin-protective acids, on salads. The only other omega-6 oil that I recommend consuming is evening primrose oil, as it is rich in GLA (gamma-linolenic acid), which is anti-inflammatory.

Fats can be hard to digest for some people, which is why it is vital to look after your liver (where bile that breaks down fats is made) and gall bladder (where it is stored) and also your digestive system, which helps make enzymes that break it down. Poor fat digestion and absorption can contribute to dry, flaky, crepey skin.

SUGAR

While our bodies require some sugar to survive, too much of it and too much of the wrong kind of sugar is not good for gut health, cellular health or skin health – in fact, pathogenic bacteria in your gut feed on refined sugar! Additionally, too much sugar can lead to acne, weight gain, insulin resistance and can reduce the efficiency of your immune system and, even worse, advanced glycation end (AGE) products are formed when sugar reacts with amino acids (both inside your body and within food), which can contribute to diabetes, cardiovascular disease and premature ageing of the skin. Limiting your sugar intake is therefore a great idea. However, I do use sweeteners in their natural form in my desserts and baking and some breakfast recipes. Raw honey and maple syrup are both rich in minerals and antioxidants, but I use them in moderation. Studies show that raw honey may act as a prebiotic.

A HOLISTIC APPROACH

Creating 'me time' is a wonderful way to recharge your batteries and it's also really beneficial for your skin, too. The relatively new field of psychodermatology looks at the impact of emotions on our skin and, considering that the skin is our largest organ, it's little wonder that psychological distress can negatively affect it. In fact, it has been suggested that up to 30 per cent of skin conditions can be traced back to an underlying cause of stressful emotions.

So, treating yourself to a pampering spa session or a massage is really good for your health, your soul and your skin! But you don't have to spend a fortune on fancy treatments to see the benefits – deep breathing and other relaxation techniques can often have visibly radiant results on our skin, as can meditation, yoga and walking. It is not only chemicals released in our body when we exercise, but there are health-boosting chemicals in the air when we connect with nature. I love my daily walk along Bondi Beach; studies show that sea air is charged with negative ions that accelerate our ability to absorb oxygen and help boost our levels of the feel-good hormone serotonin.

Getting good sleep is also one of the best and least expensive treatments. Lack of sleep can affect moisture levels in your skin due to decreased pH levels, plus not getting enough slumber impairs your body's ability to regulate glucose, while also increasing the levels of the stress hormone cortisol. In fact, not only does cortisol break down collagen, but some dermatologists believe it may also contribute to skin pigmentation and trigger acne, eczema and psoriasis. A long-term lack of sleep can increase the rate at which your skin (and body) ages. It's less able to recover from free-radical damage caused by toxins, both internal and external, and the sun, because your body isn't producing enough of the nightly growth hormones that stimulate cellular repair, collagen and new skin cells.

THE JOY OF FOOD

Although food is medicine, it's also about lifestyle and pleasure and finding a balance. I have learned that we have very adaptable palates. When I gave up most dairy products years ago, I couldn't imagine a diet without it. Now the thought of a glass of milk makes me feel a little nauseous! With a little time and patience, you can adjust your palate and before you know it, you will be ordering kale chips over fries with gravy and you will love how nourished and energised you feel.

For me, making and sharing food with and for those you love is one of the best things in life. Including my children in whatever is happening in the kitchen has always been important to me, from getting them to wash veggies, crack eggs, add pinches of spice to simmering pots or pick herbs from the garden in their younger years, through to now, where they are the ones cooking meals for the family. Encouraging them to get involved also spurred me on to become more inventive with recipes and ingredients, many of which you'll find in this book.

I hope you enjoy making and eating these meals as much as my family and I do, and that you too can enjoy a glowing kitchen!

Glowing kitchen tips

1   Recycle and reuse – putting things into the recycling bin is great, but there are other ways to recycle. Reuse your plastic wrap, wash zip-lock bags, reuse jars, paper bags and containers, buy produce that isn't packed in excessive packaging and take your own bags to the supermarket.

2   Use natural cleaning products – it's great that you're looking to help heal your belly by eating gut-loving foods, but if you're cleaning your house with non-natural chemical formulas, you may be undoing some of your hard work by ingesting toxins by proxy. Try to choose natural alternatives that are non-toxic and biodegradable – I use baking soda and vinegar to clean sinks (it cuts grease), vinegar to clean glass and mirrors, and I use a mix of 3 parts filtered water, 1 part white vinegar, 2 teaspoons lemon juice and a few drops of tea tree oil in a spray bottle as an all-purpose cleaner and disinfectant.

3   Use natural beauty products – why put chemicals on your skin when you can use natural oils and formulas bursting with goodness on your face and body instead? If you're stuck, The Beauty Chef makes a lovely Certified Organic night serum, a skin refiner and a wonderful balm, or you can check out my book *Feeding Your Skin* (published by Random House and available from Amazon and Book Depository), for recipes to make your own natural beauty products.

4   Drink filtered water – our bodies are around 60 per cent water, so it makes sense to drink the freshest, purest water you can find. Short of moving to the Swiss Alps, the next best thing is to invest in a good water filter that removes fluoride, chlorine (that kills the bacteria in our tap water but also the good bacteria in our tummies!) and heavy metals from tap water but leaves the good minerals in. I use mine to fill up water bottles for myself and the kids, which we take with us to work or school, and cook meals and clean my veg using filtered water.

5   Eat dirt? You don't have to meticulously scrub your organic veggies – because it may be that a little bit of dirt on your veg is actually good for you. For example, soil is full of good bacteria, including B12, so the micro bits of soil that linger on your veg are actually an extra gift from nature that's good for your health and your gut! In saying that, dirt also contains pathogens, so you don't want to overdo it either. If you don't buy organic, soak your fruits and veggies in apple cider vinegar and water to help remove the fungicides and pesticides that are often found on the surface of conventional produce.

6   Buy and eat in season – it's not only cheaper, but better for your body too. In winter, foods are naturally more insulating and in spring and summer, boast more cleansing properties, working in synergy with what the body needs to function at its optimum.

7   Cook and freeze – as a busy mum, I always try to cook in bulk so I can freeze meals to grab when I'm running late and don't have time to cook. It's also a great way to ensure that you don't turn to ready meals and fast foods, which are a temptation when you're time-strapped or don't feel like cooking.

8   Start up your own food co-op. For years, I ran organic veggie co-ops – it was the only way I could afford organic! Grab a bunch of like-minded friends and buy organic foods in bulk, then divide up the produce and split the cost.

9   Ferment your vegetables – I can't get enough fermented food in my diet and always have jars of fermented veggies in the pantry. Making and eating fermented foods is one of the best ways to harness a happy gut and glowing skin.

10 Prepare foods properly – nuts are wonderful things, full of good fats and flavour, but they can be harsh on your digestive system due to their levels of phytic acid. The good news is that you can make them gut-friendly by activating them. Soak a cup of nuts in enough filtered water (I always add a little apple cider vinegar to the water) to cover, adding a teaspoon of Himalayan salt, for at least 12 hours. Rinse and spread on a baking tray and dry in the oven on the lowest setting for at least 12 hours, or until they have a bit of crunch. It is important to remember that many plants, not just nuts and grains, contain some anti-nutrients but that by preparing them properly you can help reduce and even neutralise them. This is not just grains and nuts – kale, for example, is high in oxalates and by cooking it lightly you can improve its nutritional profile.

11 DIY beauty – most foods have excellent skin-rejuvenating properties when applied to the skin. I cleanse my skin with coconut oil, scrub my body with olive oil and sugar and rub the inside of the papaya skin (after I have eaten the papaya) on my face. Papaya is rich in papain, an enzyme that helps dissolve dead skin cells and leaves the skin feeling refined, soft and hydrated. Apple cider vinegar in water makes a brilliant skin toner and scalp and hair balancer. Most unrefined nut and vegetable oils make great skin moisturisers. Add a couple of drops of your favourite essential oil.

12 Avoid white carbs except for cauliflower – if it's white, then it's probably not alright. By white carbs, I mean refined or processed foods that are white in colour, like sugar, flour, cereals, crackers, baked goods, white bread, rice (which I do eat occasionally), white-flour pasta ... foods that make you feel tired and bloated, give you cravings and spike your blood sugar levels. These foods are best left on the shelf, not in your shopping trolley.

13 Grow herbs – from rosemary, oregano, basil and thyme to lemon verbena, mint, sage, dill, chives, parsley and more, herbs not only add flavour and goodness to my food but I also find tending my patch meditative and relaxing. Plus being around soil that is rich in microbes has gut-boosting benefits. In fact studies show that children who grow up on organic farms in Europe have less eczema and fewer allergies – they call it the 'farm effect' and one theory is that it relates to the exposure to microbial diversity in the soil.

14 Invest in a slow cooker – it is an amazing time saver, as I can literally throw things in the pot, turn on the timer and come home to beautifully cooked, nutritious, easily digested meals.

15 Find good food suppliers – finding the right butcher, grocer and fishmonger is as important as finding the right doctor. Food is medicine.

16 Chew, chew, chew – I'm a firm believer in chewing food thoroughly. The more you chew, the more saliva you mix with your food, which is a good thing because saliva contains digestive enzymes that lubricate the food and break down fats, all of which is beneficial to your digestive system.

17 No stress at dinner time – firstly, no arguing at the dinner table, it compromises digestion and secondly, no forcing anyone to eat their food – it is terrible for digestion. If possible also refrain from drinking while you eat as it dilutes your digestive enzymes that help you break down your meal.

18 Eat raw food in moderation – raw food is rich in active enzymes, which are brilliant for your health. But if your gut is compromised, raw food can aggravate this, so remember to strike a balance between raw and cooked food.

19 Drink bone broth – bone broth is one of the most healing and restorative foods for your gut, your skin and your wellbeing. It is anti-inflammatory and high in skin-clarifying, gut-healing and collagen-building amino acids and minerals.

Beauty nutrients

The added benefit of eating for gut health and cellular health is that your skin will look more glowing and radiant. Here are some of the nutrients that will help you eat your way to beautiful skin and also the foods in which you will find them.

While the nutrients below are important for skin health, it's important to remember that no nutrient is an island. They work together synergistically.

For example, iron is best absorbed in the presence of vitamin C, so you will absorb more iron by eating steak with spinach than eating steak alone. Antioxidants in certain foods, such as tomatoes and carrots, are oil soluble, so eating them with a little avocado or some olive oil helps your body utilise them. This is why eating a varied diet is so important, to increase your nutrient load and also support microbial diversity.

Nutrient	Why it's good for you	Where to find it
Biotin	This water-soluble vitamin helps regulate fatty-acid metabolism, which helps to protect cells and skin against damage and water loss. Biotin deficiency can cause dry scaly skin, dermatitis around the mouth and scalp, dandruff and cradle cap in babies.	Egg yolks, liver, chard, cos (romaine) lettuce, walnuts, almonds, legumes, peanuts, wholegrain cereals, milk and meat are all good sources of biotin, as are salmon, tuna, sardines, yeast, chicken, prawns (shrimp), spinach and unflavoured yoghurt.
Niacin (vitamin B3)	Also known as vitamin B3, niacin is essential for cell metabolism, the breakdown of carbohydrates, fats and proteins, as well as cholesterol synthesis and good blood circulation. It can relieve arthritic pain and stiffness and can dilate the blood vessels causing the skin to 'flush', plus it helps to keep skin soft, healthy and glowing. Niacin deficiency, on the other hand, can cause rashes and dermatitis.	Beef, pork, chicken, turkey, liver, yeast, tuna, salmon, peanuts, mushrooms, green peas, avocado and sunflower seeds are great sources of niacin, as are green leafy vegetables, milk, coffee and tea.
Omega-3 fatty acids	Research has shown that a diet rich in omega-3 fatty acids is essential for skin healing. It decreases inflammation, reduces the likelihood of acne and other skin problems, improves dermatitis, rosacea and psoriasis and can improve skin texture and quality. Omega-3s also protect the skin from UV damage.	Given the high levels of contamination in seafood, it is a good idea to take a good-quality fish oil supplement, and eat oily deep-water fish and seafood no more than twice a week. Flax seed (linseed) oil, chia seeds, walnuts and soy beans contain high levels, and kale, Brussels sprouts, cauliflower, broccoli, spinach and berries are also sources of omega-3 fatty acids.

Nutrient	Why it's good for you	Where to find it
Pantothenic acid (vitamin B5)	Pantothenic acid, or vitamin B5, is necessary for skin-cell regeneration and growth, wound healing, connective-tissue generation and the production of keratinocytes, which are essential for maintaining a healthy skin barrier ('chicken skin' is often caused by a lack of keratinocytes). It also helps to boost levels of glutathione, which is a powerful antioxidant that can help protect against sun damage and reduce the signs of ageing and the look of wrinkles and fine lines. It is also required by the adrenal gland to make stress hormones. Long-term stress will increase the need for B5.	Most foods contain some pantothenic acid, but egg yolk, royal jelly, wholegrain cereals, broccoli, mushrooms, avocado, sweet potato, liver, kidney, shellfish, fish, chicken and dairy foods are the richest sources. High heat can reduce the amount of B5 your body receives, so be mindful of cooking methods.
Selenium	This trace mineral is important for good health and glowing skin, yet many of us are often deficient in it without realising. Selenium also helps to create glutathione peroxidase, an enzyme necessary for the antioxidant function of glutathione, which helps protect against cellular damage from free radicals, inflammation, acne and skin ageing.	Organ meats and seafood are the richest sources, followed by fish (salmon, sardines, cod, tuna), beef, turkey, lamb and Brazil nuts.
Silica	This trace mineral is essential for the formation of connective tissue, including collagen (vital for firm, wrinkle-free skin), hyaluronic acid, which has been shown to increase skin-cell turnover, and retinoic acid, which is important for skin hydration and slowing down skin ageing and improving skin elasticity.	Leeks, green beans, celery, asparagus, strawberries, cucumber, mango, rhubarb and chickpeas are full of silica, as are apples, cherries, almonds, oranges, fish and seeds.
Sulphur	Crucial for skin health and overall wellness, sulphur is the third most abundant mineral in the human body and is essential for collagen synthesis, which gives skin structure and strength and prevents skin and cellular ageing. It's also necessary for the synthesis of the antioxidant glutathione, which helps prevent damage caused by free radicals and can reduce inflammatory skin conditions.	Egg yolks, wheat germ, red meat, chicken, turkey, fish, garlic, onions, kale and asparagus are rich in sulphur, as are fermented foods like sauerkraut and natto. Broccoli, cauliflower, turnips, bok choy (pak choy), kohlrabi and leeks are also full of skin-loving sulphur.
Vitamin A	Vitamin A is vital for healthy skin and has been used for years to treat acne, eczema and psoriasis (it's also good for sunburn). It is not only a potent antioxidant that helps fight free radicals, but it also helps regulate the production of pore-clogging sebum. Rough, dry skin that is scaly or keratinised is often due to a lack of vitamin A in the diet. Additionally, vitamin A helps promote the growth of healthy new skin cells and strengthens skin tissue.	Cod liver oil is the gold standard, but organic cream and butter from grass-fed animals are also rich in vitamin A. As are liver, egg yolks (organic and grass-fed), tuna and vegetables rich in carotenoids that convert to vitamin A in the body including: sweet potato, carrots, squash, cos (romaine) lettuce, papaya, mango, rockmelon, pumpkin (winter squash), dark leafy greens, squash, Brussels sprouts, dried apricots, melon, tomatoes, capsicums (bell pepper) and *Dunaliella salina* (a micro-algae).

Nutrient	Why it's good for you	Where to find it
Vitamin C	Vitamin C protects the skin from free radical damage as well as being vital for the formation and synthesis of collagen, which has been shown to firm the skin. It is also necessary for good skin health and wound healing, has anti-ageing effects on fine lines and wrinkles, can treat sun damage and helps to prevent dry skin.	Kiwi fruit, broccoli, dark leafy greens, tomatoes, Brussels sprouts, citrus fruits, strawberries and capsicums (bell pepper) all contain high levels of vitamin C, as do herbs such as basil, coriander (cilantro), chives and parsley. Vitamin C can be destroyed through cooking so eat these foods raw or only lightly cooked where possible.
Vitamin E	Vitamin E is a powerful anti-inflammatory that also fights free radical damage. When you consume food high in vitamin E, around seven days later that vitamin E is secreted through sebum (the oil on the surface of your skin) to provide a protective layer. Vitamin E is stored in our fat cells, so for our skin to receive the benefit, we must keep our levels of the vitamin high via a diet full of vitamin E-rich foods.	Greens such as kale, broccoli, spinach, asparagus, Brussels sprouts, silverbeet (Swiss chard) and green capsicums (bell pepper), as well as avocado; kiwi fruit; sunflower, sesame and pumpkin seeds (pepitas); almonds and hazelnuts; wheatgerm oil and olive oil.
Vitamin K2	K2 is one of the most powerful vitamins you can consume for preventing premature ageing, plus it also inhibits calcification of the skin's elastin, which helps to keep skin plump and springy, in addition to improving skin conditions such as acne. It also helps to protect the body from heart disease, aids the formation of strong bones, promotes healthy brain function, and supports cell growth and healthy skin.	Some of the best sources of vitamin K2 are fermented foods, including sauerkraut, natto and fermented vegetables. Other sources include high-fat dairy products and butter from grass-fed cows, egg yolks, liver and cheeses such as brie and gouda.
Zinc	This mineral helps the body form proteins and enzymes and carry vitamin A in the blood, plus it aids the immune system, wound healing and cell turnover and also has anti-inflammatory effects and protects skin against UV damage. Studies suggest zinc can also help reduce acne and, interestingly, people with low serum levels of zinc often suffer from acne.	Animal sources contain the most zinc – think liver, kidney, beef, lamb, shellfish, oysters and scallops – while pumpkin seeds (pepitas) and nuts are also high in zinc but should be soaked first.
Prebiotics or soluble fibre	Prebiotics are basically ingestible food ingredients that stimulate the growth and maintenance of beneficial gut bacteria.	Legumes, grains, berries, bananas, seeds, Jerusalem artichokes, onions, garlic, dandelion greens, leeks, chicory root, apples, celery, cruciferous vegetables (broccoli, cabbage, cauliflower, kale), carrots, sweet potato, asparagus, green beans and peas.
Thiamine (vitamin B1)	Thiamine helps to increase levels of hydrochloric acid in the gut, low levels of which are implicated in skin problems such as acne and rosacea and digestive issues.	Jerusalem artichokes, beef, liver, seafood, nuts (especially macadamias), green peas, oranges, pork, seeds (especially sunflower), legumes, oats, squash, asparagus and green beans.

Nutrient	Why it's good for you	Where to find it
Vitamin D	Vitamin D plays an integral role in cell differentiation and proliferation and therefore skin protection and rejuvenation. It contributes to skin cell growth, repair and metabolism and helps to optimise the skin's immune system and helps destroy free radicals that can cause premature ageing.	Fatty fish (salmon, and mackerel) and fish liver oils. Small amounts are found in beef liver, mushrooms, cheese and egg yolks.
Copper	Copper is an essential mineral required by the body for collagen production and bone health. It's also important for helping to code specific enzymes that help stop free radicals producing pigmentation.	Liver, seafood, oysters, lobster, crab, octopus, sesame seeds, cacao and dark chocolate, kale, mushrooms, seeds, cashews, Brazil nuts, walnuts, pine nuts, chickpeas, soybeans, adzuki beans, kidney beans, white beans, dried fruit (prunes, apricots, currants, figs), avocado, goat's cheese and fermented soy (miso, tempeh).
Manganese	Manganese is a required co-factor for collagen production and also functions as an antioxidant in skin cells. It's also an important mineral for healthy bones.	Cloves, saffron, wheatgerm, bran, rice bran, oats, nuts, chickpeas, brown rice, spinach, pineapple, mussels, oysters, clams (vongole), cocoa powder, dark chocolate, roasted pumpkin (winter squash), squash seeds, flax seeds (linseeds), sesame seeds and chilli powder.
Potassium	Potassium helps keep blood vessels healthy by protecting them against oxidative damage and also keeps cells plump and hydrated.	Sweet potato, tomatoes (tomato paste/ concentrated purée and purée are better sources), beetroot (beet) greens, silverbeet (Swiss chard), avocado, spinach, potatoes, white beans, kidney beans, broad (fava) beans, lentils, split peas, yoghurt, clams (vongole), prunes and carrots.
Iron	Iron is important for skin health. It is also especially important for hair as a deficiency of iron can cause hair loss. The hair follicle and root are fed by a nutrient-rich blood supply.	Oysters, dark green leafy veggies, beef, lamb, cashews, mussels, eggs, prunes, liver, chicken, fish, veal, soybeans, lentils, spinach, sesame seeds, chickpeas, broad (fava) beans, olives, haricot beans, silverbeet (Swiss chard) and kidney beans.
Ellagic acid	Ellagic acid inhibits an enzyme generated by free radicals that causes a breakdown of collagen.	Strawberries, raspberries, blackberries, pomegranates, walnuts, pecans and cranberries.

Nutrient	Why it's good for you	Where to find it
Antioxidants	Antioxidants come in many forms – in vitamins A, C and E for example, and in plant compounds as carotenoids, flavonoids, isothiocyanates, resveratrol and tannins, and they protect healthy cells from being attacked and damaged by free radicals. Free-radical damage causes inflammation and the breakdown of collagen and elastin as well as damage to our DNA. They are crucial in slowing the ageing process as well as protecting the skin from sun damage, pollutants, and other environmental toxins. We need a broad range of different types of antioxidants found in different foods to help protect our skin and body from the broad range of free radicals we are exposed to daily.	Antioxidants are abundant in vibrantly coloured fruits and vegetables, some meats, poultry and fish, mushrooms, legumes, seeds, leeks, onions and garlic, grains, green tea and black tea.
Probiotics	Probiotics help keep the gut microbiota in balance, which then helps reduce oxidative stress on the skin and body. Probiotics also help with glycaemic control and can help treat acne, rosacea, atopic dermatitis and psoriasis by reducing systemic inflammation. When the gut is healthy, radiant skin follows and probiotics are at the frontline for keeping the gut happy and in check. Look for probiotics that offer a broad spectrum of strains, the proven strains being *Lactobacillus* and *Bifidobacterium* species alongside beneficial yeasts such as *Saccharomyces boulardii* and *Saccharomyces cerevisiae*.	Fermented foods such as kefir, natto, sauerkraut, kombucha, kimchi and yoghurt are your best sources of probiotics, along with probiotic supplements or fermented superfood supplements like The Beauty Chef's GLOW.
Magnesium	Magnesium helps to detoxify and cleanse the skin, making it excellent for breakouts. A lack of magnesium is implicated in eczema as well as an acceleration of the ageing of human cells and also reduces levels of fatty acids in the skin, therefore moisture and elasticity. A deficiency can also affect hair growth and hair loss.	Dark leafy greens, nuts, seeds, fish, beans, whole grains, avocados, yoghurt, bananas, dried fruit, cacao and chocolate.
Enzymes	Good health is not only about what you eat, but what you digest, and enzymes in foods help our bodies digest beauty nutrients. The enzymes themselves, such as proteolytic enzymes found in papaya, are also anti-inflammatory, immune-boosting, detoxifying and healing in the body. All raw foods contain some enzymes, but certain foods like the ones suggested are the most powerful.	Lacto-fermented foods like sauerkraut and kimchi, sprouted seeds and legumes, papaya, figs, mango, kiwi, grapes, pumpkin (winter squash), apricots, melons, pineapple, avocados, bananas, raw honey, bee pollen, extra-virgin olive oil and coconut oil, raw meat and dairy.

Breakfast

....

Breakfast is our culinary introduction to the day and should delight, satisfy, sustain and nourish us for the morning. I always try to incorporate protein into my breakfast (and meals generally) as it helps keep me satiated until lunch. It also helps keep blood sugar levels balanced, which is one of the best ways to maintain metabolic efficiency (our body's ability to burn fat) as well as protect collagen, the protein that keeps our skin lovely, firm and bouncy.

Begin with a shot of apple cider vinegar in water just after waking – it will help to fire up your digestive system and increase acids in the gut, which aid digestion of your breakfast.

Then, if you have time, go for an invigorating walk or swim before you eat: there is nothing more satisfying than earning your morning fare.

I try to mix up my breakfasts, alternating between sweet and savoury, although personally I love savoury the best – I even enjoy a leftover soup or stew for breakfast.

TIPS

——— For extra gut-boosting power, add The Beauty Chef Inner Beauty Powders and Boosts to your smoothies and smoothie bowls. Other beneficial ingredients include slippery elm, marshmallow root, grass-fed gelatin, bone broth and liquorice root.

Get glowing breakfast smoothie bowl

This health-giving bowl is fibre-rich, vitamin-rich, antioxidant-rich, lipid-rich and full of skin-protective and glow-giving minerals selenium, copper and zinc, plus it has the added boost of GLOW Inner Beauty powder with pre- and probiotics to keep your gut happy and skin radiant.

SERVES 2

125 g (4½ oz) frozen blueberries

100 g (3½ oz) frozen unsweetened açai pulp, coarsely chopped

1 very ripe frozen banana, coarsely chopped

½ cup (125 g/4½ oz) coconut kefir or natural yoghurt

2 teaspoons The Beauty Chef GLOW Inner Beauty Powder (optional)

¼ teaspoon ground cinnamon

2 teaspoons chia seeds

2 teaspoons cacao nibs*

Topping

1 small ripe banana, peeled and sliced

6–10 fresh blueberries

2 tablespoons granola (see recipe page 329)

1 tablespoon finely chopped pistachios

1 tablespoon goji berries

1 teaspoon bee pollen* (not suitable for those with bee allergies)

1 teaspoon hemp seeds (optional)

To make the smoothie, blend the blueberries, açai, banana, kefir or yoghurt and GLOW powder, if using, cinnamon, chia seeds and cacao nibs in a high-speed blender, until smooth and creamy. Pour the smoothie into two wide shallow serving bowls.

Decorate with toppings.

Eat immediately.

NOTE

The topping ingredients can be substituted according to personal taste or availability.

* Available from health food stores.

Creamy millet porridge with honey-roasted figs and almond and seed toffee

This recipe is pure comfort food: both for our senses and also for the good bacteria in our gut as both millet and figs act as prebiotics – food for our healthy bugs.

SERVES 2

Porridge
½ cup (100 g/3½ oz) hulled millet*, soaked in water overnight and drained
2 cups (500 ml/17 fl oz) water
1 cup (250 ml/8½ fl oz) almond milk (or any nut milk), plus extra to serve (optional)
1 teaspoon ground cinnamon
½ teaspoon vanilla bean powder*

Almond and seed toffee
2 tablespoons almonds
3 teaspoons raw honey
1 tablespoon pumpkin seeds (pepitas)
1 tablespoon sunflower seeds
1 teaspoon black sesame seeds

Honey-roasted figs
2 ripe figs
1 teaspoon raw honey

Preheat the oven to 180°C (350°F). Line two small baking trays (baking sheets) with baking paper.

Place the millet in a medium saucepan, add the water and milk, cinnamon and vanilla and bring to the boil. Decrease the heat and gently simmer over low heat, stirring frequently, for 20–25 minutes, until the millet is tender, with a slight bite remaining, and most of the liquid has been absorbed to make a creamy porridge consistency.

Meanwhile to prepare the almond and seed toffee, scatter the almonds on one of the prepared trays. Drizzle with 2 teaspoons of the honey and bake for 5 minutes. Scatter the pumpkin, sunflower and sesame seeds over the almonds, drizzle with the remaining honey and bake for a further 5 minutes, or until the almonds and seeds are golden and the honey is caramelised. Set aside to cool, until the honey toffee hardens. Break into shards or coarsely chop.

To prepare the honey-roasted figs, tear the figs in half from the stem to the base. Place, torn side up, on the remaining tray and drizzle with honey. Bake for 15 minutes, or until softened and juicy.

Serve the porridge hot topped with warm honey-roasted figs and shards of almond and seed toffee. Serve with additional milk, if desired.

* Available from health food stores and specialty grocers.

Autumn spice smoothie bowl
with pear, banana and turmeric cream

This rich, creamy and spicy bowl of deliciousness is rich in silica from the oats, which helps with skin elasticity, and is brimming with anti-inflammatory and antioxidant spices.

SERVES 1 (MAKES 1½ CUPS)

⅓ cup (30 g/1 oz) gluten-free rolled (porridge) oats, soaked in water overnight
1 frozen banana, coarsely chopped
30 g (1 oz) almond butter
1 medjool date, pitted
½ teaspoon ground nutmeg
½ teaspoon ground turmeric
¼ teaspoon ground cinnamon
⅛ teaspoon freshly ground black pepper
½ cup (125 ml/4 fl oz) almond milk

Poached pears
2 cups (500 ml/17 fl oz) water
1½ tablespoons raw honey
1½ tablespoons apple cider vinegar (unpasteurised)
½ teaspoon vanilla bean powder*
2 beurre bosc pears, peeled

Topping
2 tablespoons granola (see recipe page 329)
1 teaspoon bee pollen* (not suitable for those with bee allergies)
marigold petals (optional)

To prepare the poached pears, place the water, honey, apple cider vinegar and vanilla in a small saucepan and bring to the boil. Decrease the temperature to low. Add the pears, cover the surface with a sheet of baking paper and weigh down with an upturned plate to keep the pears submerged. Poach for 20–25 minutes, until just tender. Turn off the heat and leave the pears in the poaching liquid to cool.

To prepare the smoothie bowl, drain the excess liquid from the oats and place them, together with the remaining ingredients, in a high-speed blender. Blend until smooth.

Pour the smoothie into a shallow bowl. Slice one of the pears (you can keep the other pear to use another day) and place on top of the smoothie. Add bee pollen and marigold petals, if using.

NOTE
The poached pears can be prepared in advance and stored in the refrigerator for up to 1 week. You only need one pear for this recipe.

You can also use fresh pears or figs, in place of the poached fruit.

* Available from health food stores.

Chocolate sprouted buckwheat, coconut and seed granola

*I love the earthy, rich combination of chocolate and buckwheat in this recipe.
By sprouting the buckwheat, a complete protein, we make it more easily digestible.*

SERVES 8–10 (MAKES 6 CUPS)

1 cup (200 g/7 oz) buckwheat groats*
½ cup (75 g/2¾ oz) sunflower seeds
½ cup (75 g/2¾ oz) pumpkin seeds (pepitas)
2 tablespoons black sesame seeds
1 cup (100 g/3½ oz) desiccated (shredded) coconut
¼ cup (30 g/1 oz) ground flax seeds (linseeds)
2 tablespoons cacao nibs*
2 tablespoons cacao powder*
1½ teaspoons ground cinnamon
1 overripe banana
4 medjool dates, pitted and coarsely chopped
2 tablespoons coconut oil, warmed
1 tablespoon maple syrup, or to taste
natural yoghurt and fruit, to serve

Place the buckwheat groats in a medium bowl and cover with cold water. Soak for 15 minutes, then drain through a fine-mesh sieve. Rinse. Place the sieve containing the buckwheat over a bowl. Cover with a clean tea towel (dish towel) and set aside at room temperature for 1–3 days**, until tail-like sprouts appear. Rinse the buckwheat under cold running water morning and night until sprouted. Alternatively place the groats in a sprouting jar and rinse twice daily.

Once the buckwheat has sprouted, soak the sunflower, pumpkin and sesame seeds in cold water for 1 hour.

Preheat the oven to 60°C (140°F), or the lowest temperature setting on your oven. Alternatively you can use a dehydrator if you have one.

Drain and rinse the soaked seeds. Place in a blender and process until finely chopped.

Combine the sprouted buckwheat, finely chopped seeds, coconut, ground flax seed, cacao nibs, cacao powder and cinnamon together in a large bowl. Mix well.

Blend the banana, dates, coconut oil and maple syrup together to make a smooth purée. Add the purée to the sprouted buckwheat mixture. Mix well using clean hands or a spoon, until combined and clumps begin to form.

Spread the mixture out onto two large baking trays (baking sheets), leaving the mixture in rough clusters.

Bake, turning once or twice, for 2½–3 hours, until crisp and completely dried out. Remove from the oven and set aside to cool. Serve with your choice of nut milk, yoghurt or coconut milk kefir (see recipe page 304) and fresh fruit.

NOTE
You can store the granola in an airtight container for up to 4 weeks.

* Available from health food stores.
** The length of time for buckwheat to sprout will depend on the temperature of your kitchen.

Puffed millet and buckwheat muesli with nuts, dried figs and goji berries

This gluten-free muesli (granola) features macadamias, which are rich in anti-inflammatory oleic acid and omega-7, a fatty acid that helps our skin remain hydrated and moisturised.

SERVES 8–10 (MAKES 6 CUPS)

½ cup (90 g/3 oz) almonds, soaked in cold water for
  1 hour, drained and rinsed
½ cup (85 g/3 oz) macadamias
1 cup (60 g/2 oz) flaked coconut
1 cup (20 g/¾ oz) puffed millet*
1 cup (12 g/¼ oz) puffed buckwheat*
75 g (2¾ oz) dried figs (approx 3 large), finely diced
½ cup (55 g/2 oz) quinoa flakes
½ cup (55 g/2 oz) pecans, coarsely chopped
⅓ cup (35 g/1¼ oz) goji berries
¼ cup (35 g/1¼ oz) sunflower seeds
1½ teaspoons ground cinnamon
1 teaspoon ground ginger
½ teaspoon ground nutmeg

Preheat the oven to 150°C (300°F).

Spread the almonds out on a small baking tray (baking sheet). Bake for 40–45 minutes, until dried out and crisp. Set aside to cool. Chop coarsely.

Roast the macadamias on a separate tray for 10 minutes, or until lightly roasted. Set aside to cool. Chop coarsely.

Lightly toast the coconut in the oven for 5 minutes, or until golden. Set aside to cool.

Combine the chopped roasted nuts and toasted coconut with the remaining ingredients in a large bowl. Stir to combine and coat evenly in the spices.

Serve with your choice of nut milk, yoghurt or coconut milk kefir (see recipe page 304) and fresh fruit.

Store in an airtight container for up to 4 weeks.

NOTE
You can substitute ¼ cup (35 g/1¼ oz) dried currants for the goji berries, if desired.

* Available from health food stores.

Chocolate sprouted buckwheat, coconut and seed granola

Puffed millet and buckwheat muesli with nuts, dried figs and goji berries

Quinoa, spiced apple and pecan bircher

Known in its native South America as chisaya mama *(mother grain), quinoa is actually a seed and is a complete protein. The apple is high in soluble fibre to help keep our digestive system healthy, and the pecans are high in cell-protective antioxidant vitamin E.*

SERVES 2

⅓ cup (65 g/2¼ oz) quinoa, rinsed

⅔ cup (150 ml/5 fl oz) water

1 teaspoon ground cinnamon

½ teaspoon ground nutmeg

⅛ teaspoon ground cloves

1 tart green apple, such as Granny Smith,
    peeled, cored and coarsely grated

½ cup (125 g/4½ oz) natural or coconut yoghurt
    (or coconut kefir), plus extra to serve

½ orange, juiced

½ cup (60 g/2 oz) pecans, coarsely chopped,
    plus extra to serve (optional)

2 medjool dates, pitted and coarsely chopped

1 tablespoon raw honey, warmed,
    plus extra to serve (optional)

raspberries, to serve

Place the quinoa, water, cinnamon, nutmeg and cloves in a small saucepan and bring to the boil. Decrease the heat to low and gently simmer for 10 minutes, or until almost all of the water has been absorbed and holes appear on the surface. Cover and remove from the heat to finish cooking for a further 5 minutes, or until tails have sprouted and all of the water has been absorbed. Transfer into a medium bowl and set aside to cool slightly. Alternatively you can use 1½ cups (200 g/7 oz) of cooked quinoa.

Add the apple, yoghurt, orange juice, pecans, dates and honey and stir to combine. Transfer into an airtight container and refrigerate overnight.

To serve, top with additional yoghurt and raspberries, plus pecans and an extra drizzle of honey, if desired.

NOTE

This can be stored in the refrigerator in an airtight container for up to 3 days.

Vanilla chai–spiced chia breakfast puddings with blackberries and choc-nut crunch

Sweet, succulent blackberries help to protect your body from oxidative stress and inflammation. Here they are combined with chia seeds, a good source of soluble fibre.

SERVES 2

½ cup (125 ml/4 fl oz) water
2 teaspoons loose chai mix or 2 good-quality chai tea bags
1 cup (250 ml/8½ fl oz) almond milk
1½ teaspoons raw honey
½ teaspoon vanilla bean powder*
⅓ cup (50 g/1¾ oz) chia seeds
natural or coconut yoghurt, to serve
10 fresh (or frozen and thawed) blackberries, to serve

Choc-nut crunch
2 tablespoons coarsely chopped hazelnuts
2 tablespoons flaked coconut
2 tablespoons buckwheat groats*
1 tablespoon cacao nibs*
2 teaspoons cacao powder*
2 teaspoons raw honey
1 teaspoon coconut oil, warmed
¼ teaspoon vanilla bean powder*
pinch of Himalayan salt

Preheat the oven to 200°C (400°F).

To prepare the chia puddings, gently simmer the water and chai mix in a small saucepan for 5 minutes, or until reduced by half. Add the almond milk, honey and vanilla and bring back to a simmer. Set aside to infuse for 10 minutes.

Meanwhile to prepare the choc-nut crunch, combine all of the ingredients in a medium bowl and mix well to combine. Spread onto a baking tray (baking sheet) lined with baking paper and place in the oven. Bake for 10 minutes, stirring occasionally, or until darkened. Set aside to cool completely. The mixture will become crunchy once it cools.

Strain the infused milk through a tea strainer or squeeze out the tea bags and discard. Add the chia seeds and stir to combine. Set aside for 10–15 minutes, stirring occasionally to break up any lumps, until the seeds swell and absorb all of the liquid, to make a thick pudding consistency.

To serve, spoon the chia pudding into two serving glasses or small bowls. Top with yoghurt, blackberries and choc-nut crunch.

NOTE
You can use either of the granolas on pages 36 and 329 in place of the choc-nut crunch.

The chia puddings can be made in advance and stored in serving glasses in the refrigerator for up to 3 days. Add the choc-nut crunch when ready to serve.

* Available from health food stores and specialty grocers.

Amaranth, apple and miso porridge

SERVES 2

Miso is one of my favourite condiments, both for flavour and its nutrient-rich ingredients, including genestein (a powerful, health-giving phytonutrient). Amaranth, cultivated by the Aztecs 8000 years ago, is a true superfood – its high levels of protein and minerals rival many animal-based foods.

½ cup (100 g/3½ oz) amaranth*, soaked in cold water overnight, drained and rinsed
¾ cup (180 ml/6 fl oz) water
1 cup (250 ml/8½ fl oz) almond milk (or any nut milk), plus extra to serve (optional)
1 tart green apple, such as Granny Smith, cored and diced
1 teaspoon ground cinnamon
pinch of Himalayan salt
2 teaspoons white (Shiro) miso paste
2 teaspoons maple syrup, plus extra for drizzling (optional)
⅓ cup (35 g/1¼ oz) walnuts, chopped
1 medjool date, pitted and chopped (optional)

Combine the amaranth, water, almond milk, apple, cinnamon and salt in a medium saucepan and bring to a simmer over medium heat.

Decrease the heat and gently simmer, stirring occasionally, for 25–30 minutes, or until the amaranth is tender and almost all of the liquid has been absorbed to make a creamy porridge consistency. Remove from the heat.

Stir in the miso and maple syrup.

Divide between two serving bowls. Scatter each bowl with walnuts and dates, if desired. Serve with a little additional milk, if desired.

* Available from health food stores or specialty grocers.

Buckwheat porridge with mushroom, spinach and hazelnuts

SERVES 2

Delicious and nourishing. Spinach, mushrooms and buckwheat all contain riboflavin, a deficiency of which is implicated in acne-prone skin. Together they also offer a good dose of selenium, manganese and zinc, all of which are also helpful for clarifying skin.

40 g (1½ oz) cultured butter (see recipe page 303)
½ onion, thinly sliced
150 g (5½ oz) mushrooms, thinly sliced
2 large handfuls baby spinach
2 tablespoons coarsely chopped roasted hazelnuts

Buckwheat porridge
½ cup (100 g/3½ oz) buckwheat groats*, soaked in cold water overnight
3 cups (750 ml/25½ fl oz) beef, chicken or vegetable broth (see recipes pages 300–302)
20 g (¾ oz) cultured butter
Himalayan salt and freshly ground black pepper

To prepare the buckwheat porridge, drain the buckwheat and place in a small saucepan with the broth. Bring to the boil then decrease the heat and simmer, stirring occasionally, for 25–30 minutes, or until the buckwheat is tender and a creamy porridge consistency. Add the butter and stir to melt and combine. Season with salt and pepper.

Meanwhile, melt the butter in a frying pan over low–medium heat. Cook the onion until golden brown. Add the mushrooms and cook until softened and golden brown. Add the spinach and stir through until it is wilted. Spoon the porridge into serving bowls. Top with the mushroom and spinach mixture and scatter over the hazelnuts.

* Available from health food stores or specialty grocers.

Amaranth, apple and miso porridge

Buckwheat porridge with mushroom, spinach and hazelnuts

Sticky black rice with mango, strawberries and coconut cream

This lovely dish is made with black rice, the only rice that contains anti-inflammatory anthocyanins, and mango, which is rich in digestive enzymes.

SERVES 2

½ cup (100 g/3½ oz) black glutinous rice, soaked in cold water overnight
1½ cups (375 ml/12½ fl oz) water
⅔ cup (160 ml/5½ fl oz) coconut cream
large pinch of Himalayan salt
1½ tablespoons maple syrup
1 ripe mango, cut into cubes
6 strawberries, sliced

Drain and rinse the rice.

Place the rice and water in a medium saucepan and bring to the boil. Decrease the heat to the lowest possible temperature. Gently simmer for 20 minutes, or until the rice is tender and all of the water has been absorbed. Remove from the heat, cover and set aside for 10 minutes, to finish cooking.

Meanwhile, gently simmer the coconut cream and salt together for 2–3 minutes, until thickened slightly. Set aside.

Once the rice is cooked, add the maple syrup and stir to combine. Set aside to cool slightly.

Serve the sticky rice warm or at room temperature drizzled with the salted coconut cream and topped with fresh mango and strawberries.

Almond meal English muffins

*I'm a little partial to an English muffin and, as a child, would eat the packet variety
with lots of butter and honey. Today I prefer those that don't bloat my tummy;
this healthier version is full of protein-rich almonds. Pair them with chia jam – yum!*

MAKES 4

1½ cups (150 g/5½ oz) almond meal
¼ cup (30 g/1 oz) coconut flour
2 teaspoons gluten-free baking powder
½ teaspoon bicarbonate of soda (baking soda)
pinch of Himalayan salt
4 large eggs
½ cup (125 ml/4 fl oz) almond milk (or any nut milk)
2 tablespoons coconut oil, melted
2 teaspoons raw honey, warmed

Preheat the oven to 180°C (350°F). Lightly grease
and line a large baking tray (baking sheet) with
baking paper.

Combine the almond meal, coconut flour, baking
powder, bicarbonate of soda and salt in a medium
bowl and mix well. Make a well in the centre.

Beat the eggs and milk in a small bowl.

Pour the egg mixture into the well. Stir in the dry
ingredients to make a thick batter. Pour in the
coconut oil and honey and stir to combine. Set the
batter aside for 10 minutes to allow the coconut flour
to rehydrate before shaping.

Divide the mixture in quarters and shape into
four 8 cm (3¼ in) discs on the prepared tray.

Bake for 20–30 minutes, turning halfway, until
golden brown. Leave on the tray for 5 minutes
to cool slightly.

Eat warm or place on a rack to cool completely.

To serve, slice the muffins in half horizontally.
Serve plain or toast until golden brown.

Top with your choice of spreads, such as cultured
butter (see recipe page 303) and chia jam (see recipe
page 335) or nut butter and honey. For a savoury
option, try topping them with scrambled egg and
avocado with fermented salsa (see recipe page 320)
or chilli sauce (see recipe page 320).

NOTE

The muffins can be made in advance and frozen.
They are ideal for a quick breakfast, lunch or
afternoon snack.

Chicken congee with soft-boiled egg

Congee is pure winter comfort food – warming, nourishing and grounding. I love this recipe with buckwheat as it adds a lovely nutty flavour, although rice also works well. Both are resistant starches that help stimulate beneficial bacteria in your gut.

SERVES 4

Congee

1 cup (200 g/7 oz) short-grain rice or buckwheat groats*
splash of apple cider vinegar (unpasteurised)
4 cups (1 litre/34 fl oz) water
1 organic skinless chicken breast
4 cups (1 litre/34 fl oz) chicken bone broth (see recipe page 300, or use store-bought stock)
5 cm (2 in) knob of ginger, peeled and shredded
4 spring onions (scallions), green part only, thinly sliced into rounds

Topping

4 large eggs
1 tablespoon coconut oil
5 purple shallots, thinly sliced into rounds
sesame oil, for drizzling
2 tablespoons tamari, or to taste
2 large handfuls coriander (cilantro) leaves
chilli sauce, to serve (optional, see recipe page 320)

NOTE

White rice is easier on your digestive system than brown rice; however, it is high GI, which is why it is best only to eat it occasionally and in small amounts, and with protein, which helps reduce the GI load. As a lower-GI alternative, you can use quinoa, basmati or buckwheat groats and use kuzu starch as a thickening agent.

Studies show that adding a little coconut oil to the water while cooking rice converts the starch to resistant starch. Chilling the cooked rice in the fridge overnight reduces the calorie content.

The chicken breast can be poached in the chicken broth to infuse it with extra flavour, if desired.

* Available from health food stores.

Soak the rice or buckwheat groats overnight in cold water with the splash of vinegar.

If using rice, drain and rinse the rice. Place the rice and water in a medium heavy-based saucepan and bring to the boil. Reduce the heat and simmer over low–medium heat, uncovered, for 30 minutes, stirring occasionally to prevent the rice from sticking to the pan, or until most of the water has been absorbed.

Bring a small saucepan of water to a simmer. Add the chicken breast and gently simmer for 6 minutes. Turn off the heat and leave the chicken in the water for 15 minutes, to finish cooking. Once cool enough to handle, shred the chicken into strips and set aside.

Add the broth, 1 cup (250 ml/8½ fl oz) at a time, to the rice (if using buckwheat instead of rice, add the drained buckwheat to a saucepan and add the broth 1 cup (250 ml/8½ fl oz) at a time), stirring occasionally until the rice or buckwheat is soft and most of the liquid has been absorbed to make a creamy porridge consistency. Remove from the heat. Add the shredded chicken, ginger and spring onion to the congee and stir to combine. Cover and set aside.

Place the eggs in a small saucepan and cover with cold water. Simmer for 3 minutes. Transfer into a bowl of iced water for 2 minutes to cool slightly.

Meanwhile heat the coconut oil in a small frying pan over medium heat. Fry the shallots until crisp and golden. Place on kitchen paper to drain.

Peel the eggs. To serve, divide the congee between four serving bowls. Drizzle with the sesame oil and tamari. Top each bowl of rice with a soft-boiled egg, coriander leaves and fried shallots. Drizzle with some chilli sauce, if desired.

Savoury custards with shiitake mushrooms and spring onion

These tasty, nutrient-dense pots star the wonderful flavour of shiitake mushrooms,
which are good for heart health, weight loss, help protect our DNA and boost immunity.

MAKES 4

4 dried shiitake mushrooms
6 large eggs
2 teaspoons finely grated ginger
½ teaspoon sesame oil
1¾ cups (430 ml/14½ fl oz) chicken bone broth
    (see recipe page 300)
2 spring onions (scallions), thinly sliced diagonally
tamari, to serve
chilli sauce (see recipe page 320), to serve (optional)

Soak the shiitake mushrooms in hot water for 20 minutes, or until rehydrated. Drain. Remove and discard the woody stems. Slice the caps.

Preheat a wide-based steamer pot over medium-high heat.

Gently whisk the eggs, ginger, sesame oil and chicken broth together in a medium bowl. Add the shiitake mushrooms and spring onion and mix through.

Pour the egg mixture into four 1½-cup (375 ml/12½ fl oz)-capacity ovenproof ramekins, distributing the shiitake and spring onion evenly.

Cook the custards in batches, arranging the ramekins in the preheated steamer set over medium heat. Steam for 10 minutes, or until the custards are just set with a slight wobble remaining in the centre. Remove from the steamer and set aside to cool slightly.

Serve warm or at room temperature. Drizzle with tamari to serve, and chilli sauce, if desired.

Baked eggs with hazelnut dukkah

Baked eggs are a hit in our house – they're chock-full of skin-, eye-, mood- and body-boosting nutrients. I make fresh dukkah, an Egyptian condiment of seeds, nuts and spices, every few weeks and it adds a healthy zest to this dish.

SERVES 2

1 tablespoon olive oil

½ red capsicum (bell pepper), seeded and very thinly sliced lengthways

1 small red onion, thinly sliced

1 clove garlic, finely chopped

½ teaspoon cumin

½ teaspoon sweet paprika

¼ teaspoon chilli flakes

400 g (14 oz) can chopped tomatoes

Himalayan salt and freshly ground black pepper

4 large eggs

100 g (3½ oz) marinated goat's cheese, crumbled

1 large handful coriander (cilantro) leaves, coarsely chopped

Hazelnut dukkah

1 teaspoon sesame seeds

1 teaspoon coriander seeds

½ teaspoon cumin seeds

2 tablespoons roasted hazelnuts

Himalayan salt and freshly ground black pepper, to taste

Preheat the oven to 200°C (400°F).

Heat the oil in a medium ovenproof frying pan over low–medium heat. Cook the capsicum, onion and garlic, stirring occasionally, for 10 minutes, or until softened. Add the spices and cook until fragrant. Add the tomato and simmer for 10–15 minutes, until reduced to make a sauce. Season with salt and pepper.

Meanwhile to make the dukkah, dry-fry the sesame, coriander and cumin seeds in a small frying pan over low heat, until the sesame seeds are lightly toasted and the spices are fragrant. Lightly crush the toasted seeds and hazelnuts together, using a small mortar and pestle or a spice grinder. Season with salt and pepper and set aside.

Make four wells in the cooked tomato sauce and crack an egg inside each one. Bake in the oven for 15 minutes or until the white is just set and the egg yolk is still runny, or until cooked to your liking.

To serve, scatter with goat's cheese, hazelnut dukkah and coriander leaves.

NOTE

The eggs can also be baked and served in individual ramekins. Simply transfer the hot sauce into two approximately 1½-cup (375 ml/12½ fl oz)-capacity ovenproof ramekins. Make two wells in each and crack in the eggs. Bake for 10–15 minutes, until cooked to your liking.

Green eggs and ham

Eggs are hands-down my breakfast favourite, as they are nutrient-dense and so easy to prepare. The kale and pumpkin seed pesto is a twist on a classic and together with the eggs, this dish is a brain and beauty booster, rich in zinc, selenium and B vitamins.

SERVES 2

4 large eggs, lightly beaten

1 tablespoon ghee

2 green or heirloom tomatoes, sliced

150 g (5½ oz) shaved free-range, nitrate-free ham
   (salmon gravlax, see page 322, also works well)

1 large handful rocket (arugula) leaves

1 tablespoon pumpkin seeds (pepitas), lightly toasted

freshly ground black pepper, to taste (optional)

Kale and pumpkin seed pesto

¼ cup (35 g/1¼ oz) pumpkin seeds (pepitas),
   lightly toasted

2 tablespoons savoury yeast flakes*

½ clove garlic

finely grated zest of 1 unwaxed lemon

2 large kale leaves, deveined and coarsely chopped

1 large handful basil leaves

2 tablespoons extra-virgin olive oil

2 tablespoons freshly squeezed lemon juice

Himalayan salt and freshly ground black pepper,
   to taste

To prepare the kale and pumpkin seed pesto, place the pumpkin seeds, savoury yeast flakes, garlic and lemon zest in a small food processor and blend to coarsely chop. Add the kale and basil and blend, gradually adding the oil and lemon juice, to finely chop. Season with salt and pepper. Transfer into a small bowl and set aside.

Whisk the eggs together in a medium bowl.

Melt the ghee in a small non-stick saucepan over low–medium heat. Add the eggs and cook for 30 seconds without stirring, or until they begin to set. Cook for a further 1 minute, stirring occasionally, until the egg begins to set in big curds, but is still wet. Gently stir through 2 tablespoons of the prepared pesto, trying not to break up the egg too much. Remove from the heat.

To serve, arrange the tomato slices and ham on serving plates. Spoon over the green scrambled egg. Scatter with the rocket and toasted pumpkin seeds. Top with black pepper, if desired.

NOTE

The pesto can be stored in an airtight container in the refrigerator for up to 1 week. Drizzle a little olive oil over the surface to prevent discolouration.

You can also add the kale and pumpkin seed pesto to pasta dishes, salads, on top of soups or as a spread on crackers or wraps.

* Available from health food stores and specialty grocers.

Asian-style spring onion omelette with kimchi and crab

For years I constantly craved crab; then I discovered I was low in vitamin B12 and that crab is high in B12. I love crab with eggs, and kimchi gives this recipe a delicious Asian spark.

MAKES 2

6 large eggs
1 spring onion (scallion), green part only, very thinly sliced
1 tablespoon coconut oil, melted
chilli sauce, to serve (optional, see recipe page 320)

Filling
200 g (7 oz) fresh crabmeat
1½ cups (225 g/8 oz) kimchi, coarsely chopped (see recipe page 315)
2 large handfuls coriander (cilantro) stems and leaves
1 large handful bean sprouts
fresh chilli, thinly sliced (optional)

To prepare the filling, combine the crabmeat, kimchi, coriander, bean sprouts, and fresh chilli, if using, in a medium bowl and toss to combine. Set aside.

To prepare the omelette mixture, using a fork, lightly beat the eggs together in a medium bowl to just combine so the whites marble through the yolks. Stir through the spring onion.

Preheat a wok or large frying pan over medium–high heat. Add 2 teaspoons of the coconut oil and swirl to coat. Once the oil is shimmering, pour half of the egg mixture into the wok, tilting and turning to coat the wok, making a thin omelette.

Cook for 20–30 seconds, until golden on the base and just set. Spread half of the filling over one side of the omelette and fold over to enclose. Transfer onto a serving plate. Serve immediately.

Repeat using the remaining coconut oil, egg mixture and filling to make a second omelette and serve immediately, with chilli sauce if desired.

Sweet potato latkes with goat's cheese cream, sautéed spinach and poached egg

Potato latkes make a great base for everything from eggs to chicken to veggies, and sweet potatoes, as well as being delicious, contain prebiotics, which feed the good bacteria in your gut.

SERVES 4 (MAKES 8)

splash of white vinegar
4 large eggs
1 tablespoon ghee
250 g (9 oz) English spinach, coarsely chopped
juice of ½ lemon
Himalayan salt and freshly ground black pepper, to taste
chilli sauce, to serve (see recipe page 320)
micro herbs, to garnish (optional)

Sweet potato latkes
350 g (12½ oz) sweet potato, (approx 1 medium)
½ small red onion, thinly sliced
Himalayan salt and freshly ground black pepper
1 large egg, lightly beaten
ghee, for frying

Goat's cheese cream
150 g (5½ oz) soft goat's cheese
¼ cup (60 ml/2 fl oz) coconut cream
1½ tablespoons freshly squeezed lemon juice
1 small clove garlic, crushed

Preheat the oven to 150°C (300°F).

To make the goat's cheese cream, mix the goat's cheese, coconut cream, lemon juice and garlic together in a small bowl until smooth. Season with salt. Set aside.

To prepare the sweet potato latkes, peel and coarsely grate the sweet potato. Squeeze out in a clean tea towel (dish towel) to remove any excess moisture.

Combine the sweet potato and onion in a medium bowl. Season with salt and pepper. Add the egg and stir to combine.

Heat a tablespoon of ghee in a large non-stick frying pan over low–medium heat. Cook the latkes in batches, spooning 2 heaped tablespoons of mixture into the pan for each and flattening slightly. Cook for 3 minutes on each side, or until crisp and golden brown. Transfer onto a plate and place in the oven to keep warm while you cook the remaining latkes.

Bring a medium saucepan of water to a gentle simmer. Add a splash of vinegar. Create a whirlpool in the water and carefully crack the eggs, one at a time, into the centre. Poach the eggs for 2–3 minutes, until the whites are firm but the yolks are still soft. Remove using a slotted spoon and set on clean kitchen paper to drain.

At the same time, heat a teaspoon of ghee in the frying pan and cook the spinach until just wilted. Add a squeeze of lemon and season with salt and pepper.

Serve the latkes topped with the goat's cheese cream, wilted spinach and poached eggs. Drizzle with chilli sauce (or fresh or dried chilli if chilli sauce is unavailable), and micro herbs, if desired.

Brussels sprout and kale fritters with nut cheese and avocado, pea and mint smash

Avocado, one of my favourite skin foods, is rich in good oils, which make the oil-soluble antioxidants in the kale and Brussels sprouts more available for your body to use.

SERVES 4

olive oil, for cooking
cultured nut 'cheese' (see recipe page 308)*
lemon wedges, to serve

Fritters
200 g (7 oz) Brussels sprouts, shredded
4 large stems kale, deveined and finely shredded
3 spring onions (scallions), thinly sliced
⅓ cup (15 g/½ oz) savoury yeast flakes**
1 large handful mint leaves, coarsely chopped
1 large handful dill leaves, coarsely chopped
2 cloves garlic, finely chopped
3 teaspoons capers, finely chopped
finely grated zest of 1 unwaxed lemon
1½ tablespoons arrowroot
½ teaspoon Himalayan salt
¼ teaspoon freshly ground black pepper
4 large eggs, lightly beaten

Avocado, pea and mint smash
½ cup (70 g/2½ oz) frozen peas
1 large avocado, halved, stone removed and
    flesh scooped out
½ lemon, juiced
1 small handful mint leaves, thinly sliced
Himalayan salt and freshly ground black pepper

Preheat the oven to 150°C (300°F).

To prepare the avocado, pea and mint smash, bring a small saucepan of water to the boil. Blanch the peas for 20 seconds. Drain and refresh in a bowl of iced water. Drain.

Place the peas and avocado in a medium bowl. Using a potato masher, coarsely mash together. Add the lemon juice and mint and stir to combine. Season with salt and pepper.

To prepare the fritters, place the Brussels sprouts, kale, spring onion, savoury yeast flakes, mint, dill, garlic, capers, lemon zest, arrowroot, salt and pepper in a medium bowl. Mix well to combine. Add the eggs and stir to coat.

Preheat a large non-stick frying pan over medium heat. Drizzle with oil. Cook the fritters in batches, spooning 2–3 heaped tablespoons of mixture into the pan for each and flatten slightly to make 1 cm (½ in)-thick fritters. Cook for 2 minutes on each side, or until golden brown. Transfer onto a plate and place in the oven to keep warm while you cook the remaining fritters.

To serve, spread cultured nut cheese over the fritters and top with the avocado, pea and mint smash. Serve with lemon wedges.

* Substitute labneh (see recipe page 306) if preferred.
** Available from health food stores and specialty grocers.

Buckwheat pancakes with horseradish cream and smoked salmon

The flavours of this dish marry beautifully and horseradish, an anti-inflammatory with disease fighting compounds, will help clear your sinuses if you have a cold.

SERVES 2 (MAKES 4 PANCAKES)

200 g (7 oz) sliced smoked salmon (or gravlax,
    see recipe page 322)
1 large avocado, halved, stone removed and
    flesh thickly sliced
fermented beetroot (beets) and onion, to serve
    (optional, see recipe page 310),
1 small handful dill, to serve
freshly ground black pepper, to serve

Buckwheat pancakes
½ cup (80 g/2¾ oz) buckwheat flour
1 tablespoon arrowroot
½ teaspoon gluten-free baking powder
½ cup (125 g/4½ oz) natural yoghurt
1 large egg, separated
2 teaspoons melted ghee, plus extra for greasing

Horseradish cream
½ cup (125 g/4½ oz) natural yoghurt
1 tablespoon freshly squeezed lemon juice
1 tablespoon freshly grated horseradish
Himalayan salt, to taste

To prepare the buckwheat pancakes, place the buckwheat flour, arrowroot and baking powder in a medium bowl and mix well to combine. Add the yoghurt and egg yolk and whisk to make a smooth batter.

In a separate bowl, whisk the egg white to soft peaks. Fold the whites through the buckwheat mixture. Add the melted ghee and stir to combine. Cover and refrigerate for 30 minutes.

To make the horseradish cream, combine the yoghurt, lemon juice and horseradish in a small bowl. Season with salt.

Brush a large frying pan with ghee and set over medium heat.

Cook the pancakes, using approximately ¼ cup (60 ml/2 fl oz) of batter for each one and spreading out slightly to make 1 cm (½ in)-thick discs. Cook for 1–2 minutes on each side, until golden brown.

Serve the pancakes warm, topped with smoked salmon, avocado, horseradish cream and fermented beetroot and onion, if desired. Top with dill and freshly ground black pepper.

Coconut and lime hotcakes with yoghurt and berries

A relaxed Sunday brunch calls for these lovely discs of goodness – and they're also popular with kids. The good news is that coconut flour is not only a great source of fibre, but it's also low GI. The berries in this dish are also low GI, and rich in collagen-protective ellagic acid.

SERVES 4 (MAKES 12)

natural yoghurt, to serve
1 cup (125 g/4½ oz) fresh raspberries
1 cup (125 g/4½ oz) fresh blueberries

Pancakes
6 large eggs
1 small overripe banana, coarsely chopped
½ cup (125 ml/4 fl oz) coconut cream
2 tablespoons melted ghee, plus extra for cooking
2 tablespoons maple syrup,
    plus extra to serve (optional)
1 teaspoon apple cider vinegar (unpasteurised)
¾ cup (90 g/3 oz) coconut flour
1½ teaspoons gluten-free baking powder
½ teaspoon bicarbonate of soda (baking soda)
finely grated zest of 2 unwaxed limes

To prepare the pancakes, blend the eggs, banana, coconut cream, ghee, maple syrup and vinegar together in a food processor or blender until smooth.

Transfer into a medium bowl. Add the coconut flour, baking powder, bicarbonate of soda and lime zest and mix to make a thick batter. Set aside for 10 minutes, to hydrate the flour.

Brush a large non-stick frying pan with ghee and set over very low heat.

Cook the hotcakes in batches, spooning approximately 2 tablespoons of batter per hotcake into the pan. Spread out slightly to make 1 cm (½ in)-thick cakes. Cook for 4–5 minutes, until the surface begins to dry out and the base is golden brown. Carefully turn the cakes (they will still be quite soft). Cook for a further 2–3 minutes, or until golden brown, slightly puffed and cooked through.

Serve warm topped with yoghurt and berries. Drizzle with additional maple syrup, if desired.

Lunch

....

When people think of lunch, they generally envisage sandwiches: a myriad of filling choices in between two pieces of bread. While I enjoy a good sandwich, for many of us, overdoing it with gluten is not conducive to good gut health. Happily, there is an abundance of other options. In summer, salads are an excellent choice – a little prep work on a Sunday or at the beginning of the week will make assembling salads a breeze: wash salad leaves, make aioli, pesto or dressings, grill some chicken or make some gravlax and you're set. Savoury tarts, dolmades and wraps are also nourishing lunch options.

Making superfood bowls is another good way to satiate and nourish yourself during the day: combine a selection of nutrient-charged ingredients such as seasonal vegetables, seaweeds, seeds, herbs, spices, fermented foods, some sweet potato and a protein of your choice, and top it with a tahini dressing or chilli sauce. In winter, however, I really love to put my vacuum flask to good work, keeping leftover stews, curries and soups warm for lunch.

TIPS

—— Have a warm lemon juice before you eat lunch to increase acids in the gut, which will help digest your meal.

—— Instead of drinking coffee, try peppermint, fennel or liquorice teas to help aid digestion after your meal.

Green minestrone

I love a traditional tomato-based minestrone, but this is a gentle and nourishing alternative, with cleansing and alkalising properties. Green veggies boost glutathione, oxygenate the blood and support the liver. Substitute the stock for chicken stock to enhance the restorative properties of this soup.

SERVES 4-6

2 tablespoons olive oil
1 leek, white part only, thinly sliced
2 sticks celery, diced
3 cloves garlic, finely chopped
1 small head broccoli, broken into small florets and stalk diced
1 zucchini (courgette), diced
6 cups (1.5 litres/51 fl oz) vegetable broth (see recipe page 302)
150 g (5½ oz) green beans, trimmed and halved crossways
3 large stems kale, deveined and coarsely chopped
1 cup (140 g/5 oz) fresh or frozen peas
2 large handfuls flat-leaf (Italian) parsley, coarsely chopped
1 large handful mint leaves, coarsely chopped
1 large handful basil leaves, coarsely chopped
finely grated zest of 1 unwaxed lemon
Himalayan salt and freshly ground black pepper
freshly grated parmesan cheese, to serve (optional)

Heat the oil in a large saucepan over low heat. Cook the leek, celery and garlic until softened. Add the broccoli and zucchini and stir to combine.

Pour in the broth and bring to the boil. Decrease the heat and simmer for 10 minutes. Add the beans and simmer for a further 5 minutes, or until the vegetables are just tender.

Add the kale, peas, parsley, mint, basil and lemon zest and simmer for 5 minutes, or until the kale has wilted and the peas are tender. Season with salt and pepper.

Serve topped with freshly grated parmesan, if desired.

Pho with healthy hoisin

The Bondi Markets have the most exquisite pho I have ever had the pleasure to eat, but I feel this version does this restorative Vietnamese soup justice. Often, it's the commercially made condiments that we eat that have the most additives, so here I have made a delicious, healthy version of hoisin.

SERVES 4

1 cinnamon stick

3 star anise

5 whole cloves

2 teaspoons coriander seeds

6 cups (1.5 litres/51 fl oz) beef bone broth (see recipe page 301)

1 small carrot, peeled and coarsely chopped

2 spring onions (scallions)

5 cm (2 in) knob of ginger, bruised

2 strips mandarin peel (optional)

150 g (5½ oz) beef fillet

250 g (9 oz) dry rice noodles, or zucchini (courgette) noodles

1 tablespoon tamari

1½ tablespoons freshly squeezed lime juice

4 large handfuls (approx 1⅔ cups/150 g/5½ oz) bean sprouts

2 large handfuls Thai basil leaves

2 large handfuls Vietnamese mint leaves

2 large handfuls coriander (cilantro) sprigs

2 red birds-eye chillies, thinly sliced

lime wedges, to serve

chilli sauce, to serve (optional, see recipe page 320)

Hoisin sauce (Makes ¾ cup/185 ml/6 fl oz)

3 medjool dates, pitted

¼ cup (60 ml/2 fl oz) boiling water

⅓ cup (90 g/3 oz) brown (Genmai) miso paste

1 tablespoon apple cider vinegar (unpasteurised)

1 tablespoon honey

2 teaspoons tamari

1 clove garlic, peeled and coarsely chopped

2 cm (¾ in) knob of ginger, peeled and chopped

1 teaspoon five spice powder

Place the spices in a medium saucepan and toss over low heat for 3–4 minutes, until fragrant. Add the bone broth, carrot, spring onions, the ginger and mandarin peel, if using, and bring to the boil over high heat. Decrease the heat and gently simmer for 30 minutes.

Wrap the beef fillet tightly in plastic wrap, to make a nice round shape. Freeze for 30 minutes, or until partially frozen, firm but not solid. This helps to make it easier to slice thinly, for serving.

Meanwhile to prepare the hoisin sauce, soak the dates in the boiling water for 10 minutes. Combine the dates and their soaking liquid with the remaining ingredients in a high-speed blender. Blend until smooth.

Soak the noodles in boiling water, or according to the packet instructions, until softened. Strain.

Strain the broth, discarding the solids. Return to the pan. Add the tamari and lime juice.

Unwrap the partially frozen beef. Using a sharp knife, slice into very thin rounds.

To assemble, divide the noodles among four serving bowls. Top with slices of raw beef, bean sprouts, fresh herbs and chilli. Ladle over the hot broth.

Serve with lime wedges. Drizzle with chilli and hoisin sauces, as desired.

NOTE

The hoisin sauce can be stored in an airtight container in the refrigerator for up to 3 weeks. It makes a wonderful marinade for meats, especially pork and beef.

Chicken broth with chicken and almond meal 'matzoh' balls

In winter as a child I would devour matzoh ball soup. It is comforting, simple and great for when you are feeling under the weather. Here is my gluten-free version.

SERVES 4

6 cups (1.5 litres/51 fl oz) chicken bone broth
   (see recipe page 300), or store-bought stock
1 carrot, peeled and sliced diagonally 5 mm (¼ in)
   thick
1 stick celery, sliced 5 mm (¼ in) thick
½ onion, roughly cut into 2 cm (¾ in) pieces
Himalayan salt, to season
dill fronds, to garnish

Chicken and almond meal 'matzoh' balls
200g (7 oz) organic skinless chicken breast,
   any sinew removed, coarsely chopped
½ cup (50 g/1¾ oz) almond meal
2 large egg whites
large pinch of Himalayan salt
¼ teaspoon ground white pepper
1 small handful dill fronds, coarsely chopped

To prepare the matzoh balls, place the chicken in a food processor and blend to finely chop. Add the almond meal, egg whites, salt and pepper and blend to combine. Transfer into a medium bowl. Add the dill and stir to combine. Cover and refrigerate for 15 minutes.

Heat the chicken broth in a medium saucepan over medium heat, until simmering. Add the carrot, celery and onion and gently simmer for 15 minutes, or until tender. Season the broth with salt.

Meanwhile bring a medium saucepan of salted water to the boil over high heat. Decrease the heat to just below simmering.

Using two dessertspoons, shape the chicken mixture into 12 walnut-sized balls. Poach in the salted water for 5–8 minutes, until they float to the surface, are firm but still slightly springy, and completely cooked through.

Using a slotted spoon, transfer the cooked chicken balls into serving bowls. Ladle over the hot broth with some of the cooked vegetables. Garnish with dill fronds.

Warm cauliflower couscous salad with roasted roots, hazelnuts and crispy spiced chickpeas

Cauliflower makes a great base in place of grains. According to Traditional Chinese Medicine, root veggies are very balancing to your chi *(vital energy), especially in winter.*

SERVES 4

400 g (14 oz) can chickpeas, drained and rinsed*
2 tablespoons coconut oil, warmed
1 teaspoon ground cumin
½ teaspoon ground turmeric
½ teaspoon ground coriander
¼ teaspoon Himalayan salt
1 sweet potato, peeled and cut into 2 cm (¾ in) chunks
1 parsnip, peeled and cut into 2 cm (¾ in) chunks
1 beetroot (beet), peeled and cut into 2 cm (¾ in) chunks
¼ cup (40 g/1½ oz) hazelnuts
1 (600–800 g/1 lb 5 oz–1 lb 12 oz) cauliflower, trimmed and broken into chunks
⅓ cup (80 ml/2½ fl oz) extra-virgin olive oil
2 large handfuls coriander (cilantro) leaves, chopped
juice of 1 lemon
2 cloves garlic, finely chopped
Himalayan salt, to taste
micro herbs, to garnish (optional)

Preheat the oven to 200°C (400°F).

Spread the chickpeas onto a small baking tray (baking sheet). Drizzle with a little of the coconut oil. Combine the cumin, turmeric, coriander and salt in a small bowl. Scatter the spice mix over the chickpeas and toss to coat. Roast, shaking the tray occasionally, for 15 minutes, or until crisp and golden.

Place the sweet potato, parsnip and beetroot on a large baking tray. Drizzle with coconut oil and toss to coat. Roast for 20 minutes, or until tender and golden brown.

Roast the hazelnuts on a separate baking tray for 5–7 minutes, until the skins begin to peel away and the nut is golden. Set aside to cool slightly. Wrap the hazelnuts up in a clean piece of kitchen paper and rub together to remove the skins. Coarsely chop the nuts.

Place the cauliflower in a food processor and blend to finely chop into couscous-sized grains.

Heat 1 tablespoon of the olive oil in a large frying pan over medium heat. Cook the cauliflower, stirring frequently, for 3–4 minutes, until just tender. Transfer to a large bowl. Add the chickpeas, roasted root vegetables, hazelnuts and coriander and toss to combine.

Mix the remaining olive oil, lemon juice and garlic together in a small bowl. Pour over the cauliflower couscous and toss to coat. Season with salt. Garnish with micro herbs, if desired.

Serve immediately.

NOTE
You can also serve this with labneh (see recipe page 306) or natural yoghurt, if desired.

* You can soak and cook your own chickpeas if preferred.

Kale bowl with quinoa, fermented vegetables, wakame and avocado

Fresh and nutritious, this flavour-packed dish features wakame, a great source of minerals that can be lacking in conventionally grown produce and that we need for healthy, glowing skin.

SERVES 4

½ cup (100 g/3½ oz) quinoa, rinsed

1 cup (250 ml/8½ fl oz) water

7 g (¼ oz) wakame

1 tablespoon coconut oil

1 onion, thinly sliced

1 clove garlic, finely chopped

2 bunches (approx 800 g/1 lb 12 oz) kale, stemmed and coarsely chopped

2 teaspoons white sesame seeds, plus extra to serve

2 teaspoons black sesame seeds, plus extra to serve

½ teaspoon chilli flakes

1½ cups (230 g/8 oz) sweet and sour fermented vegetables (see recipe page 316)

1 avocado, halved, stone removed and flesh sliced lengthways

½ cup (75 g/2¾ oz) raw cashews, roasted and coarsely chopped

Tahini sauce

¼ cup (60 ml/2 fl oz) freshly squeezed lemon juice

¼ cup (60 g/2 oz) tahini

1 tablespoon extra-virgin olive oil

2 cm (¾ in) knob of ginger, peeled and finely grated

3 teaspoons tamari

2 teaspoons raw honey

1 teaspoon sesame oil

Place the quinoa and water in a medium saucepan and bring to the boil. Cover and decrease the heat to low and gently simmer for 15 minutes, or until almost all of the water has been absorbed and holes appear on the surface. Keep covered and remove from the heat to finish cooking for a further 5 minutes, or until tails have sprouted and all of the water has been absorbed. Keep warm.

Meanwhile, soak the wakame in cold water for 5 minutes, or until rehydrated. Drain and squeeze out excess water. Slice into strips. Set aside.

To prepare the sauce, place all of the ingredients in a jar and seal with a lid. Shake vigorously to combine.

Heat the coconut oil in a large frying pan or wok over low–medium heat. Cook the onion and garlic, until softened. Add the kale and cook, stirring occasionally, for 4–5 minutes, until wilted. Add the sesame seeds and chilli flakes and toss to combine.

To serve, arrange the kale, quinoa, wakame, fermented vegetables and avocado into serving bowls. Drizzle with the tahini sauce and scatter with roasted cashews and extra sesame seeds.

Rainbow chard, tomato and goat's cheese tart

Rainbow chard, tomato and goat's cheese tart

I love the shiny ribbed leaves of this nutrient-dense leafy green, and its slightly stronger
flavour than spinach, although both are equally good for you – full of skin-clarifying
riboflavin and zinc, as well as biotin, essential for healthy skin, hair and nails.
Goat's cheese is lovely and is easier on the digestive system than cow's.

SERVES 8

Buckwheat and hazelnut pastry
1 cup (150 g/5½ oz) buckwheat flour
1 cup (100 g/3½ oz) finely ground hazelnuts
¼ cup (30 g/1 oz) arrowroot
½ teaspoon Himalayan salt
2½ tablespoons macadamia oil
1 large egg, lightly beaten
1½ tablespoons water
1 tablespoon apple cider vinegar (unpasteurised)

Filling
1 tablespoon olive oil
1 small brown onion, thinly sliced
2 cloves garlic, thinly sliced
200 g (7 oz) rainbow chard, coarsely chopped
finely grated zest of 1 lemon
Himalayan salt and freshly ground black pepper
100 g (3½ oz) soft goat's cheese
150 g (5½ oz) cherry tomatoes, halved
1 small handful basil leaves, coarsely chopped
1 small handful thyme leaves, coarsely chopped
6 large eggs
⅔ cup (160 ml/5½ fl oz) almond milk

Preheat the oven to 200°C (400°F). Lightly grease a 23 cm (9 in) loose-based fluted flan (tart) tin with coconut oil. Refrigerate.

To prepare the pastry, place the buckwheat flour, ground hazelnuts, arrowroot and salt in a large bowl and stir to combine. Add the macadamia oil, egg, water and vinegar and stir to form a sticky dough.

Press the dough evenly into the base and sides of the prepared tin. Prick the base several times with a fork. Bake for 15 minutes, or until crisp and golden brown.

To prepare the filling, heat the oil in a large frying pan over low heat. Cook the onion and garlic, stirring occasionally, for 10 minutes, or until softened and beginning to caramelise. Add the chard and cook for 1–2 minutes, until wilted. Remove from the heat. Add the lemon zest and season with salt and pepper.

Scatter half of the goat's cheese over the base of the tart. Arrange the chard and onion mixture over the top. Scatter with the tomatoes, basil and thyme. Scatter with the remaining goat's cheese.

Lightly beat the eggs together in a medium bowl. Add the almond milk and beat to combine. Season with salt and pepper. Pour the egg mixture into the tart.

Bake for 25–35 minutes, until the egg is set and the top is golden brown. Leave in the tin for 10 minutes to cool slightly.

Remove from the tin and slice to serve.

NOTE
The tart can be served warm, at room temperature or chilled.

Lemon and herbed quinoa dolmades

This take on traditional Greek parcels of goodness is delicious as it is, although the herby, lemony flavour of the vine leaves also works well with the addition of lamb mince, marinated peppers, zucchini (courgettes) or eggplants (aubergines). Vine leaves are a staple in a Mediterranean diet and are nutritive and anti-inflammatory.

SERVES 6 (MAKES APPROXIMATELY 24)

30–40 vine leaves, fresh or preserved in brine
⅓ cup (80 ml/2½ fl oz) olive oil, plus extra for drizzling
4 French shallots, finely chopped
2 cloves garlic, finely chopped
1 cup (200 g/7 oz) quinoa, rinsed
1 large handful dill, finely chopped
1 small handful flat-leaf (Italian) parsley, finely chopped
1 small handful mint leaves, finely chopped
½ spiced preserved lemon, zest only, finely chopped (see recipe page 319), or 2 teaspoons grated lemon zest
1 tablespoon currants
¼ teaspoon ground cinnamon
Himalayan salt and freshly ground black pepper
3 cups (750 ml/25½ fl oz) chicken bone broth (see recipe page 300), or vegetable broth (see recipe page 302) or store-bought stock
⅓ cup (80 ml/2½ fl oz) freshly squeezed lemon juice
natural yoghurt, to serve

If using fresh vine leaves, blanch them in boiling water for 30 seconds and then refresh in cold water. If using leaves preserved in brine, soak them in warm water for 10 minutes.

Drain and separate the vine leaves. Gently pat dry, setting aside any torn ones.

Heat half of the oil in a medium saucepan over medium–low heat. Cook the shallots and garlic until softened. Add the quinoa, dill, parsley, mint, preserved lemon, currants and cinnamon and stir to coat. Remove from the heat. Season with salt and pepper.

Spread the vine leaves out flat, onto a clean kitchen surface, smooth-side down, with the stems facing you. Trim the stems and place tablespoonfuls of the mixture at the base of the leaves. Fold the sides in and roll up into little logs. Don't roll too tightly, as the quinoa needs room to swell when cooked.

Line a large wide-based saucepan with any torn and any remaining vine leaves; alternatively you can use baking paper. Pack the dolmades in tightly together, so they don't unravel.

Combine the broth, lemon juice and remaining oil in a medium bowl or jug. Pour over the dolmades. Cover with a heatproof plate, to keep them submerged. Bring the liquid just to a simmer. Cover and gently simmer for 20–30 minutes, until the quinoa is tender and most of the liquid has been absorbed. Leave in the pan to cool to room temperature.

Serve at room temperature or chilled, with natural yoghurt for dipping.

NOTE
You can decrease the quinoa by ½ cup (100 g/3½ oz) and add 150 g (5½ oz) browned lamb mince, 1 teaspoon of cumin and 1½ tablespoons of lightly toasted pine nuts to the filling ingredients.

Lemon and herbed quinoa dolmades

Raw rainbow salad with soft-boiled egg and creamy miso dressing

This lovely salad is inspired by a Kylie Kwong recipe. It is high in health-protective carotenoids from both the veggies and the egg yolk and makes a great shared plate as part of a meal.

SERVES 4

½ large celeriac, peeled
1 beetroot (beet), peeled
1 carrot, peeled
150 g (5½ oz) large radishes (approx 4–5)
4 large eggs
1 large handful chives, cut into 5 cm (2 in) batons

Creamy miso dressing
¼ cup (60 ml/2 fl oz) brown rice vinegar
1 large egg yolk
1 tablespoon white (Shiro) miso paste
1 teaspoon tamari
2 cm (¾ in) knob of ginger, peeled and finely grated
⅓ cup (80 ml/2½ fl oz) light-flavoured extra-virgin
    olive oil
1 teaspoon sesame oil

To make the creamy miso dressing, place the brown rice vinegar, egg yolk, miso paste, tamari and ginger in a medium bowl. Whisk to combine. Gradually pour in the olive and sesame oils, whisking continuously, until incorporated.

Using a mandoline, finely shred the celeriac, beetroot, carrot and radishes. Wash the mandoline between each vegetable to prevent the colours from bleeding. Alternatively coarsely grate using a hand-held grater.

Place the eggs in a small saucepan and cover with cold water. Simmer for 3 minutes. Transfer into a bowl of iced water for 2 minutes, to cool slightly. Peel the eggs.

Combine the shredded vegetables and chives in a large bowl and toss to combine. Add three-quarters of the dressing and toss to coat.

Serve the salad topped with the soft-boiled eggs and drizzled with the remaining dressing.

NOTE
This salad pairs beautifully with salmon gravlax (see recipe page 322).

Raw cauliflower and lemon tabouli with grilled haloumi

Haloumi is a brined cheese made from a mix of goat's and sheep's milk and cooking it unleashes its salty, cheesy deliciousness. It's high in calcium, which is good for your bones. The versatile cauliflower is a great stand-in for bulgur in recipes – in fact I think it's superior.

SERVES 4

1 (600 g/1 lb 5 oz) cauliflower, trimmed and broken into chunks
250 g (9 oz) cherry tomatoes, halved
½ small red onion, finely diced
4 large handfuls flat-leaf (Italian) parsley, chopped
2 large handfuls mint leaves, chopped
100 ml (3½ fl oz) extra-virgin olive oil
2 unwaxed lemons, zest finely grated and juiced
1 clove garlic, crushed
Himalayan salt and freshly ground black pepper, to taste
180 g (6½ oz) haloumi (sheep and cow milk blend)

Place the cauliflower in a food processor and blend to finely chop into couscous-sized grains.

Combine the cauliflower, tomatoes, onion, parsley and mint in a large bowl and toss together.

Place the oil, lemon zest and juice and garlic in a glass jar and fit with a lid. Shake to combine. Season with salt and pepper.

Pour the dressing over the cauliflower mixture and toss to coat. Set aside for 10 minutes, to allow the liquid and flavours to absorb.

Meanwhile heat a large frying pan over medium heat. Slice the haloumi into eight slices. Grill for 1–2 minutes on each side, until browned.

Serve the haloumi warm with the cauliflower tabouli.

NOTE
Cauliflower tabouli can be stored in an airtight container in the refrigerator for up to 3 days.

Roasted beetroot, red cabbage, pomegranate and herb salad with labneh and lamb koftes

Pomegranate bejewels whatever meal it stars in. It's one of the most antioxidant-rich foods on the planet and, here, cuts through the richness of the lamb beautifully.

SERVES 4

3 beetroot (beets)
4 cups (300 g/10½ oz) finely shredded red cabbage
seeds from ½ pomegranate
3 large handfuls flat-leaf (Italian) parsley, chopped
2 large handfuls mint leaves, chopped
¼ cup (60 ml/2 fl oz) extra-virgin olive oil
2 tablespoons red wine vinegar (unpasteurised)
2 teaspoons maple syrup
¼ teaspoon ground cinnamon
¼ teaspoon ground cumin
Himalayan salt and freshly ground black pepper
¾ cup (180 g/6½ oz) labneh (see recipe page 306)

Koftes
500 g (1 lb 2 oz) lamb mince
½ small red onion, coarsely grated
¼ cup (35 g/1¼ oz) pine nuts
1 small handful mint leaves, finely shredded
1 small handful flat-leaf (Italian) parsley, finely shredded
1 clove garlic, minced
1 teaspoon Himalayan salt
1 teaspoon ground cumin
½ teaspoon ground cinnamon
½ teaspoon ground allspice
¼ teaspoon freshly ground black pepper

Preheat the oven to 200°C (400°F).

Place the beetroot on a small baking tray (baking sheet). Roast for 1 hour, or until tender.

Meanwhile, to make the koftes, place all of the ingredients in a medium bowl. Using clean hands, mix well to combine and bind together. Shape into 12 oval shapes approximately 8 cm (3¼ in) long. Set on a plate, cover and refrigerate, until required.

Place the cabbage, pomegranate seeds, parsley and mint in a medium bowl and toss to combine.

Place the oil, vinegar, maple syrup, cinnamon and cumin in a glass jar and fit with a lid. Shake. Season with salt and pepper.

Dress the salad and toss to coat.

Peel the beetroot (wearing food-handling gloves, if you don't want to stain your hands). Slice into 1 cm (½ in)-thick rounds.

Preheat a large frying pan over medium heat. Cook the koftes for 6–8 minutes, turning occasionally, until browned and just cooked through. Transfer to a plate to rest for a few minutes.

To serve, spread the labneh onto serving plates and arrange beetroot slices on top.

Top with salad and koftes.

Daikon noodle and grilled salmon salad with lime and ginger dressing

The vitamin C from the daikon (white radish), plus the omega-3 and selenium from the salmon, make this lovely recipe a winner when it comes to boosting skin and immune health.

SERVES 4

1 daikon (white radish), peeled and ends trimmed

1 carrot, peeled and ends trimmed

200 g (7 oz) radishes, thinly sliced into rounds

150 g (5½ oz) snow peas (mangetout), stringed and thinly sliced lengthways

2 large handfuls coriander (cilantro) stems and leaves, coarsely chopped, plus extra to garnish

1 large handful Thai basil leaves, torn, plus extra to garnish

1 long red chilli, seeded and thinly sliced

2 teaspoons black sesame seeds, toasted, plus extra to garnish

coconut oil, warmed, for drizzling

4 × 150–200 g (5½ oz–7 oz) salmon fillets

wasabi, to serve (optional)

Lime and ginger dressing

finely grated zest and juice of 2 unwaxed limes

1 tablespoon finely grated ginger

2 tablespoons macadamia oil

1 teaspoon sesame oil

Himalayan salt, to taste

Use a spiraliser to cut the daikon and carrot into noodle-like lengths. Alternatively, using a mandoline, thinly slice into long, thin strips.

Place the daikon, carrot, radish, snow peas, coriander, Thai basil, chilli and sesame seeds in a medium bowl and toss to combine.

To make the lime and ginger dressing, combine the lime zest and juice and ginger in a small bowl. Whisk in the macadamia and sesame oils. Season with salt.

Preheat a large frying pan over medium–high heat.

Drizzle and rub coconut oil over the salmon fillets. Cook the salmon, skin-side down, for 3 minutes, or until the skin is crisp and golden brown and the salmon is cooked approximately one-quarter of the way through. Turn and cook for a further 2–3 minutes, until cooked one-quarter of the way through; the centre should still be pink. Transfer onto a plate or chopping board and rest for 2 minutes.

Pour the dressing over the salad and toss to coat.

Flake the warm salmon into chunks and toss through the salad.

Serve topped with additional herbs, sesame seeds and wasabi, if desired.

Buckwheat noodles with miso-roasted pumpkin, caramelised onion and umeboshi plum salad

One of my favourite salads. Umeboshi plum is an ancient fermented Japanese medicinal food with a dramatic flavour, healing for many imbalances in the body, from coughs to fevers.

SERVES 4

2 tablespoons white (Shiro) miso paste
2 tablespoons coconut oil, melted and cooled
1½ tablespoons sesame seeds
500 g (1 lb 2 oz) pumpkin (winter squash), peeled, seeds removed and cut into 1 cm (½ in)-thick slices
1 brown onion, thinly sliced
2 cloves garlic, finely chopped
200 g (7 oz) packet buckwheat noodles
3 umeboshi plums, pitted and thinly sliced
1 large handful coriander (cilantro) leaves, torn

Dressing
¼ cup (60 ml/2 fl oz) tamari
¼ cup (60 ml/2 fl oz) freshly squeezed lemon juice
2 teaspoons sesame oil

Preheat the oven to 200°C (400°F). Place a large wire rack on a large baking tray (baking sheet).

Blend the miso paste, 1 tablespoon of the coconut oil and 1 tablespoon of the sesame seeds together in a medium bowl. Add the pumpkin and toss to coat.

Arrange the pumpkin slices on the rack. Roast for 15–20 minutes, until softened and caramelised.

Meanwhile heat the remaining oil in a medium frying pan over low heat. Cook the onion and garlic, stirring occasionally, for 15 minutes, or until caramelised. Set aside.

Bring a large saucepan of water to the boil.

Cook the buckwheat noodles, according to the packet instructions, or until al dente. Drain and refresh in iced water. Drain.

To prepare the dressing, place the tamari, lemon juice and sesame oil in a jar and seal with a lid. Shake to combine.

To assemble, place the noodles, roasted pumpkin, caramelised onion, umeboshi plums, coriander and remaining sesame seeds in a large bowl and toss to combine. Pour over the dressing and toss to coat.

Smoked trout and roasted fennel and cauliflower salad

The Romans revered fennel for its medicinal properties and it is still used today as a digestive aid, cleanser and detoxifier. Alongside watercress and parsley, beauty-giving vegetables, rich in skin-boosting vitamin K, manganese, and vitamins A and C, and omega-3 oils from the trout, this dish is both flavoursome and a skin saviour.

SERVES 4

1 (750 g/1 lb 11 oz) cauliflower,
    broken into small florets
olive oil, for drizzling
1 teaspoon cumin seeds
Himalayan salt and freshly ground black pepper
2 fennel bulbs, trimmed and cut into thin wedges
1 smoked trout
½ spiced preserved lemon (see recipe page 319)
3 large handfuls watercress, leaves picked
2 large handfuls flat-leaf (Italian) parsley, coarsely
    chopped

Maple almonds
½ cup (90 g/3 oz) almonds
2 tablespoons maple syrup
pinch of Himalayan salt

Dressing
1 lemon, juiced
1 teaspoon Dijon mustard
½ clove garlic, finely chopped
¼ cup (60 ml/2 fl oz) extra-virgin olive oil
Himalayan salt and freshly ground black pepper,
    to taste

Preheat the oven to 200°C (400°F).

Spread the cauliflower onto a medium baking tray (baking sheet). Drizzle with olive oil, scatter with the cumin seeds and season with salt and pepper. Toss to coat.

Spread the fennel onto a separate medium baking tray. Drizzle with olive oil. Roast the cauliflower and fennel, tossing occasionally, for 20–25 minutes, until tender and golden brown. Remove from the oven and set aside to cool.

Meanwhile to prepare the maple almonds, line a small baking tray with baking paper.

Cook the almonds in a small frying pan over low–medium heat, tossing occasionally, until lightly roasted. Add the maple syrup and salt. Cook, tossing to coat, until the maple syrup has reduced to a thick sticky caramel. Pour onto the prepared tray and set aside to cool.

To prepare the dressing, whisk the lemon juice, mustard and garlic together in a small bowl. Gradually pour in the extra-virgin olive oil, continuously whisking, until fully incorporated. Season with salt and pepper. Set aside.

Remove and discard the trout skin. Flake the trout into bite-sized pieces, ensuring all the bones have been removed. Set aside. Remove and discard the flesh of the preserved lemon. Thinly slice the skin lengthways into strips. Once cooled, coarsely chop the almonds.

Combine the cauliflower, fennel, maple almonds, trout, preserved lemon, watercress and parsley in a large bowl. Toss to combine. Pour over the dressing and toss to coat. Transfer to a large serving dish. Serve immediately.

Spiced fish tacos with slaw, avocado and fermented salsa

Most Mexican restaurants have their own iteration of a fish taco and here is my healthy version with a fermented salsa twist. Tacos are traditionally made from corn or wheat, but these are just as delicious and better for tummy health.

SERVES 4

coconut oil, for cooking
1 large avocado, halved, stone removed
    and flesh coarsely mashed
fermented tomato and coriander salsa
    (see recipe page 320)

Slaw
¼ small green cabbage, shredded
1 carrot, peeled and shredded
150 g (5½ oz) radishes (approx 6–8), shredded
1 large handful coriander (cilantro) leaves
juice of 1 lime
1½ tablespoons olive oil

Spiced fish
500 g (1lb 2 oz) skinless firm white fish fillets,
    such as non-oily mackerel*
2 tablespoons arrowroot
½ teaspoon Himalayan salt
½ teaspoon ground cumin
½ teaspoon sweet paprika
½ teaspoon ground coriander
½ teaspoon onion powder
¼ teaspoon garlic powder
¼ teaspoon cayenne pepper

Hard-shell tacos
1½ cups (180 g/6½ oz) quinoa flour**
½ cup (75 g/2¾ oz) millet flour**
½ teaspoon ground turmeric
½ teaspoon ground cumin
pinch of Himalayan salt
¾ cup (180 ml/6 fl oz) water
2 tablespoons olive oil

* Always opt for sustainable fish – see your fishmonger
    for advice.
** Available from health food stores and specialty grocers.

To prepare the tacos, toast the quinoa flour in a dry frying pan over low–medium heat until hot, golden and nutty. Set aside to cool.

Combine the cooled toasted quinoa flour, millet flour, turmeric, cumin and salt in a medium bowl. Add the water and olive oil and stir to form a slightly sticky dough. Add a little additional water, if required.

Divide the dough into 12 portions and roll into balls. Using a tortilla press or a rolling pin, flatten the balls one at a time between two sheets of baking paper to make thin, approximately 15 cm (6 in)-wide discs.

To cook, heat a small cast-iron or non-stick frying pan over high heat. Place the tortillas, one at a time, onto the pan and lay them down flat with the base sheet of paper still attached. Cook for 1–2 minutes (the paper will easily peel off after about 20 seconds), until the surface begins to bubble. Flip and cook for a further 1 minute, or until cooked through with golden brown spots. Immediately lay each hot taco over a rolling pin suspended over two pans or bowls, and gently bend into a U shape. Hold briefly in place. Leave to cool and firm up to hold their shape, then remove and set aside.

To prepare the slaw, combine the cabbage, carrot, radishes and coriander in a medium bowl. Add the lime juice and olive oil and toss to coat.

To prepare the fish, cut the fillets into 10 cm (4 in) strips. Combine the arrowroot, salt and spices in a medium bowl. Add the fish and toss to coat. Heat a large frying pan over medium heat. Drizzle in a little coconut oil. Cook the fish for 2 minutes on each side, or until just cooked through.

To assemble, spoon some of the avocado down the middle of the tacos. Top with slaw, spiced fish and some of the fermented tomato and coriander salsa.

Peruvian-style ceviche

Ceviche is light, fresh and easy to digest. It's very important that the fish you use is super fresh. The humble chickpea pairs so well with this dish and rounds out the flavour as well as being a source of soluble fibre, heart-protective plant compounds and high in collagen and bone-boosting manganese.

SERVES 4

400 g (14 oz) can chickpeas, drained and rinsed
olive oil, to drizzle
Himalayan salt and freshly ground black pepper
2 small sweet potatoes

Ceviche
400 g (14 oz) very fresh, skinless firm white fish*
1 small red onion, thinly sliced
juice of 3 limes, plus extra, to drizzle (optional)
½ teaspoon Himalayan salt
1 long red chilli, thinly sliced
1 small handful coriander (cilantro) leaves, finely
    chopped
1 small handful micro herbs
freshly ground black pepper

Preheat the oven to 200°C (400°F).

Spread the chickpeas out on a small baking tray (baking sheet). Drizzle with oil and season with salt and pepper. Bake for 15 minutes, or until crisp and golden brown.

Peel the sweet potatoes and slice into 2 cm (¾ in)-thick rounds. Steam for 5–7 minutes, until tender.

To prepare the ceviche, using a very sharp knife, thinly slice the fish. Place in a medium bowl. Add the onion.

Combine the lime juice and salt in a small bowl. Stir to dissolve the salt. Pour over the fish and onion and stir to coat. Set aside for 10 minutes.

Add the chilli to the fish and toss to coat.

Drain the fish, reserving the juice.

To serve, arrange the sweet potatoes and fish on a large serving plate or four individual plates. Drizzle with oil and a little additional lime juice if desired. Scatter with the crispy chickpeas, herbs and freshly ground black pepper.

*   Always opt for sustainable fish – see your fishmonger
    for advice.

Mussel toast with roast garlic aioli and herbs

Mussels are full of flavour and pair well with tomato or coconut milk or are simply delicious on toast. For me, it's important that mussels are from clean waters, as they are the filters of the ocean. Mussels contain five essential health-giving nutrients that many of us are deficient in: B12, iodine, iron, selenium and omega-3 fatty acids.

SERVES 2

buckwheat and seeded bread (see recipe page 330)

Mussels
750 g (1 lb 11 oz) mussels in their shells
1½ tablespoons olive oil
2 purple shallots, thinly sliced into rounds
2 cloves garlic, sliced
1 long red chilli, thinly sliced diagonally, seeds in
2 tablespoons apple cider vinegar (unpasteurised)
½ cup (125 ml/4 fl oz) fish stock
1 large handful flat-leaf (Italian) parsley, coarsely chopped
1 large handful basil leaves, coarsely chopped
1 small handful dill, coarsely chopped
freshly ground black pepper

Roast garlic aioli
1 bulb garlic
¾ cup (180 ml/6 fl oz) light-flavoured extra-virgin olive oil, plus extra for drizzling
2 large egg yolks
1 tablespoon white wine vinegar
1 teaspoon Dijon mustard
Himalayan salt and ground white pepper, to taste

NOTE
Aioli can be stored in an airtight container for up to 5 days in the refrigerator.

Preheat the oven to 200°C (400°F).

To prepare the roast garlic aioli, slice the tip off the garlic bulb to expose the cloves. Drizzle with a little of the extra-virgin olive oil and wrap in foil. Place on a small baking tray (baking sheet) and roast in the oven for 30 minutes, or until soft. Set aside, until cool enough to handle.

Squeeze the garlic from the skins into a medium bowl. Set aside to cool completely.

Place the roasted garlic, egg yolks, vinegar and mustard in a small food processor and blend to combine. With the motor running, gradually pour in the remaining oil, in a thin, steady stream, until fully incorporated and thick and creamy. Season with salt and pepper. Transfer to a small serving bowl and set aside.

To prepare the mussels, use the blunt side of a knife and your fingers to grasp the mussel beards. Quickly pull downwards to remove. Discard any mussels that are broken or don't close in response to being bearded or tapped on the kitchen bench. Scrub the outside of the shells clean, if necessary.

Heat the olive oil in a large saucepan over low–medium heat. Cook the shallots, garlic and chilli until softened. Add the mussels, increase the heat to medium–high and stir to coat. Add the vinegar and stock. Cover and steam for 5–10 minutes, until the mussels open.

Remove the mussels from their shells. Discard the shells and any mussels that have not opened. Return the mussels to the pan with the cooking juices. Add the herbs and stir to combine.

To serve, slice and toast 4 slices of bread. Spread with roast garlic aioli. Top with mussels and freshly ground black pepper.

Korean bibimbap

Korean food has long been a favourite of mine, it's fresh and healthy and I also love kimchi. Bibimbap is my favourite go-to Asian dish. Bibimbap means mixed rice, but I like making it with a mixture of gluten-free grains, seeds and/or cauliflower rice.

SERVES 2

1½ cups (300 g/10½ oz) quinoa, rinsed
3 cups (750 ml/25½ fl oz) water
2 large eggs
tamari, to serve
1 cup (200 g/7 oz) kimchi, to serve (optional, see recipe page 315)

Beef
150 g (5½ oz) beef mince (ground beef)
1 tablespoon coconut oil
1 tablespoon tamari
1 teaspoon sesame oil
1 teaspoon maple syrup
1 clove garlic, finely chopped

Chilli sauce
3 tablespoons Korean chilli powder (kochukaru/gochugaru)*
1½ tablespoons tamari
1 tablespoon maple syrup
1 tablespoon apple cider vinegar (unpasteurised)
2 cloves garlic, finely chopped

Toppings
½ small carrot, peeled and cut into thin strips
4 shiitake mushrooms, thinly sliced
1 spring onion (scallion), halved or quartered lengthways, depending on thickness, then cut into 5 cm (2 in) batons
3 large handfuls baby spinach
2 small handfuls bean sprouts
sesame oil, to taste
Himalayan salt, to taste
1 teaspoon white sesame seeds

To prepare the beef, combine all of the ingredients in a medium bowl and mix well to combine. Cover and set aside for 15 minutes to marinate.

Place the quinoa and water in a medium saucepan and bring to the boil. Decrease the heat to low and gently simmer, uncovered, for 10 minutes, or until almost all of the water has been absorbed and holes appear on the surface. Cover and remove from the heat to finish cooking for a further 5 minutes, or until tails have sprouted and all of the water has been absorbed. Keep warm.

To prepare the chilli sauce, combine all of the ingredients in a small bowl. Set aside.

To cook the beef mince, heat a medium frying pan over low heat. Cook the marinated beef, stirring with a wooden spoon to break up any lumps, for 4–5 minutes, or until browned. Cover and set aside to keep warm.

To prepare the toppings, cook each ingredient separately in a small frying pan with a dash of water over low–medium heat, until just softened. Drizzle all with a little sesame oil and season with salt. Add sesame seeds to the spinach. Transfer each topping into separate small bowls.

Fry the eggs until cooked to your liking.

To assemble, serve the quinoa in deep bowls. Arrange the toppings in clusters around the edge. Spoon the beef in the centre and top with an egg. Serve with chilli sauce, tamari and kimchi, if desired.

* Available from Asian grocers.

Pickled papaya and chilli chicken salad

Papaya is rich in an enzyme called papain, which is healing, detoxifying and helps our bodies digest proteins and fats. It's brilliant with protein as it helps us digest whatever we consume it with. This dish is delectable and the chilli in the chicken mixture helps to stimulate digestive fire.

SERVES 4

⅓ cup (55 g/2 oz) macadamia, lightly roasted, coarsely chopped

Pickled papaya salad
1 kg (2 lb 3 oz) green papaya
2 tablespoons Himalayan salt
1 carrot, peeled and thinly shredded into 7 cm (2¾ in) strips
½ red capsicum (bell pepper), thinly sliced into 7 cm (2¾ in) strips
1 small white onion, thinly sliced
4 cloves garlic, thinly shredded
3 cm (1¼ in) knob of ginger, peeled and thinly shredded
1 large handful mint leaves, shredded
1 large handful Vietnamese mint leaves, shredded

Pickling liquid
1 cup (250 ml/8½ fl oz) apple cider vinegar (unpasteurised)
⅓ cup (80 ml/2½ fl oz) raw honey
1 tablespoon black peppercorns
½ teaspoon Himalayan salt

Chilli chicken
¼ cup (40 g/1½ oz) macadamias, lightly roasted
2 long red chillies, coarsely chopped
1 clove garlic, coarsely chopped
juice of 1 lime
2 tablespoons raw honey
1 tablespoon coconut oil
2 teaspoons tamari
2 organic skinless chicken breast

NOTE
Start this recipe 1–2 days before you plan to eat it.

To prepare the pickled papaya salad, peel the papaya and scoop out the seeds. Using a mandoline, thinly shred the papaya into approximately 7 cm (2¾ in)-long strips. Place the strips in a large bowl. Scatter with the salt and toss to coat. Cover and refrigerate overnight. Rinse the papaya thoroughly under cold water. Set aside to drain.

For the pickling liquid, place all the ingredients in a small saucepan and set over low–medium heat. Bring to a simmer, stirring to dissolve the honey. Set aside to cool.

Combine the papaya, carrot, capsicum, onion, garlic and ginger in a large bowl. Pour over the cooled pickling liquid. Massage the liquid into the vegetables to soften slightly. Press down the papaya mixture to completely cover with liquid. Cover with a plate and weigh down if necessary. Refrigerate for at least 8 hours, or overnight.

Meanwhile to prepare the chilli chicken, place the macadamias, chillies and garlic in a small food processor and blend to finely chop. Transfer into a large bowl, add the lime juice, honey, coconut oil and tamari and mix to combine. Add the chicken and coat in the marinade. Cover and refrigerate for at least 4 hours or overnight.

Preheat the oven to 180°C (350°F). Line a small baking tray (baking sheet) with baking paper. Place the marinated chicken on the prepared tray. Bake, basting occasionally with juices, for 20–25 minutes, until just cooked through. Set aside to cool slightly.

To serve, shred the cooled chicken into strips. Strain the papaya salad and return to the bowl. Add the chicken, mint and Vietnamese mint leaves and macadamias to the bowl and toss to combine.

Lunch wraps with poached chicken and celeriac and roasted almond remoulade

These gluten-free wraps work well with any number of fillings, but this nutrient-charged combination, topped with remoulade, is one of my favourites.

SERVES 4

1 organic skinless chicken breast
4 millet and linseed and spinach wraps (see recipe page 326)
2 large handfuls snow pea (mangetout) sprouts
4 medium radishes, coarsely grated

Celeriac and roasted almond remoulade
300 g (10½ oz) celeriac, peeled and coarsely grated
⅓ cup (80 g/2¾ oz) mayonnaise (see recipe below)
2 tablespoons freshly squeezed lemon juice
1 tablespoon extra-virgin olive oil
¼ cup (45 g/1½ oz) roasted almonds, coarsely chopped
Himalayan salt and freshly ground black pepper

Mayonnaise (Makes 1 cup, 250 g/9 oz)
2 large egg yolks
1 tablespoon white wine vinegar
1 teaspoon Dijon mustard
¾ cup (180 ml/6 fl oz) light-flavoured extra-virgin olive oil, plus extra for drizzling
Himalayan salt and ground white pepper, to taste

To prepare the mayonnaise, place the egg yolks, vinegar and mustard in a small food processor and blend to combine. With the motor running, gradually pour in the oil in a thin, steady stream, until fully incorporated and thick and creamy. Season with salt and pepper. Transfer into a small serving bowl and set aside.

To poach the chicken, bring a small saucepan of water to a simmer. Add the chicken breast and gently simmer for 6 minutes. Turn off the heat and leave the chicken in the water for 15 minutes, to finish cooking. Once cool enough to handle, shred the chicken into strips and set aside.

To prepare the celeriac and roasted almond remoulade, combine the celeriac, mayonnaise, lemon juice and oil in a medium bowl and mix well. Add the shredded chicken and roasted almonds and stir to combine. Season with salt and pepper.

To assemble, spread the remoulade down the centre line of the wraps. Top with snow pea sprouts and radish. Fold the sides in and roll up to enclose.

NOTE

Try other filling ideas such as smoked or seared salmon, gravlax (see page 322), hard-boiled eggs, cooled thin omelettes, cultured nut 'cheese' (see recipe page 308), dips (see recipes page 126–127), avocado, grated carrot and beetroot (beet), sprouts such as alfalfa, coleslaw, baby cos (romaine), baby spinach, rocket (arugula) and other lettuce mixes.

Leftover mayonnaise can be stored in an airtight container in the refrigerator for up to 5 days.

Southern-style baked chicken pieces

These scrumptious, finger-licking-good chicken pieces show you that you can incorporate fried chicken as part of a healthy diet! There are seldom, if ever, leftovers of these in our house, but when there are, they make a great cold lunch. Perfect served with creamy coleslaw.

SERVES 4

400 ml (13½ fl oz/1⅔ cups) can coconut milk
½ brown onion, coarsely grated
12 chicken pieces – drumsticks, thighs and wings, skin on
coconut oil, for frying

Spice coating
½ cup (60 g/2 oz) arrowroot
¼ cup (30 g/1 oz) coconut flour
1½ teaspoons onion powder
1½ teaspoons garlic powder
1½ teaspoons sweet paprika
1½ teaspoons ground cumin
½ teaspoon Himalayan salt
¼ teaspoon freshly ground black pepper

Lime mayonnaise
2 large egg yolks
finely grated zest and juice of 1 unwaxed lime
1 teaspoon Dijon mustard
1 cup (250 ml/8½ fl oz) light-flavoured extra-virgin olive oil
Himalayan salt and ground white pepper, to taste

Begin this recipe at least 4 hours ahead of time.

Preheat the oven to 200°C (400°F).

Combine the coconut milk and onion in a large zip-lock bag. Add the chicken to the coconut milk mixture and seal the bag. Lay flat on a tray and refrigerate, turning once, for at least 4 hours or up to overnight.

To prepare the spice coating, combine all of the ingredients in a large zip-lock bag.

Drain the chicken and place it, a few pieces at a time, in the coating mix and shake to coat. Place on a tray while you coat the remaining pieces. Refrigerate, uncovered, for 30 minutes to dry out slightly.

Pour enough coconut oil in a large heavy-based frying pan to a depth of 2 cm (¾ in). Heat over medium–high heat.

Cook the chicken pieces in batches for 5–7 minutes, turning occasionally, until golden all over. Take care as the chicken can cause the oil to spit. Transfer onto a baking tray (baking sheet) lined with kitchen paper, to drain.

Discard the paper and spread the chicken out onto the tray.

Bake the chicken for 25–30 minutes, until crisp, golden brown and cooked through.

Meanwhile to prepare the mayonnaise, place the egg yolks, lime zest and juice and mustard in a small food processor. Blend to combine. With the motor running, gradually pour in the oil, in a thin, steady stream, until fully incorporated and thick and creamy. Season with salt and pepper. Transfer into a small serving bowl.

Serve the chicken with lime mayonnaise for dipping.

Lamb and liquorice root soup with parsnip dumplings

I'm a bit of a soup and dumpling devotee and this recipe ticks all the boxes of being warming, nourishing and nutrient-charged, with liquorice root great for balancing digestive health and supporting adrenals. The flavours of the lamb and liquorice also work beautifully together.

SERVES 4

2 tablespoons coconut oil

3 lamb shanks

1 large onion, roughly diced

1 medium carrot, peeled and roughly diced

1 leek, white part only, roughly diced

2 sticks celery, roughly diced

4 cm (1½ in) knob of ginger, peeled and finely grated

3 cloves garlic, finely chopped

1 teaspoon liquorice root powder*

1 teaspoon ground cinnamon

1 teaspoon ground cumin

½ teaspoon ground turmeric

400 g (14 oz) can chopped tomatoes

8 cups (2 litres/68 fl oz) chicken bone broth (see recipe page 300) or store-bought stock

juice of ½ lemon

1 large handful coriander (cilantro) leaves, coarsely chopped

1 large handful flat-leaf (Italian) parsley, coarsely chopped

1 large handful mint leaves, coarsely chopped

Himalayan salt and freshly ground black pepper

Parsnip dumplings

1 parsnip, peeled and cut into 3 cm (1¼ in) pieces

1 tablespoon olive oil

½ cup (50 g/1¾ oz) almond meal

1½ tablespoons arrowroot

¼ teaspoon gluten-free baking powder

¼ teaspoon bicarbonate of soda (baking soda)

¼ teaspoon Himalayan salt

1 large egg white

To prepare the soup, heat the coconut oil in a large heavy-based saucepan over high heat. Cook the lamb shanks, turning occasionally, for 5 minutes, or until browned all over. Transfer onto a plate and set aside.

Decrease the heat to low–medium. Cook the onion, carrot, leek, celery, ginger and garlic, stirring occasionally, for 10–15 minutes, until golden brown. Add the liquorice root powder and spices and cook until fragrant. Return the shanks to the pan. Add the tomato, pour in the broth and bring to the boil. Decrease the heat to a simmer. Cover and cook for 2–2½ hours, until the meat is falling off the bone.

Preheat the oven to 200°C (400°C). Grease a large baking tray (baking sheet) and line with baking paper.

To prepare the parsnip dumplings, steam the parsnip for 15 minutes, or until tender. Mash the parsnip and oil together in a medium bowl. Add the almond meal, arrowroot, baking powder, bicarbonate of soda and salt and stir to combine.

Whisk the egg white in a medium bowl, until soft peaks form. Stir through the parsnip mixture. Using wet hands, roughly shape into 8 even-sized balls. Place on the prepared tray. Bake for 20 minutes, or until golden brown and dumplings spring back when pressed. Set aside.

When the meat is almost falling off the bone remove the shanks from the soup and set aside until cool enough to handle. Pull the meat off the bones. Coarsely shred, discarding any fat and sinew. Return the meat to the soup and heat through. Add the lemon juice and herbs and stir to combine. Season with salt and pepper. Ladle into serving bowls and top with the dumplings.

* Available from Asian grocers.

Jerusalem artichoke salad
with seared tuna and ponzu sauce

*Tuna is rich in zinc and selenium, both wonderful skin rejuvenators, and Jerusalem artichoke
is a very effective prebiotic food, paired here with piquant ponzu: lovely!*

SERVES 4

400 g (14 oz) tuna loin*
Himalayan salt and freshly ground black pepper
2 tablespoons white sesame seeds
2 tablespoons black sesame seeds
1 tablespoon coconut oil

Jerusalem artichoke salad
juice of ½ lemon
450 g (1 lb) Jerusalem artichokes (approx 6–8), peeled
2 carrots, peeled and halved crossways
2 large handfuls sunflower seed sprouts
½ bunch chives, cut into 5 cm (2 in) lengths

Ponzu sauce
¼ cup (60 ml/2 fl oz) instant dashi stock (premade)
¼ cup (60 ml/2 fl oz) tamari
2 tablespoons freshly squeezed lemon juice
2 tablespoons freshly squeezed lime juice
1½ tablespoons mirin

Chilli mayo
2 tablespoons chilli sauce (see recipe page 320)
¼ cup (60 ml/2 fl oz) whole-egg mayonnaise

To make the ponzu sauce, whisk all of the ingredients together in a small bowl. Set aside.

To make the chilli mayo, mix the chilli sauce and mayonnaise together in a small bowl. Set aside.

To prepare the Jerusalem artichoke salad, fill a medium bowl with cold water and add the lemon juice. Using a mandoline, thinly slice the artichokes and place in the lemon water, to prevent discolouration.

Thinly slice the carrots and place in another medium bowl. Add the sprouts and chives. Toss to combine.

Cut the tuna into four 100 g (3½ oz) rectangular batons. Season with salt and pepper. Spread the white and black sesame seeds onto a large plate. Roll the tuna in sesame seeds to coat.

Heat a medium frying pan over medium–high heat, until hot. Add the coconut oil and tilt the pan to coat. Sear the tuna for 10–15 seconds, on each side, until the outside edge is evenly cooked, leaving the centre pink.

Rest on a chopping board for 2 minutes, then cut into 1.5 cm (½ in)-thick slices.

Drain the Jerusalem artichoke slices and add to the remaining salad ingredients. Pour half of the ponzu sauce over the salad and toss to coat.

Serve the salad and tuna slices drizzled with additional ponzu sauce and chilli mayo.

NOTE
Ponzu sauce can be made in advance and stored in an airtight container in the refrigerator for up to 1 month.

* I recommend eating tuna only occasionally, due to its potentially high mercury levels.

Snacks

······

Snacking is where we often stumble in our pursuit of a healthy skin and body. Mid-morning or afternoon slumps in energy can clamour for high-energy snacks full of simple sugars. Rather than reaching for such high-carb snacks, opt instead for those high in nutrients, protein, good fats and slow release, complex carbohydrates – these will give you sustained energy throughout the morning or afternoon. In addition, nutrient-dense snacks help to combat cravings for unhealthier foods.

Healthy snacks, such as seeded crispbreads topped with sardines and avocado, apple slices with nut butter, healthy dips with carrot and celery sticks, kale or sweet potato chips (crisps), smoothies and nutrient-dense pâtés, all help keep our blood sugar levels balanced and our skin nourished from within.

Can you have healthy sweet snacks? Yes! Although, if your snack contains an added natural sweetener (even the good ones), they are best eaten in moderation. When I eat a piece of chocolate I always try and eat it with nuts to help balance spikes in blood sugar, plus it is such a delicious combination. When opting for sweeter healthy snacks, ensure they contain plenty of protein as well, which will help balance blood sugar levels.

You can snack on all the recipes in this book: soups also make great snacks, and leftovers from lunch or dinner the day before can make for scrumptious pickings.

Spiced and seeded crispbreads

The seeds in these moreish crispbreads are rich in minerals including copper and manganese, essential for collagen production, and iron that helps maintain healthy hair and keep nails lovely and strong. Top with tomato, as vitamin C aids iron absorption.

MAKES 16 LARGE CRACKERS

¼ cup (40 g/1½ oz) chia seeds
1½ tablespoons ground flax seeds (linseeds)
¾ cup (180 ml/6 fl oz) water
1½ teaspoons coriander seeds
1 teaspoon cumin seeds
1 teaspoon fennel seeds
1 teaspoon chilli flakes
⅓ cup (50 g/1¾ oz) pumpkin seeds (pepitas)
¼ cup (35 g/1¼ oz) sesame seeds
¼ cup (35 g/1¼ oz) sunflower seeds
¼ cup (50 g/1¾ oz) unhulled millet*
¼ cup (40 g/1½ oz) flax seeds
1 teaspoon Himalayan salt
½ teaspoon freshly ground black pepper

Preheat the oven to 120°C (250°F).

Place the chia and ground flax seeds in a medium bowl. Add the water and stir to combine. Set aside for 10 minutes, to hydrate and swell to a thick gel.

Preheat a small frying pan over low–medium heat. Toast the coriander, cumin and fennel seeds and chilli flakes for 20 seconds, or until fragrant. Remove from the heat. Crush using a mortar and pestle or spice grinder, until coarsely ground.

Add the spice mix, pumpkin, sesame, sunflower, millet, flax seeds, salt and pepper to the chia and ground linseed mixture. Mix well.

Roll the seed mixture out between two pieces of baking paper, to make a 40 × 25 cm (15 × 10 in) rectangle, approximately 2 mm (1/16 in) thick. Discard the top sheet of paper.

Using a large knife, score the seed mixture to make 16 large crackers. Transfer the whole sheet of baking paper onto a large baking tray (cookie sheet).

Bake for 1¾–2 hours, or until crisp and completely dried out. Alternatively, the crackers can be dried out using a dehydrator at 60°C (140°F), but the time will need to be increased to approximately 4 hours.

Remove from the oven or dehydrator and cut through the scored lines to make individual crackers. Leave to cool completely.

Serve topped with nut spreads, avocado, tomato, sardines, sliced boiled egg or any other of your favourites for breakfast, lunch or as a snack.

NOTE
The crackers can be stored in an airtight container for up to 1 month.

* Available from health food stores.

Mushroom and walnut pâté

This nourishing and delicious pâté is a great beauty booster: rich in skin-hydrating omega-3s from the walnuts, hair-boosting iron from the lentils, immune-boosting beta-glucans and vitamin D, as well as niacin (vitamin B3) from the mushrooms, which helps maintain good circulation and keeps the skin soft, healthy and glowing.

MAKES 2 CUPS (SERVES 6–8)

2 cups (500 ml/17 fl oz) vegetable broth (see recipe page 302)
1 bay leaf
½ cup (110 g/4 oz) Puy lentils, soaked in cold water overnight, drained and rinsed
¼ cup (60 g/2 oz) ghee
1 small onion, coarsely chopped
2 cloves garlic, finely chopped
200 g (7 oz) button mushrooms, sliced
1 teaspoon finely chopped thyme leaves
½ cup (60 g/2 oz) walnuts, lightly roasted
1 small handful flat-leaf (Italian) parsley, coarsely chopped
1½ tablespoons red wine vinegar (unpasteurised)
1 tablespoon tamari
Himalayan salt and freshly ground black pepper
fresh herbs, to garnish

Place the vegetable broth and bay leaf in a medium saucepan and bring to the boil. Add the lentils, cover and simmer for 30–35 minutes, until tender but still retaining their shape and all of the liquid has been absorbed. Cover and set aside.

Heat 2 tablespoons of the ghee in a large frying pan over low–medium heat. Cook the onion until golden brown. Add the garlic and cook until softened. Add the mushrooms and thyme and cook for 10–15 minutes, until softened and golden brown.

Remove from the heat. Add the lentils, walnuts, parsley, vinegar, tamari and remaining ghee and stir to combine. Set aside to cool slightly.

Transfer the mixture into a food processor or high-speed blender. Blend until smooth. Season with salt and pepper.

Spoon the pâté into a 2 cup (500 ml/17 fl oz)-capacity plastic wrap–lined mould. Press down and smooth out to make sure there are no air bubbles. Alternatively you can spoon it into one medium or two small serving bowls. Cover the surface with plastic wrap. Cover and refrigerate for 1 hour, to firm up slightly.

To serve, if using a mould turn the pâté out onto a serving plate. Garnish with herbs.

Serve with crackers or crudités to accompany.

Jewish-style chicken liver pâté

*One of my favourite snacks and probably one of the most nutrient-dense foods of all,
liver contains a plethora of nutrients including biotin, a lack of which can cause brittle hair
and dry skin. Eating liver also gives your own liver the nutrients it needs to detoxify properly.*

MAKES 3 CUPS (SERVES 6–8)

4 large eggs
¼ cup (60 g/2 oz) ghee
500 g (1 lb 2 oz) organic chicken livers
1 small onion, finely chopped
½ clove garlic, finely chopped
1 teaspoon red wine vinegar (unpasteurised)
pinch of ground nutmeg
Himalayan salt and freshly ground black pepper
1 tablespoon coarsely chopped flat-leaf (Italian)
  parsley

Place the eggs in a medium saucepan. Cover with
cold water and bring to a simmer over medium heat.
Simmer for 8 minutes. Remove the eggs and plunge
into a bowl of iced water to chill.

Heat 2 tablespoons of the ghee in a large frying pan
over medium–high heat. Sauté the chicken livers for
2 minutes on each side, or until almost completely
cooked through and only slightly pink inside.
Remove from the pan and set aside on a plate to cool.

Add the remaining ghee to the pan. Decrease the
heat to medium and cook the onion until golden.
Add the garlic and cook until softened and the onion
is dark golden brown. Set aside to cool.

Peel the eggs. Coarsely chop three of the eggs and
set the remaining egg aside.

Place the chicken livers, coarsely chopped eggs,
red wine vinegar and nutmeg in a food processor and
blend to finely chop. Add the onion mixture and any
ghee remaining from the pan and blend until smooth
with flecks of onion. Season with salt and pepper.

Spoon the mixture into a 2 cup (500 ml/17 fl oz)-
capacity plastic wrap–lined mould. Press down and
smooth out to make sure there are no air bubbles.
Alternatively you can spoon it into one medium
or two small serving bowls. Cover the surface with
plastic wrap, to prevent discolouration. Refrigerate
for 12 hours, or overnight to firm up.

To serve, if using a mould turn the pâté out onto
a serving plate. Chop or coarsely grate the remaining
egg. Scatter the egg and parsley over the pâté to
garnish. Top with freshly ground black pepper.

Serve with crackers, gherkins, pickled vegetables,
sauerkraut and crudités.

'Cheesy' almond, olive and rosemary crackers

CLOCKWISE FROM LEFT: Raw beetroot and sprouted chickpea hummus | Minty broad bean, pea and yoghurt dip | Roasted pumpkin, chilli and tahini dip

'Cheesy' almond, olive and rosemary crackers

MAKES 24

The combination of olive, rosemary and cheese is a delight. However, in this dish I have used yeast flakes instead of cheese, which are rich in B vitamins and a great substitute for the flavour of cheese.

1 cup (100 g/3½ oz) almond meal
⅓ cup (15 g/½ oz) savoury yeast flakes*
¼ cup (45 g/1½ oz) chopped pitted Kalamata olives
1 tablespoon finely chopped rosemary leaves
½ teaspoon Himalayan salt, plus extra for sprinkling
¼ teaspoon freshly ground black pepper
1 large egg white
1 tablespoon coconut oil, melted

Preheat the oven to 150°C (300°F). Combine the almond meal, savoury yeast flakes, olives, rosemary, salt and pepper in a medium bowl. Add the egg white and oil and mix well to combine.

Roll the almond mixture out between two pieces of baking paper, to make a 24 cm (9½ in) square, approximately 2 mm (1/16 in) thick. Discard the top sheet of paper. Using a large knife, score the almond mixture to make 24 crackers. Press the ends of a fork into the centre of each cracker to mark. Transfer the crackers on the sheet of baking paper onto a large baking tray (cookie sheet). Sprinkle with additional salt. Bake for 10–15 minutes, until light golden.

Remove from the oven and cut through the scored marks. Separate into individual crackers. Remove the outer crackers that are crisp and golden and set onto a rack to cool. Cook the remaining crackers for a further 5 minutes, or until golden but not browned. Transfer onto the rack and leave to cool completely.

Serve with dips, spreads, or as part of a meal.

* Available from health food stores.

Raw beetroot and sprouted chickpea hummus

MAKES 1½ CUPS (SERVES 4)

Beetroot (beet) is a unique source of betaine, which helps protect the liver and support fat metabolism – making it an excellent food for detoxification, as well as helping good fats get to the skin.

⅓ cup (65 g/2¼ oz) dried chickpeas
1 medium beetroot (beet), peeled and cut into small chunks
1 clove garlic
2 teaspoons finely chopped fresh rosemary leaves
1 teaspoon ground cumin
juice of ½ lemon
2 tablespoons tahini
2 tablespoons extra-virgin olive oil
Himalayan salt and black pepper, to taste

Start this recipe at least 3 days ahead of time.

Soak the chickpeas in cold water for 8–12 hours, or overnight. Drain and rinse. Discard any discoloured chickpeas.

To sprout the chickpeas, place them in a sieve set over a bowl. Cover with a clean tea towel (dish towel) and set aside at room temperature. Rinse the chickpeas under cold running water morning and night, so they don't dry out. Tail-like sprouts will appear in 1–2 days, depending on the temperature of your kitchen. Grow sprouts to 1 cm (½ in)-length. Alternatively you can use a sprouting jar.

Blend the sprouted chickpeas, beetroot, garlic, rosemary and cumin together in a high-speed blender, to finely chop. Add the lemon juice, tahini and oil and blend to a smooth consistency. Season with salt and pepper.

Serve with crudités, crackers or as part of a meal.

Roasted pumpkin, chilli and tahini dip

MAKES 1½ CUPS (SERVES 4)

A flavour-packed dip, starring pumpkin (winter squash), which is a great source of skin-rejuvenating vitamin A. And did you know that when you consume foods high in vitamin E – such as tahini (made from sesame seeds) – around seven days later vitamin E is secreted through your sebum to provide a protective layer?

350 g (12½ oz) peeled pumpkin (winter squash), cut into 5 cm (2 in) chunks
1 medium tomato, halved
2 tablespoons extra-virgin olive oil, plus extra for drizzling
4 cloves garlic, in their skins
2 long red chillies
2 tablespoons tahini
juice of ½ lemon
1½ teaspoons ground cumin
Himalayan salt, to taste

Preheat the oven to 200°C (400°F).

Place the pumpkin and tomato on a baking tray (baking sheet). Drizzle with olive oil and roast for 30 minutes.

Turn the pumpkin, add the garlic and chilli and roast for a further 15 minutes, or until the garlic and chilli are soft and the pumpkin is tender and caramelised. Set aside to cool slightly.

Squeeze the garlic out of its skin. Peel the tomato and chillies. Scrape the seeds out of the chillies and discard.

Place the pumpkin, tomato, 2 tablespoons extra-virgin olive oil, garlic and chilli in a high-speed food processor. Add the remaining ingredients and blend until smooth. Season with salt.

Serve with crudités, crackers or as part of a meal.

Minty broad bean, pea and yoghurt dip

MAKES 1½ CUPS (SERVES 4)

This fresh green dip is the perfect spring snack and digestive booster. It is rich in soluble fibre, and peas and beans are also a great source of silica and potassium, which keep the skin supple and hydrated, as well as thiamine and Lactobacillus *in the yoghurt, which both help with skin breakouts.*

2 cups (300 g/10½ oz) fresh and podded or frozen broad (fava) beans
¾ cup (100 g/4 oz) fresh or frozen peas
1 large handful fresh mint leaves
1 clove garlic, finely chopped
finely grated zest of 1 unwaxed lemon
¼ cup (60 g/2 oz) natural yoghurt
¼ cup (60 ml/2 fl oz) freshly squeezed lemon juice
1 tablespoon extra-virgin olive oil
Himalayan salt and freshly ground black pepper, to taste

Bring a medium saucepan of water to the boil.

Blanch the broad beans and peas for 20 seconds. Strain. Refresh in iced water, to chill. Drain.

Peel the grey tough outer skin off broad beans to expose the bright green inside bean.

Combine the peeled broad beans, peas, mint, garlic and lemon zest in a food processor. Blend to coarsely chop. Add the yoghurt, lemon juice and oil and blend to combine, to a textured consistency. Season with salt and pepper.

Serve with crudités, crackers or as part of a meal.

NOTE
These dips can be stored in an airtight container in the refrigerator for up to 5 days.

Roasted kale, beetroot, almond and seed chips

Who would have thought you could say 'nutrient dense' and 'chips' (crisps) in the same sentence? These scrumptious, addictive chips don't last long in our house and make great additions to lunchboxes. They are spiced with cumin, a wonderful digestive aid and skin cleanser.

SERVES 4

1 bunch (approx 250 g/9 oz) curly kale

¼ cup (60 ml/2 fl oz) coconut oil, melted

2 tablespoons freshly squeezed lemon juice

2 medium beetroots (beets), peeled and coarsely chopped

½ cup (50 g/1¾ oz) almond meal

2 tablespoons pumpkin seeds (pepitas)

2 tablespoons sunflower seeds

1 tablespoon sesame seeds

3 teaspoons sweet smoked paprika

2 teaspoons onion powder

1 teaspoon garlic powder

1 teaspoon ground cumin

2 teaspoons Himalayan salt

Preheat the oven to 70°C (160°F).

Strip the kale leaves off the ribs then tear the leaves into 10 cm (4 in) lengths. Place in a medium bowl. Drizzle with coconut oil and lemon juice and rub to coat.

Place the beetroot in a high-speed food processor and blend to coarsely chop. Add the almond meal, pumpkin and sunflower seeds and process until finely ground and combined.

Scatter the beetroot and almond mixture, sesame seeds, spices and salt over the kale. Rub and clump together, to coat and stick.

Spread out onto two large baking trays (baking sheets). Bake, turning occasionally, for 2½–3 hours, until dried out and crisp. Set aside to cool.

Eat immediately or store in an airtight container for up to 3 days.

Sweet potato and beetroot chips with matcha, lime and chilli salt

These zesty chips (crisps) are rich in vitamins A and C, which are essential for skin cell regeneration and maintaining a healthy skin barrier.

SERVES 4

1 sweet potato, washed and dried
1 large beetroot (beet), trimmed, washed and dried
1½ tablespoons coconut oil, warmed, plus extra
    for greasing

Matcha, lime and chilli salt
finely grated zest of 1 lime
½ teaspoon Himalayan salt
¼ teaspoon matcha green tea powder
pinch of chilli flakes

Preheat the oven to 160°C (320°F).

Lightly grease two large baking trays (baking sheets) with coconut oil.

Using a mandoline, thinly slice the sweet potato into rounds and place in a medium bowl. Drizzle with half of the oil and rub to coat. Thinly slice the beetroot in the same manner and place in a separate bowl. Drizzle and coat in the remaining oil.

Arrange the sweet potato and beetroot slices in a single layer onto the prepared trays.

Bake for 20 minutes, checking frequently and turning occasionally, until crisp and lightly coloured. Transfer onto a rack to cool completely. Bake any remaining sweet potato or beetroot slices.

To prepare the matcha, lime and chilli salt, blend the ingredients together, using a mortar and pestle or in a spice grinder, to lightly crush the chilli and infuse the flavours into the salt.

Sprinkle the salt over the chips to serve.

NOTE
Any remaining flavoured salt can be dried out at room temperature or in a low oven. Store in an airtight container for future use.

Mushroom, cauliflower and kuzu 'arancini' balls

Arancini balls, with their crisp outside and gooey inside, are delicious, but they always make me feel slightly bloated. This more easily digested version is wonderfully cheesy and makes a great, satisfying snack and lunchbox addition.

SERVES 6 (MAKES 18)

15 g (½ oz) dried porcini mushrooms, soaked in ⅓ cup (80 ml/2½ fl oz) boiling water for 15 minutes

1 (600 g/1 lb 5 oz) cauliflower, broken into florets

2 tablespoons ghee

½ small brown onion, finely chopped

2 cloves garlic, finely chopped

200 g (7 oz) Swiss brown or button mushrooms, finely chopped

1 tablespoon fresh thyme leaves

Himalayan salt and freshly ground black pepper, to taste

3 teaspoons kuzu (crushed to a powder between two spoons)*

100 g (3½ oz) marinated goat's cheese, cut into 18 cubes

coconut or macadamia oil, for shallow-frying

lime wedges, to serve

Coating

⅓ cup (30 g/1 oz) arrowroot

1 egg, lightly beaten

splash nut milk or water

1 cup (100 g/3½ oz) quinoa flakes

Chilli mayo

2 tablespoons chilli sauce (see recipe page 320)

¼ cup (60 g/2 oz) whole egg mayonnaise

finely grated zest of 1 unwaxed lime

NOTE

The arancini can be kept warm in a 150°C (300°F) oven prior to serving, if required.

* Available from health food stores.

Drain the porcini, reserving the liquid, and finely chop. Place the cauliflower in a food processor and blend to chop into rice-sized pieces, or coarsely grate. Heat the ghee in a medium frying pan over low–medium heat. Cook the onion and garlic until softened. Add the porcini and Swiss brown or button mushrooms and thyme, cook until golden brown. Add the cauliflower and cook until just tender. Season.

Heat the reserved porcini liquid in a small saucepan over low heat, until hot. Blend the kuzu powder with a little cold water in a small bowl, until dissolved. Stir kuzu into the hot porcini liquid. Gently simmer for a few minutes until thickened and the kuzu turns clear. Pour into the mushroom mixture and stir to combine. Transfer the mixture to a shallow tray and spread out. Refrigerate for 20 minutes, or until firm enough to roll.

Meanwhile to make the chilli mayo, combine all of the ingredients in a small bowl. Set aside.

Roll the mushroom mixture into 18 walnut-sized balls. Press your finger into the centre of each ball and insert a cube of cheese and reshape to cover.

To coat, place the arrowroot, egg whisked with a splash of milk and quinoa flakes in three separate bowls. Roll the balls one or two at a time in the arrowroot to coat, then dip in egg mixture and finally coat in quinoa flakes.

Add oil to a medium frying pan so it is 2 cm (¾ in) deep. Set over medium heat and heat until a quinoa flake can be dropped in and it floats straight to the surface, bubbling and gently browning. Cook the arancini in batches for 6–8 minutes, turning frequently, until golden brown all over. Transfer onto kitchen paper, to drain. Season with salt.

Serve with chilli mayo and lime wedges.

Chocolate, orange and buckwheat crunch balls

I would feel guilty about eating so many of these crunchy, flavourful, enticing treats if I didn't know that they were so healthy. Buckwheat is rich in rutin, a powerful antioxidant that helps to protect your body and brain from inflammation and collagen degradation.

MAKES 18

6 medjool dates, pitted
½ cup (125 ml/4 fl oz) boiling water
1 cup (200 g/7 oz) buckwheat groats*
½ cup (40 g/1½ oz) cacao powder
1 cup (100 g/3½ oz) desiccated (shredded) coconut
2 tablespoons almond butter
2 tablespoons tahini
1 teaspoon vanilla bean powder*
½ teaspoon ground cinnamon
finely grated zest of 1 unwaxed orange
pinch of Himalayan salt
⅓ cup (60 g/2 oz) raisins, coarsely chopped
2 tablespoons cacao nibs*

Coating
¼ cup (20 g/¾ oz) cacao powder
⅓ cup (30 g/1 oz) desiccated (shredded) coconut
½ cup (70 g/2½ oz) pistachios, finely ground

Soak the dates in water for 10 minutes, or until softened.

Toast the buckwheat groats in a dry frying pan over low–medium heat for 3–4 minutes, until golden brown and nutty. Set aside to cool.

Place the dates and any remaining liquid, cacao powder, coconut, almond butter, tahini, vanilla, cinnamon, orange zest and salt in a high-speed blender. Blend until the mixture begins to bind together.

Transfer into a medium bowl. Add the cooled toasted buckwheat, raisins and cacao nibs and stir to combine.

Divide the mixture into 18 even portions. Roll into balls.

Roll six balls in cacao powder, six in desiccated coconut and six in finely ground pistachios to coat. Place on a tray and refrigerate for 1 hour, or until firm.

NOTE
These can be stored in an airtight container for up to 3 weeks in the refrigerator. Alternatively, you can freeze them for up to 3 months.

*   Available from health food stores.

Chilli-spiked stuffed date truffles

Truffles are delightful balls of chocolate, spiced here with cayenne pepper to help spark your digestive fire. Cacao and almonds are rich in skin-strengthening magnesium, potassium and copper, and almonds are also a great source of vitamin E and biotin, which helps protect the skin from dryness and dehydration.

MAKES 12

12 medjool dates

Filling
¼ cup (20 g/¾ oz) desiccated (shredded) coconut,
    plus extra to decorate (optional)
30 g (1 oz) almond butter
1 tablespoon finely chopped roasted almonds,
    plus extra to decorate (optional)
3 teaspoons maple syrup
½ teaspoon cayenne pepper, plus extra
    to decorate (optional)
¼ teaspoon ground cinnamon
¼ teaspoon vanilla bean powder*
⅛ teaspoon ground nutmeg
pinch of Himalayan salt, plus extra
    to decorate (optional)

Raw chocolate coating
⅔ cup (50 g/1¾ oz) cacao powder
50 g (1¾ oz) cacao butter, coarsely chopped
1 tablespoon maple syrup
1 tablespoon coconut oil

Line a medium baking tray (baking sheet) with baking paper.

Cut the dates down the centreline, going halfway through to expose the pit. Remove and discard the pits.

To prepare the filling, combine all of the ingredients in a small bowl and stir to combine.

Stuff the dates with the filling, pressing the cut edges back together to seal. Arrange on the prepared tray. Refrigerate for 30 minutes, or until firm.

To make the chocolate coating, half-fill a small saucepan with water and bring to a simmer. Place all of the ingredients in a heatproof bowl. Take the pan off the heat and set the bowl over the top. Ensure the base of the bowl does not touch the water. Leave for 5 minutes, or until the cacao butter and coconut oil melts. Stir to combine.

Holding the stuffed dates on a fork, or using toothpicks, dip and roll the dates one at a time in the chocolate, to coat evenly. Place back on the lined tray.

To decorate, sprinkle a little desiccated coconut, roasted almond, cayenne pepper and/or Himalayan salt alternately on top of the dates, if desired. Refrigerate for 30 minutes, or until set.

NOTE
You can store these in an airtight container for up to 1 month.

* Available from health food stores.

Chocolate and peppermint crunch

When I was a kid, my dad would hide after-dinner mint chocolates at the back of the fridge,
but every Sunday morning when everyone was asleep, I would find them and eat them.
This is a healthy version of a much-loved childhood treat. The buckwheat gives
a nutritious and scrumptious crunch.

MAKES 24 SQUARES

Base
½ cup (100 g/3½ oz) buckwheat groats*
⅓ cup (25 g/1 oz) cacao powder
1½ cups (210 g/7½ oz) pecans
¼ cup (60 ml/2 fl oz) maple syrup
40 g (1½ oz) nut butter
½ teaspoon vanilla bean powder*
pinch of Himalayan salt

Filling
1 medium avocado, halved, stone removed and
    flesh scooped out
125 g (4½ oz) coconut butter, melted
2 tablespoons maple syrup
3 teaspoons The Beauty Chef Cleanse powder or
    barley grass powder
pinch of Himalayan salt
4–6 drops of essential food-grade peppermint oil,
    to taste

Raw chocolate
35 g (1¼ oz) cacao powder
35 g (1¼ oz) cacao butter, coarsely chopped
3 teaspoons maple syrup
3 teaspoons coconut oil

Lightly grease a 25 × 16 × 3 cm (10 × 6¼ 1¼ in) baking tray (baking sheet) and line it with baking paper.

To prepare the base, lightly toast the buckwheat groats in a medium frying pan over low–medium heat for 2 minutes, or until golden and crisp. Set aside to cool.

Place the remaining base ingredients in a high-speed blender. Blend until finely chopped and mixture begins to bind together. Transfer to a medium bowl. Add the toasted buckwheat and stir to combine. Press into the base of the prepared tray. Smooth over with the back of a spoon. Refrigerate for 30 minutes, or until firm.

To prepare the filling, combine all of the ingredients in a high-speed blender. Blend until smooth. Spread the 'filling over the set base. Refrigerate for 15 minutes.

To make the raw chocolate, half-fill a small saucepan with water and bring to a simmer. Place all of the ingredients in a heatproof bowl. Take the pan off the heat and set the bowl over the top. Ensure the base of the bowl does not touch the water. Leave for 5 minutes, or until the cacao butter and coconut oil melt. Stir to combine.

Pour the raw chocolate over the filling, tilting the tray or spreading to cover in an even layer. Refrigerate for 15 minutes, or until set.

Using a hot knife, cut into 24 squares.

Store in an airtight container in the refrigerator for up to 5 days. Alternatively, you can freeze for up to 3 months.

* Available from health food stores.

Vanilla, date and tahini salted caramels

How can a caramel be so 'naughty', yet so sustaining? A hit in our household, these lovely squares of buttery, sweet and salty–tasting joy are mineral-rich from the tahini.

MAKES 16 SMALL SQUARES

6 medjool dates, pitted
½ cup (50 g/1¾ oz) almond meal
40 g (1½ oz) coconut butter, melted
2 tablespoons tahini
½ teaspoon vanilla bean powder*
½ teaspoon Himalayan salt
salt flakes, for sprinkling

Place all of the ingredients, except the salt flakes, in a high-speed blender. Blend until you have a smooth, thick, fudge-like consistency.

Transfer the mixture onto a sheet of baking paper. Using your hands, shape into a 2 cm (¾ in)-thick square. It will feel a little oily, but don't worry, the oils will set when refrigerated. Cover with another sheet of baking paper. Roll out, smoothing the surface, to make an approximately 1 cm (½ in)-thick square.

Leave on the baking paper and transfer onto a tray. Refrigerate for 30 minutes, or until firm.

Cut into 16 squares. Sprinkle with salt flakes.

NOTE
The caramels can be stored in an airtight container in the refrigerator for up to 2 weeks.

* Available from health food stores.

Dinner

....

Dinner gives us a platform from which to conclude the day, with a nourishing meal and conversation with family and friends. Sometimes, however, for me that can look a little chaotic, with everyone arriving home at different times from meetings or school activities, and, as a result, we all eat separately, in different locations around the house and at different times. Dinner, then, may mean a meal that is very simple and thrown together – eggs and kimchi on toast or a piece of meat and salad are often on our menu. Such informality can be refreshing, but I do cherish the times when we are all home together, sitting, eating, sharing food that I have put some love into – it always tastes so much better.

I have two strict rules when it comes to dinner: no arguing and no forcing anyone to eat the food; stress is not conducive to good digestion!

I try to eat as early as possible – around 6 pm – which allows good digestion of food and means I don't go to bed on a full stomach, something that may well will wake you at around 3 am – according to Traditional Chinese Medicine, this is around the time your liver will wake you if it is overloaded.

TIPS

—— Chew your food slowly; this helps digestion.

—— Have a shot of apple cider vinegar or lemon juice in water before dinner to help build the acids in your stomach to aid the digestion of your food.

—— Finish dinner with a cup of fennel or dandelion tea to both support the liver and aid digestion.

Cauliflower and oyster soup

Cauliflower and oyster soup

This soup is a dinner-party favourite of mine and the flavours of cauliflower and oyster together are creamy and superb. It is luscious and nutritious, giving your body a good helping of skin- and immune-boosting vitamin C and zinc.

SERVES 6

2 tablespoons ghee
1 leek, white part only, thinly sliced
1 onion, thinly sliced
1 clove garlic, coarsely chopped
1 (1.2 kg/2 lb 10 oz) cauliflower, broken into florets
4 cups (1 litre/34 fl oz) chicken bone broth (see recipe page 300) or store-bought stock
pinch of saffron threads
1 cup (250 ml/8½ fl oz) warm water
½ cup (75 g/2¾ oz) raw cashews, soaked in cold water for at least 4 hours, or overnight
Himalayan salt and ground white pepper, to taste
12 shucked fresh oysters, with their liquid
chervil or micro herbs, to garnish

Melt the ghee in a large saucepan over low–medium heat. Cook the leek, onion and garlic, until softened and golden. Add the cauliflower and stir to combine. Pour in the broth and bring to the boil. Reduce the heat and gently simmer for 20 minutes, or until tender.

Meanwhile, crush the saffron in a small bowl. Add the warm water and set aside to soak for 20 minutes.

Drain and rinse the cashews.

Place the cashews and saffron liquid in a high-speed blender. Blend until smooth and creamy. Add to the soup and stir to combine. Gently simmer for 5 minutes.

Using a hand-held blender, blend the soup until smooth. Add a little additional broth or water if you find your soup is too thick. Season with salt and pepper.

Reheat soup until hot.

Remove from the heat. Add the oysters and their juice to the soup and stir to combine. Let stand for 2–3 minutes, until the oysters are heated through.

Serve garnished with chervil or micro herbs.

Chicken and prawn laksa with sweet potato noodles

I love making homemade laksa, as it fills our home with the fragrance of coconut and aromatic spices. Coconut milk is rich in lauric acid, which is anti-fungal, anti-inflammatory and brilliant for gut health. This marries beautifully and healthily with the sweet potato noodles.

SERVES 4

2 × 400 ml (13½ fl oz) cans coconut milk

4 kaffir lime leaves

1 cup (250 ml/8½ fl oz) chicken bone broth (see recipe page 300) or store-bought stock

2 organic skinless chicken breasts, thinly sliced

2 tablespoons fish sauce

2 tablespoons lime juice

1 tablespoon raw honey

8 large raw prawns (shrimp), shelled and deveined, tails left on

250 g (9 oz) bean sprouts

2 large handfuls coriander (cilantro) leaves, picked

1 large handful Vietnamese mint leaves, picked

1 large handful mint leaves, picked

1 lime, cut into wedges

Spice paste

2 tablespoons coconut oil

2 purple shallots, coarsely chopped

4 cloves garlic, coarsely chopped

¼ cup (40 g/1½ oz) macadamias, coarsely chopped

2 stalks lemongrass, white part only, coarsely chopped

3 long red chillies, coarsely chopped (seeds in)

2 coriander (cilantro) roots, coarsely chopped

2 cm (¾ in) knob of ginger, peeled and coarsely chopped

1 teaspoon ground turmeric

Sweet potato noodles

1 sweet potato, peeled

To make the spice paste, blend all of the ingredients together using a small food processor, to make a smooth paste.

Heat a large saucepan over low–medium heat. Fry the paste for 2 minutes, or until softened and fragrant. Add the coconut milk and lime leaves and bring to the boil. Decrease the heat and gently simmer for 10–15 minutes, until the oil separates from the milk and floats to the surface. Pour in the broth and bring to the boil. Decrease the heat and gently simmer for 10 minutes.

Meanwhile to prepare the sweet potato noodles, use a spiraliser to cut the sweet potato into noodle-like lengths. Alternatively, using a mandoline, thinly slice into long strips.

Add the chicken, fish sauce, lime juice and honey to the broth and stir to combine. Gently simmer for 5 minutes, until the chicken is almost cooked.

Add the prawns and cook for 3–5 minutes, until the prawns turn pink and are just cooked through.

To serve, divide the noodles among four deep serving bowls and top with bean sprouts. Ladle the broth over the top, distributing the chicken and prawns evenly. Garnish generously with coriander, Vietnamese mint and mint. Serve with lime wedges.

Chicken and prawn laksa with sweet potato noodles

Pulled eggplant with seeded slaw and quinoa

Pulled eggplant with seeded slaw and quinoa

This is a seriously moreish, fibre-rich vegetarian meal, great for tantalising the taste buds. The slaw is high in gut-promoting soluble fibre and is mineral-rich, including silica, which is found in the seeds, parsley and cabbage, which helps promote skin elasticity and healthy hair.

SERVES 4

5 large eggplants (aubergines)
1 tablespoon olive oil
1 tablespoon maple syrup
1½ cups (300 g/10½ oz) quinoa, rinsed
3 cups (750 ml/25½ fl oz) water

Spice rub
2 teaspoons sweet paprika
2 teaspoons onion powder
1 teaspoon dried oregano
½ teaspoon garlic powder
½ teaspoon smoked paprika
½ teaspoon freshly ground black pepper
½ teaspoon ground cumin
½ teaspoon mustard powder
¼ teaspoon cayenne pepper
¼ teaspoon Himalayan salt

Mop sauce
¼ cup (60 ml/2 fl oz) apple cider vinegar
    (unpasteurised)
1½ tablespoons maple syrup
1 tablespoon white vinegar
½ teaspoon chilli sauce (see recipe page 320)
½ teaspoon chilli flakes
¼ teaspoon Himalayan salt
⅛ teaspoon cayenne pepper

Slaw
2 tablespoons pumpkin seeds (pepitas)
2 tablespoons sunflower seeds
1 tablespoon sesame seeds
⅛ red cabbage
⅛ white cabbage
1 carrot, peeled
2 spring onions (scallions), thinly sliced diagonally
2 large handfuls coriander (cilantro) stems and
    leaves, coarsely chopped
1 large handful flat-leaf (Italian) parsley, coarsely
    chopped
¼ cup (60 ml/2 fl oz) olive oil
1 unwaxed lime, zest finely grated and juiced
1 teaspoon Dijon mustard
1 teaspoon maple syrup
1 teaspoon sesame oil
Himalayan salt and freshly ground black pepper,
    to taste

Preheat the oven to 180°C (350°F).

Place the eggplants on a large baking tray (baking sheet) and cover with foil. Bake for 1½ hours, or until collapsing and very tender. Set aside to cool enough so they can be handled easily.

Meanwhile to prepare the spice rub, combine all of the ingredients in a small bowl. Mix well. Set aside.

To prepare the mop sauce, combine all of the ingredients in a bowl and set aside.

Decrease the oven temperature to 150°C (300°F).

Once cool enough to handle, trim and peel the eggplants. Shred the flesh into long, thick strips. Place in a medium bowl. Add the olive oil, maple syrup and spice mix. Toss to coat. Spread out onto a large baking tray (baking sheet). Cook for 20 minutes, or until slightly dried out and firmed up.

Meanwhile to prepare the slaw, place the pumpkin, sunflower and sesame seeds in a small frying pan and toast over low heat, until golden brown. Set aside to cool.

Finely shred the red and white cabbage and carrot and place in a large bowl. Add the spring onions, coriander and parsley and cooled toasted seeds.

Place the remaining ingredients in a small jar to make the dressing. Seal with a lid and shake to combine. Season with salt and pepper and set aside.

Place the quinoa and water in a medium saucepan and bring to the boil. Cover, decrease the heat to low and gently simmer for 15 minutes, or until almost all of the water has been absorbed and holes appear on the surface. Keep covered and remove from the heat to finish cooking for a further 5 minutes, or until tails have sprouted and all of the water has been absorbed.

To serve, pour the mop sauce over the semi-dried eggplant and toss to coat. Pour the dressing over the slaw and toss.

Serve the pulled eggplant with the slaw and quinoa.

Lebanese-style stuffed eggplants

Cooked eggplant (aubergine) has a luscious creamy texture and is a great source of fibre, as well as containing a number of brain-boosting nutrients. It lends itself to many cuisines, though it is my favourite when used in Middle Eastern food – as baba ganoush – or stuffed, as here.

SERVES 4

4 eggplants (aubergines)
½ cup (125 ml/4 fl oz) water
¼ cup (20 g/¾ oz) flaked almonds, lightly toasted
1 small handful mint leaves, chopped
1 small handful flat-leaf (Italian) parsley,
    roughly chopped

Spiced lamb
1 tablespoon olive oil
1 onion, thinly sliced
2 cloves garlic, finely chopped
500 g (1 lb 2 oz) lamb mince (ground lamb)
2 teaspoons ground cumin
2 teaspoons ground cinnamon
1 teaspoon ground coriander
3 tomatoes, chopped
Himalayan salt and freshly ground black pepper

Cumin and preserved lemon yoghurt
⅔ cup (160 g/5½ oz) natural yoghurt
¼ spiced preserved lemon, rind only, thinly chopped
    (see recipe page 319), or substitute grated zest
    of ½ unwaxed lemon
2 tablespoons freshly squeezed lemon juice
1 tablespoon extra-virgin olive oil
1 teaspoon ground cumin
Himalayan salt, to taste

Preheat the oven to 170°C (340°F).

Place the eggplants in a medium roasting tray and pour in the water. Cover with foil. Bake for 1 hour, or until they are soft and beginning to collapse.

Meanwhile to prepare the spiced lamb, heat the oil in a medium frying pan over low heat. Cook the onion and garlic until softened. Increase the heat to medium. Add the lamb and spices and cook, stirring with a wooden spoon to break up any lumps, for 10 minutes, or until browned and fragrant. Add the tomatoes and gently simmer for 20 minutes, or until reduced to a thick sauce. Season with salt and pepper.

Increase the oven temperature to 190°C (375°F).

Slice down the centreline of the eggplants, to expose the soft flesh. Open up slightly. Spoon the lamb mixture over the eggplants to cover and partially fill. Bake for 20 minutes, or until the lamb is browned.

To prepare the cumin and preserved lemon yoghurt, mix all of the ingredients together in a small bowl.

To serve, drizzle the eggplants with the cumin and preserved lemon yoghurt and scatter with the toasted flaked almonds and fresh herbs.

Creamy mushroom, pea and mint spaghetti

As a child, carbonara was my favourite pasta sauce, but it wasn't kind to my tummy.
In this recipe you will barely notice the coconut, but its creaminess complements
the mushrooms and peas, which are a great source of energy-giving B vitamins.
The mint adds a delightful, fresh flavour.

SERVES 4

500 g (1 lb 2 oz) gluten-free spaghetti
2 tablespoons extra-virgin olive oil
2 purple shallots, thinly sliced
2 cloves garlic, finely chopped
350 g (12½ oz) button mushrooms, thinly sliced
1½ cups (375 ml/12½ fl oz) coconut cream
¼ cup (10 g/¼ oz) savoury yeast flakes*
½ cup (70 g/2½ oz) frozen peas
1 small handful chives, cut into batons,
    plus extra to garnish
1 small handful mint leaves, thinly sliced
Himalayan salt and freshly ground black pepper

Place a large saucepan of water over high heat and bring to the boil.

Cook the spaghetti according to the packet instructions, or until al dente.

Heat the oil in a large frying pan over low heat. Cook the shallots and garlic, until softened. Add the mushrooms and cook, stirring occasionally, until softened and golden brown.

Add the coconut cream and yeast flakes, stirring to combine. Bring to a simmer. Add the peas and cook for 30 seconds. Add the chives and mint and stir to combine. Season with salt and pepper.

Drain the pasta.

Add the pasta to the prepared sauce and stir through to coat.

Serve hot, topped with additional chives and black pepper.

NOTE
Seek out gluten-free pastas that have a higher protein content, such as amaranth and quinoa.

* Available from health food stores.

Buckwheat pizza with mushrooms and roasted bone marrow

Besides being highly nutritious, with plenty of skin-loving collagen and helping to boost immunity, the creamy, nutty combination of the roasted bone marrow and mushrooms is delicious.

SERVES 2 (MAKES TWO 20 CM/8 IN PIZZAS

½ cup (125 ml/4 fl oz) tomato passata (puréed tomatoes)
1 clove garlic, finely chopped
300 g (10½ oz) button mushrooms, thinly sliced
Himalayan salt and freshly ground black pepper
500 g (1 lb 2 oz) grass-fed beef thigh bones filled with marrow*
¼ cup (60 g/2 oz) salsa verde (see recipe page 325)
2 large handfuls baby beetroot (beet) or rocket (arugula) leaves

Base
1 cup (160 g/5½ oz) buckwheat flour
1½ tablespoons arrowroot
¼ teaspoon bicarbonate of soda (baking soda)
¼ teaspoon Himalayan salt
100 ml (3½ fl oz) water, at room temperature
1 tablespoon olive oil
1 teaspoon apple cider vinegar (unpasteurised)

Preheat the oven to 200°C (400°F).

Place two 20 cm (8 in) pizza trays or 2 large flat baking trays (baking sheets) in the oven to preheat for 15 minutes.

To prepare the base, place the ingredients in a medium bowl and stir to form a thick batter. Divide the batter in half.

Spoon half of the batter on a large sheet of baking paper. Cover with another sheet and roll out to form a 20 cm (8 in) disc. Leave on the baking paper and set aside. Repeat with the remaining batter.

Combine the passata and garlic in a small bowl. Spread the passata over the bases and scatter with the mushrooms. Season with salt and pepper.

Place the bones in a small roasting tray. Roast for 20 minutes, or until the marrow is golden brown and gelatinous.

Transfer the pizzas on the baking paper onto the preheated trays.

Cook for 20 minutes, or until the bases are crisp and mushrooms golden brown.

To serve, scoop the roasted marrow out of the bones and spread over the mushrooms. Drizzle with salsa verde. Top with baby beetroot or rocket leaves.

* Ask your butcher for these.

Mediterranean cauliflower pizza

*Can you imagine eating pizza without the gut luggage and lethargy that follows,
but still with all the classic toppings of olives, capsicum and cheese? Enter the incredibly
versatile cauliflower, in brilliant disguise here, as a delicious, nutritious base for
this much-loved favourite dish.*

SERVES 2 (MAKES ONE 23 CM/9 IN PIZZA)

Cauliflower base

1 (600 g/1 lb 5 oz) cauliflower

¼ cup (25 g/1 oz) finely grated parmesan cheese

¼ cup (25 g/1 oz) almond meal

1 large egg

1 tablespoon olive oil

½ teaspoon onion powder

½ teaspoon Himalayan salt

¼ teaspoon garlic powder

Pizza sauce

2 teaspoons extra-virgin olive oil

1 clove garlic

2 small tomatoes, coarsely chopped

½ teaspoon dried oregano or dried basil

Himalayan salt and freshly ground black pepper

Topping

½ roasted red capsicum (bell pepper), peeled, seeded
   and sliced

4 marinated artichoke halves, thickly sliced

150 g (5½ oz) marinated goat's cheese, broken into
   lumps

¼ cup (45 g/1½ oz) pitted Kalamata olives

1 large handful rocket (arugula) leaves

1 tablespoon pine nuts, lightly toasted

extra-virgin olive oil, for drizzling

NOTE

Vegans or those avoiding dairy can substitute
savoury yeast for the parmesan in the base and
cultured nut 'cheese' (see recipe page 308) for the
goat's cheese topping.

Place a pizza stone or upturned baking tray (baking
sheet) in the oven and preheat the oven to 220°C
(430°F). Lightly grease and line a 26 cm (10¼ in)
pizza tray with baking paper.

Bring a large saucepan of water to the boil. Line a
colander with muslin (cheesecloth) or a clean tea
towel (dish towel).

Place the cauliflower in a food processor and blend
until finely chopped into tiny grains.

Cook the cauliflower for 1 minute, so it still has a bite
to it but is not completely raw. Pour into the prepared
colander and set aside to drain and cool slightly.

To prepare the pizza sauce, heat the oil in a small
saucepan over low heat. Cook the garlic until
softened. Add the tomatoes and herbs and cook for
15 minutes, or until softened and the liquid has reduced
to make a thick sauce. Purée using a stick blender or
food processor. Season with salt and pepper.

Bundle the cauliflower up in the muslin cloth or tea
towel (dish towel) and squeeze out any excess liquid.

To prepare the base, place the cauliflower and the
remaining ingredients in a medium bowl and mix
well to combine. Spoon the mixture in the centre of
the pizza tray and press out to make an even base.
Place the pizza tray onto the preheated pizza stone
or upturned baking tray. Bake for 15–20 minutes,
until golden brown and beginning to crisp up.

Spread the prepared sauce over the base. Scatter the
roasted capsicum, artichoke, goat's cheese and olives
on top. Cook for a further 10 minutes, or until the
cheese softens and begins to turn golden brown.

Remove from the oven, top with rocket and scatter
with pine nuts. Drizzle with oil. Slice to serve.

Middle Eastern–spiced walnut and white bean balls with cauliflower rice and fried onion

A beautifully fragrant and gratifying dish, rich in protein, good fats and lots of herbs and spices that are anti-inflammatory and help promote good digestion.

SERVES 4

¼ cup (60 ml/2 fl oz) olive oil, for cooking
1 large handful flat-leaf (Italian) parsley, chopped
1 large handful coriander (cilantro) leaves, chopped

Walnut and white bean balls
1 tablespoon olive oil
2 purple shallots, finely chopped
2 cloves garlic, finely chopped
1 teaspoon ground cumin
1 teaspoon ground coriander
1 teaspoon sweet paprika
2 cups (240 g/8½ oz) walnuts
400 g (14 oz) can cannellini (lima) beans, drained
    and rinsed
1 large handful flat-leaf (Italian) parsley
1 large handful coriander (cilantro) leaves and stems
Himalayan salt and freshly ground black pepper

Sauce
1 tablespoon olive oil
1 clove garlic, finely chopped
1 teaspoon sweet paprika
1 teaspoon ground cumin
3 cups (750 ml/25½ fl oz) tomato passata
    (puréed tomatoes)
½ cup (125 ml/4 fl oz) water
¾ cup (180 g/6½ oz) natural yoghurt
1½ tablespoons maple syrup

Fragrant cauliflower rice
1 (800 g/1 lb 12 oz) cauliflower
1 tablespoon ghee
⅓ cup (30 g/1 oz) flaked almonds
½ teaspoon ground cinnamon
¼ teaspoon ground cloves
Himalayan salt and freshly ground black pepper

Fried onion
2 tablespoons coconut oil
1 red onion, thinly sliced into rounds

To prepare the walnut and white bean balls, heat the oil in a medium frying pan over low heat. Cook the shallots and garlic until softened. Add the spices and cook until fragrant. Add the walnuts and cook until lightly toasted. Set aside to cool slightly.

Transfer the walnut mixture into a food processor. Add the beans and herbs. Process to finely chop. Season. Shape into 20 walnut-sized balls.

Heat half of the oil in a large frying pan over medium heat. Cook half of the walnut and bean balls for 4–5 minutes, turning frequently, until browned all over. Transfer onto a large plate and set aside. Repeat with the remaining oil and balls.

To prepare the sauce, heat the oil in a large deep frying pan over low heat. Cook the garlic until softened. Add the paprika and cumin and cook until fragrant. Add the passata, water, yoghurt and maple syrup and bring to a simmer. Simmer over low–medium heat for 10 minutes. Season to taste. Add the browned walnut and bean balls to the sauce. Simmer for 5 minutes, or until heated through.

Meanwhile to prepare the fried onion, heat the oil in a medium frying pan over medium–high heat. Cook the onion until golden brown. Drain on kitchen paper.

Meanwhile to prepare the cauliflower rice, place the cauliflower in a food processor and blend until finely chopped into rice-sized grains. Heat the ghee in a large frying pan over medium heat. Cook the flaked almonds until golden. Add the cauliflower and spices and cook, stirring occasionally, for 3–4 minutes, until cauliflower is just tender and heated through and spices are fragrant. Season with salt and pepper. Cover and keep warm.

Serve walnut and bean balls with fragrant cauliflower rice, scattered with chopped herbs and fried onion.

Spanish seafood stew

This has to be one of my favourite recipes of all time. The high zinc and B vitamin content of seafood always make me feel energised and happy. Saffron contains 150 health-giving plant compounds, and its flavour blends beautifully in this classic dish with the smoked paprika, tomato, seafood and wine.

SERVES 4

5 Roma (plum) tomatoes, halved lengthways

¼ cup (60 ml/2 fl oz) olive oil, plus extra for drizzling

4 cloves garlic, coarsely chopped

¼ cup (25 g/1 oz) almond meal

2 large handfuls flat-leaf (Italian) parsley

1 onion, halved and sliced

1 large red chilli, seeded and finely chopped

1 teaspoon smoked paprika

2 bay leaves

⅓ cup (80 ml/2½ fl oz) dry white wine

1 teaspoon saffron threads, soaked in 2 tablespoons water

1 tablespoon tomato paste (concentrated purée)

2 cups (500 ml/17 fl oz) fish stock

700 g (1 lb 9 oz) skinless non-oily mackerel fillets, or other firm white fish*, cut into 5 cm (2 in) chunks

12 mussels in their shells, scrubbed and de-bearded

12 raw prawns (shrimp), shelled and deveined, tails left on

Himalayan salt and freshly ground black pepper

cooked quinoa, to serve

lemon wedges, to serve

Preheat the oven to 180°C (350°F).

Place the tomatoes on a baking tray (baking sheet) and drizzle with a little oil. Roast for 20 minutes, or until softened and beginning to caramelise. Set aside.

Heat half of the oil in a large deep frying pan over low–medium heat. Cook the garlic until softened. Add the almond meal and cook for 3–4 minutes, until golden brown. Set aside to cool.

Place the almond mixture and half of the parsley in a food processor and blend to make a paste. Transfer into a small bowl and set aside.

Heat the remaining oil in a large heavy-based saucepan over low–medium heat. Cook the onion until softened. Add the chilli, paprika and bay leaves and cook for 30 seconds, or until fragrant. Pour in the wine. Add the saffron water, roasted tomatoes and tomato paste and stir to combine. Pour in the fish stock. Simmer for 10 minutes.

Add the almond and parsley paste and stir to combine. Add the fish and mussels. Cover and cook for 3–4 minutes, until the mussels open. Add the prawns and cook, uncovered, for a further 3 minutes, or until the prawns are pink and the rest of the seafood is cooked through. Discard any mussels that have not opened. Stir in the remaining parsley and season with salt and pepper.

Serve with quinoa and lemon wedges.

* Always opt for sustainable fish – see your fishmonger for advice.

Chermoula-baked barramundi

Chermoula-baked barramundi

Making baked fish is so easy and never fails to impress my dinner guests.
Chermoula, a herb, spice and oil marinade, originates from North Africa and there are
many different variations, depending on the region. I also enjoy it on grilled meats,
veggies and haloumi and eggs – on everything actually.

SERVES 4

1 × 2–2.2 kg (4 lb 6 oz–5 lb) OR 2 × 700–800 g
  (1 lb 9 oz–1 lb 12 oz) whole barramundi, or other
  firm, white fish

Preserved lemon and herb salad
1 small red onion, thinly sliced
½–1 spiced preserved lemon, thinly sliced lengthways
  (see recipe page 319)
3 large handfuls coriander (cilantro) leaves
2 large handfuls flat-leaf (Italian) parsley
1 large handful mint leaves
2 long red chillies, seeded and thinly sliced lengthways
juice of ½ lime

Chermoula paste
¼ cup (60 ml/2 fl oz) extra-virgin olive oil
2 tablespoons freshly squeezed lemon juice
4 cm (1½ in) knob of ginger, peeled and finely
  chopped
2 cloves garlic, finely chopped
2 teaspoons ground coriander
2 teaspoons ground cumin
½ teaspoon sweet paprika
½ teaspoon chilli flakes
¼ teaspoon freshly ground black pepper

To make the chermoula paste, place all of the
ingredients in a small bowl and stir to combine.

Rinse the barramundi under cold running water,
removing any remaining scales. Pat dry with
kitchen paper.

Score the fish twice in the thickest part near the head
to ensure even cooking. Place the fish in a large non-
reactive dish and coat in chermoula paste, filling the
cavity and cuts where it has been scored. Cover and
marinate in the refrigerator for at least 4 hours,
or overnight.

Preheat the oven to 200°C (400°F).

Cut sheets of foil large enough to wrap and enclose
your fish. Line the foil with baking paper and lay
the fish on top. If cooking two small fish create
two separate parcels. Wrap and enclose in foil.

Bake for 25 minutes if cooking 1 large fish or
15 minutes if cooking two smaller fish, or until
cooked through and the flesh flakes easily.

Meanwhile to prepare the preserved lemon and
herb salad, combine the red onion, preserved lemon,
coriander, parsley, mint and chilli in a medium bowl.
Squeeze over the lime juice and toss to coat.

To serve, transfer the fish onto large serving plates
and scatter with preserved lemon and herb salad.

Grilled sardines with fennel, asparagus and olive salad

This dish is a veritable skin and brain booster, with the folate in the asparagus working synergistically with the B12 from the sardines to help improve cognitive health. Sardines are also one of the richest sources of omega-3s, and asparagus is a nutrient superhero, which we all should eat more of for radiant skin and good health.

SERVES 4

1 kg (2 lb 3 oz) large whole fresh sardines (approx 16–20)
olive oil, for drizzling
Himalayan salt and freshly ground black pepper

Fennel, asparagus and olive salad
1 large fennel bulb, trimmed
finely grated zest and juice of 1 unwaxed lemon
2 bunches asparagus
½ cup (90 g/3 oz) pitted Kalamata olives, coarsely chopped
1 large handful flat-leaf (Italian) parsley, coarsely chopped
1 large handful dill fronds, coarsely chopped
1 clove garlic, finely chopped
2 tablespoons extra-virgin olive oil

Chilli oil
1 long red chilli, coarsely chopped, seeds in
1 tablespoon extra-virgin olive oil

To prepare the salad, using a mandoline or peeler, very thinly slice the fennel into lengthways strips. Place in a medium bowl. Add the lemon zest and juice and toss to coat.

Bring a medium saucepan of water to the boil.

Snap the woody ends off the asparagus and discard. Cut the asparagus stalks in half crossways. Depending on their thickness, cut in half or quarters lengthways, to make thin sticks. Blanch the asparagus for 10 seconds, or until just tender. Drain and refresh in iced water. Drain.

Add the asparagus and remaining ingredients to the fennel and toss to combine.

To prepare the chilli oil, combine the chilli and oil in a small bowl and set aside.

Rinse the sardines under cold running water to remove any remaining scales. Pat dry with kitchen paper.

Heat a chargrill pan over medium–high heat.

Drizzle the sardines with oil and season with salt and pepper. Grill the sardines for 2–3 minutes on each side, until golden brown and just cooked through.

Arrange the salad on serving plates, top with sardines and drizzle with chilli oil.

Grilled sardines with fennel, asparagus and olive salad

Fragrant barramundi curry with cauliflower rice

*Spices are rich in protective plant compounds and work as wonderful digestive aids,
which is why I use them daily in my cooking. I love a white fish curry made with
the earthy flavour of lentils; they are a great source of resistant starch, which feeds
the beneficial bacteria in your colon.*

SERVES 4-6

⅓ cup (80 ml/2½ fl oz) coconut oil
1 sweet potato, peeled and cut into 2.5 cm (1 in) chunks
1 carrot, peeled and coarsely chopped
Himalayan salt and black pepper
1 brown onion, diced
4 cm (1½ in) knob of ginger, peeled and finely grated
1 long red chilli, thinly sliced
1 clove garlic, finely chopped
2 teaspoons black mustard seeds
2 teaspoons ground turmeric
1½ teaspoons cumin seeds
1½ teaspoons ground cumin
1½ teaspoons ground coriander
1 teaspoon garam masala
½ teaspoon ground chilli
seeds from 2 green cardamom pods, crushed
5 ripe tomatoes, diced
150 g (5½ oz) split peas or lentils, soaked in cold
    water for 1 hour, drained and rinsed
5 cups (1.25 litres/42 fl oz) water
600 g (1 lb 5 oz) barramundi, or other firm white fish,
    cut into 2.5 cm (1 in) chunks
1 large handful baby spinach
juice of 1 lemon
coriander (cilantro) sprigs, to serve

Cauliflower rice
1 (1 kg/2 lb 3 oz) cauliflower, cut into small florets
2 tablespoons coconut oil
½ onion, diced
1 tablespoon finely grated ginger
1 small clove garlic
Himalayan salt and freshly ground black pepper,
    to taste

Preheat the oven to 200°C (400°F).

Heat half of the coconut oil in a heavy-based roasting tray in the oven. Add the sweet potato and carrot and toss to coat. Season with salt and pepper. Roast for 20–30 minutes, until very tender.

Meanwhile heat the remaining coconut oil in a large saucepan over medium heat. Cook the onion, ginger, chilli and garlic until light golden. Stir in the mustard seeds and cook until they begin to pop. Add the remaining spices and stir until fragrant. Add the tomatoes and cook for 5 minutes, or until pulpy. Add the split peas and water and bring to the boil. Decrease the heat and simmer for 30 minutes, or until the split peas break down and thicken the sauce slightly.

Meanwhile to prepare the cauliflower rice, place the cauliflower in a food processor and blend to finely chop into rice-sized grains.

Heat the coconut oil in a large frying pan over medium heat. Cook the onion, ginger and garlic until softened. Add the cauliflower and cook, stirring occasionally, for 3–4 minutes, until the cauliflower is just tender and heated through. Season with salt and pepper. Cover and keep warm.

Add the roasted sweet potato and carrot to the curry mixture and stir to combine. Add the barramundi and gently simmer for 3–4 minutes, until the fish is just cooked through. Add the spinach and lemon juice. Season with salt and pepper.

Serve curry with cauliflower rice and garnished with coriander sprigs.

Cashew butter chicken

My kids love butter chicken and when you make it yourself you can be assured that you know exactly what's in it. This recipe is rich and creamy and the cashews give a soft kiss of sweetness as well as being a good source of good fats, zinc, selenium and tryptophan, making it a wonderful skin- and mood-boosting dish.

SERVES 4

1 kg (2 lb 3 oz, or approx 8) skinless chicken thigh fillets, quartered
2 tablespoons coarsely chopped roasted cashews
1 large handful coriander (cilantro) leaves, coarsely chopped to garnish
cooked quinoa, to serve

Chicken marinade
½ cup (125 g/4½ oz) natural yoghurt
juice of ½ lemon
2 cloves garlic, finely chopped
4 cm (1½ in) knob of ginger, peeled and coarsely grated
1 teaspoon garam masala
½ teaspoon ground turmeric
½ teaspoon ground cumin
½ teaspoon chilli powder
½ teaspoon Himalayan salt

Sauce
½ cup (75 g/2¾ oz) raw cashews, soaked in cold water for 4 hours
1 cup (250 ml/8½ fl oz) coconut cream
2 tablespoons ghee
3 cloves garlic, finely chopped
4 cm (1½ in) knob of ginger, peeled and finely grated
1 teaspoon ground cumin
½ teaspoon ground cinnamon
½ teaspoon garam masala
½ teaspoon chilli powder
1½ cups (375 ml/12½ fl oz) tomato passata (puréed tomatoes)
⅔ cup (160 ml/5½ fl oz) water

To prepare the marinade, combine all of the ingredients in a medium bowl. Mix well. Add the chicken and stir to coat. Cover and refrigerate for 4 hours.

To make the sauce, drain and rinse the cashews and place in a high-speed blender or food processor. Blend to finely chop. Add the coconut cream and blend until smooth. Set aside.

Heat the ghee in a large frying pan over low heat. Cook the garlic and ginger until the garlic is softened. Add the spices and cook until fragrant. Add the passata and simmer for 5 minutes. Add the cashew cream and water and gently simmer for 10 minutes.

Meanwhile, preheat a large frying pan or heavy-based saucepan over high heat. Once very hot, cook the marinated chicken pieces in batches for 2 minutes on each side, or until browned.

Add the chicken to the sauce and stir to coat. Cook for 20 minutes, or until the chicken is cooked through.

Serve the cashew butter chicken scattered with roasted cashews and coriander. Accompany with quinoa.

Za'atar chicken with cauliflower rice and raisin and pine nut stuffing

This nutritious, fragrant dish stars za'atar, a delightful, anti-inflammatory spice blend with an orchestra of flavours. It's a great Sunday night dish to nourish you for the week ahead.

SERVES 4

1.5 kg (3 lb 5 oz) organic chicken
2 red onions, thickly sliced into rounds
olive oil, for drizzling
2 tablespoons za'atar spice mix
Himalayan salt and freshly ground black pepper
1 cup (250 ml/8½ fl oz) water

Stuffing
300 g (10½ oz) cauliflower florets
3 large handfuls flat-leaf (Italian) parsley, coarsely
    chopped
40 g (1½ oz) cultured butter (see recipe page 303)
2 cloves garlic, finely chopped
¼ cup (35 g/1¼ oz) pine nuts, lightly toasted
¼ cup (35 g/1¼ oz) raisins, coarsely chopped
1 tablespoon sesame seeds, lightly toasted
finely grated zest and juice of 1 unwaxed lemon
Himalayan salt and freshly ground black pepper

Preheat the oven to 200°C (400°F).

To prepare the stuffing, place the cauliflower in a food processor. Blend until finely chopped into rice-sized grains. Transfer into a medium bowl. Add the remaining ingredients and stir to combine. Season with salt and pepper.

Wash the chicken under cold running water, cleaning out the cavity. Pat dry with kitchen paper.

Pack the stuffing into the chicken cavity.

Arrange the onion slices in the base of a roasting tin. Place the chicken on top. Drizzle the chicken with oil and rub to coat. Scatter over the za'atar and season with salt and pepper.

Pour the water into the base of the tray. Roast the chicken for 30 minutes.

Decrease the heat to 180°C (350°F).

Roast the chicken for a further 1 hour, or until the skin is crisp and golden brown and the juices run clear when a skewer is inserted into the thickest part of the thigh.

Remove from the oven. Place the chicken on a platter and cover with foil. Rest for 10–15 minutes before serving, accompanied by your choice of side dishes.

Baked chicken with celeriac, rosemary and juniper

I cook a baked chicken most Sunday nights; it's a much-loved family tradition.
This is a seriously delicious and nourishing recipe: celeriac is beneficial for digestion,
rosemary helps protect against oxidative damage and juniper berries are anti-microbial,
antioxidant and a wonderful, fragrant addition to meat.

SERVES 4

4 chicken marylands (chicken leg quarters)
olive oil, for drizzling
Himalayan salt and freshly ground black pepper
2 tablespoons cultured butter (see recipe
    page 303), plus extra to butter bread
1 large brown onion, thinly sliced
2 cloves garlic, thinly sliced
1½ cups (375 ml/12½ fl oz) dry white wine
1½ cups (375 ml/12½ fl oz) chicken bone broth
    (see recipe page 300) or store-bought
½ cup (125 ml/4 fl oz) thickened (double/heavy)
    cream (optional for those who are avoiding dairy –
    or add 2 teaspoons of cultured butter)
400 g (14 oz) peeled celeriac, cut into wedges
4 large sprigs rosemary
3 bay leaves
1 tablespoon juniper berries, cracked
1 strip orange zest
thyme sprigs (optional)

Preheat the oven to 180°C (350°F).

Preheat a medium-sized Dutch oven or heavy-based ovenproof saucepan with a lid, over medium–high heat.

Drizzle the chicken marylands with oil and season with salt and pepper. Cook for 3–4 minutes on each side, until browned all over. Transfer onto a plate.

Decrease the heat to low–medium. Add the butter and cook the onion and garlic, until softened and golden. Pour in the wine, bring to the boil and simmer for a few minutes. Add the chicken broth and cream and bring to a simmer. Remove from the heat. Return the chicken to the pan. Add the celeriac wedges, rosemary, bay leaves, juniper berries, orange zest and thyme sprigs, if using.

Cover and bake in the oven for 40 minutes, or until juices run clear when a skewer is inserted into the thickest part of the chicken legs and celeriac is tender.

Remove the chicken and celeriac from the pan and set on a plate. Cover to keep warm.

Place the pan over medium heat and simmer the liquid for 3–4 minutes, until thickened slightly to coat the back of a spoon.

Return the chicken and celeriac to the pan and coat in sauce before serving.

Cabbage and pork rolls baked in tomato sauce

Who would have thought these traditional Eastern European rolls were a super beauty food? Cabbage and tomato are rich in collagen-producing vitamin C and pork is a great strengthening and mood-boosting food – high in protein, B vitamins and zinc – good for the nervous system, cardiovascular health and a radiant complexion.

SERVES 4

8 large green cabbage leaves
1 large handful flat-leaf (Italian) parsley, coarsely
    chopped

Tomato sauce
3 cups (750 ml/25½ fl oz) tomato passata (puréed
    tomatoes)
1 cup (250 ml/8½ fl oz) chicken bone broth
    (see recipe page 300) or store-bought stock
1 tablespoon maple syrup
Himalayan salt and freshly ground black pepper

Filling
2 tablespoons olive oil
1 small onion, finely chopped
2 cloves garlic, finely chopped
750 g (1 lb 11 oz) pork mince (ground pork)
1 cup (135 g/5 oz) cooked quinoa
⅔ cup (65 g/2¼ oz) finely grated parmesan cheese,
    plus extra to serve
1 large handful sage leaves, finely chopped
1 teaspoon Himalayan salt
½ teaspoon freshly ground black pepper

Preheat the oven to 180°C (350°F).

To prepare the filling, heat the oil in a large frying pan over low heat. Cook the onion and garlic until softened. Transfer to a large bowl and set aside to cool slightly.

Add the remaining ingredients to the cooled onion mixture. Mix well to combine.

Place a large saucepan of water over high heat and bring to the boil.

Trim the hard stems from the cabbage leaves and discard. Blanch the leaves for 10 seconds, or until wilted. Refresh in iced water. Drain and pat dry with kitchen paper.

Divide the filling into eight equal portions.

Place the filling portions at the base of the cabbage leaves. Fold in the sides and roll up to form a log-shaped parcel. Arrange the cabbage parcels snugly, seam-side down, in a medium ovenproof dish.

To prepare the sauce, combine the passata, chicken broth and maple syrup in a large bowl or jug. Season with salt and pepper.

Pour the sauce over the cabbage rolls. Cover with foil and bake for 50–60 minutes, until the filling is cooked through (insert a knife into the centre of the filling of one of the rolls, leave for 5 seconds, pull out and feel if it is warm–hot) and the sauce has thickened.

Scatter with parsley and additional parmesan cheese to serve.

Slow-roasted pork belly with pickled cabbage, apple and radish salad

The sulphur-rich cabbage and radish in this delicious dish help to support the hard-working liver, as well as being a great source of fibre to support bowel and digestive health.

SERVES 4

1.2 kg (2 lb 10 oz) free-range pork belly
olive oil, for drizzling
2 teaspoons sea salt

Pickled cabbage, apple and radish salad
⅛ medium red cabbage, shredded,
    outer leaves reserved
⅛ medium white cabbage, shredded
1 large tart green cooking apple, such as
    Granny Smith, thinly sliced
250 g (9 oz) radishes (approx 8), thinly sliced
3 spring onions (scallions), thinly sliced diagonally
1 large handful oregano leaves, finely chopped

Pickling liquid
1 teaspoon chilli flakes
1 teaspoon fennel seeds
½ teaspoon mustard seeds
½ cup (125 ml/4 fl oz) water
1 cup (250 ml/8½ fl oz) apple cider vinegar
    (unpasteurised)
2 teaspoons raw honey
2 teaspoons Himalayan salt

Start this recipe at least 3 hours in advance.

To prepare the pickling liquid, toast the chilli flakes, fennel and mustard seeds in a small saucepan over low heat for 30 seconds, or until fragrant and mustard seeds begin to pop. Pour in the water, then the vinegar. Add the honey and salt. Gently heat, stirring until the salt dissolves. Set aside to cool.

To prepare the salad, place all of the ingredients in a medium bowl and toss to combine. Pour over the cooled pickling liquid and toss to coat. Cover with the reserved cabbage leaves. Place a large plate on top and weigh down to submerge the salad in liquid. Refrigerate, tossing occasionally, for at least 2 hours or up to overnight.

Place a large wire rack inside a large roasting tin.

Using a very sharp knife, score the pork skin crossways at 1 cm (½ in) intervals. Place the pork, skin-side up, on the rack in the roasting tin. Lightly drizzle and rub oil into the skin. Scatter salt over the skin and rub in well. Set aside at room temperature for 30 minutes, to dry the skin out.

Preheat the oven to 160°C (320°F). Then roast the pork for 2 hours or until the fat has rendered down.

Increase the oven temperature to 220°C (430°F) and roast the pork for a further 15–20 minutes, or until the skin is crisp and golden brown. Alternatively crisp up the skin under an overhead grill (broiler) for approximately 5 minutes. If grill is in the oven leave the door ajar.

Transfer the pork to a large chopping board and rest, uncovered, in a warm place for 15 minutes.

Cut the pork into portions and serve with the pickled salad.

Baked smoky barbecue ribs

Eating ribs is a truly tactile, visceral experience and nothing short of a culinary delight, with sweet, sticky, saucy and savoury flavours and textures. This recipe is perfect for the primal or paleo among us and my version offers you a traditional flavour with healthful ingredients.

SERVES 4

2 kg (4 lb 6 oz) American-style pork spare ribs
   (4–6 slabs)

Spice mix
3 teaspoons smoked sweet paprika
3 teaspoons ground cumin
1½ teaspoons Himalayan salt
½ teaspoon ground cinnamon
½ teaspoon ground allspice
¼ teaspoon cayenne pepper

Braising liquid
½ cup (125 ml/4 fl oz) apple juice
½ cup (125 ml/4 fl oz) water
2 tablespoons apple cider vinegar (unpasteurised)
4 cm (1½ in) knob of ginger, peeled and coarsely
   grated
1 clove garlic, finely chopped

Smoky barbecue sauce
1 tablespoon olive oil
½ small onion, coarsely grated
2 cloves garlic, finely chopped
1 tablespoon smoked paprika
2 teaspoons ground cumin
¼ teaspoon cayenne pepper
1 cup (250 ml/8½ fl oz) tomato passata (puréed
   tomatoes)
¼ cup (60 ml/2 fl oz) raw honey
1½ tablespoons apple cider vinegar (unpasteurised)
1½ tablespoons Worcestershire sauce

Begin this recipe at least 6½ hours in advance.

Remove and discard the thin membrane from the back of each slab of ribs.

Combine all of the spice mix ingredients in a small bowl, then rub the spice mix over both sides of the ribs. Lay the ribs on a large tray and cover. Refrigerate for at least 4 hours, or overnight.

Preheat the oven to 150°C (300°F).

Place the ribs, meat-side up, in two large roasting tins. Cut the slabs of ribs in half to fit, if necessary. Cover the trays with foil and pinch to seal. Bake for 1 hour.

Combine the ingredients for the braising liquid. Pour over the ribs. Cover and bake for a further 1½ hours, until very tender, but not falling off the bone.

Meanwhile prepare the smoky barbecue sauce. Heat the oil in a small saucepan over low heat. Cook the onion and garlic until softened. Add the spices and cook for 20 seconds, or until fragrant. Add the remaining ingredients and bring to the boil. Decrease the heat and gently simmer for 10 minutes, or until thickened slightly. Set aside to cool. Using a stick blender, purée until smooth.

Pour any remaining braising liquid and cooking juices from the ribs into the sauce and stir to combine.

Preheat an overhead grill (broiler) on high heat. Baste the ribs with the barbecue sauce. Grill (broil) for 3–4 minutes on both sides, until caramelised. Loosely cover with foil and leave to rest for 10 minutes.

Cut into individual ribs and serve with any remaining sauce.

Osso bucco with creamy cauliflower mash

When I was little, our family would frequent Bill and Toni's on Stanley St in Kings Cross for a bowl of minestrone or some osso bucco, always with a bottle of Lambrusco and cordial, and followed by gelato and pinball games. This dish is a more nutritious twist on a favourite childhood recipe.

SERVES 4

Osso bucco
⅓ cup (40 g/1½ oz) arrowroot
Himalayan salt and freshly ground black pepper
2 kg (4 lb 6 oz) osso bucco pieces (centre-cut veal shank)
¼ cup (60 ml/2 fl oz) olive oil
1 large onion, finely diced
2 sticks celery, finely diced
1 large carrot, peeled and finely diced
3 cloves garlic, finely chopped
2 vine-ripened tomatoes, coarsely chopped
2 cups (500 ml/17 fl oz) dry white wine
2 cups (500 ml/17 fl oz) chicken bone broth (see recipe page 300) or store-bought stock
5 sprigs thyme
2 bay leaves

Gremolata
zest of 2 unwaxed lemons, cut into fine strips
2 large handfuls flat-leaf (Italian) parsley
1 clove garlic

Creamy cauliflower mash
1 (800 g/1 lb 12 oz) cauliflower, broken into large florets
2 tablespoons ghee
Himalayan salt and freshly ground black pepper

Preheat the oven to 160°C (320°F).

Put the arrowroot on a plate. Season generously with salt and pepper and mix well. Toss the veal in the seasoned arrowroot until lightly coated.

Heat 2 tablespoons of the oil in a heavy-based ovenproof saucepan with a lid, set over medium–high heat. Cook the veal pieces for 3–4 minutes on each side, until browned all over. Transfer to a plate.

Decrease the heat to low–medium, add the remaining oil to the pan and cook the onion, celery, carrot and garlic, scraping the base of the pan to remove any browned bits, until softened and golden. Add the tomato and cook until softened. Return the veal to the pan. Pour in the wine and chicken broth and bring to the boil. Add the thyme and bay leaves. Cover and cook in the oven for 2 hours, or until tender and the meat is almost falling off the bone.

To prepare the gremolata, finely chop the lemon zest, parsley and garlic and combine in a small bowl. Set aside.

To prepare the creamy cauliflower mash, steam the cauliflower for 15 minutes, or until very tender. Transfer the cauliflower into a food processor. Add the ghee and blend until creamy. Season with salt and pepper.

Transfer the cooked veal pieces to a plate. Cover to keep warm. Set the pan over medium heat and simmer the liquid until reduced to make a coating sauce. Discard the bay leaves and thyme sprigs. Return the veal to the pan and coat in sauce. Cover and keep warm.

Sprinkle the osso bucco with gremolata and serve with creamy cauliflower mash.

Zucchini spaghetti and meatballs

Consuming organ meat along with the flesh of an animal means that we get a good balance of amino acids. Adding liver also adds a depth of flavour that makes this dish seriously delicious. Zucchini (courgette) noodles are a nutrient-rich and gut-loving alternative to pasta. The oregano gives a herbaceous note and helps to eliminate bad bacteria in the gut.

SERVES 4

2 zucchini (courgettes)
extra-virgin olive oil, for drizzling
Himalayan salt, to taste
1 small handful basil leaves
shaved parmesan cheese, to serve

Meatballs
1 tablespoon olive oil
½ onion, finely chopped
2 cloves garlic, finely chopped
350 g (12½ oz) pork mince (ground pork)
350 g (12½ oz) beef mince (ground beef)
100 g (3½ oz) organic chicken livers, finely chopped
½ cup (50 g/1¾ oz) finely grated parmesan cheese, plus extra for serving
½ cup (50 g/1¾ oz) almond meal
1 large egg
1 small handful oregano leaves, finely chopped
finely grated zest of 1 unwaxed lemon
1 teaspoon Himalayan salt
½ teaspoon freshly ground black pepper
¼ cup (60 ml/2 fl oz) olive oil

Sauce
1 tablespoon olive oil
½ onion, finely chopped
2 cloves garlic, finely chopped
2 × 400 g (14 oz) cans chopped tomatoes
¼ cup (60 ml/2 fl oz) water
1 small handful basil leaves, coarsely chopped
1 teaspoon maple syrup
½ teaspoon Himalayan salt

To prepare the meatballs, heat the oil in a small frying pan over low–medium heat. Cook the onion and garlic until softened. Transfer to a medium bowl and set aside to cool slightly.

Once cooled add the remaining ingredients except the olive oil. Using clean hands or a wooden spoon, mix together thoroughly. Shape into 24 meatballs and place on a tray. Cover and refrigerate for 20 minutes.

Heat a little of the oil in a large frying pan over medium–high heat. Cook the meatballs in batches, turning frequently, for 3–5 minutes, until browned all over. Transfer onto a clean tray and set aside.

Meanwhile, to prepare the sauce, heat the oil in a large frying pan over low–medium heat. Cook the onion and garlic until softened. Add the tomatoes and water and bring to the boil. Reduce the heat and simmer for 10 minutes, or until softened. Add the basil, maple syrup and salt and stir to combine.

Add the browned meatballs to the sauce and simmer for 15–20 minutes, until the sauce becomes thick and the meatballs are cooked through.

To prepare the zucchini spaghetti, use a spiraliser to cut the zucchini into spaghetti-like lengths. Alternatively, using a mandoline, thinly julienne into lengthways strips. Drizzle with oil, season with salt and toss to coat.

To serve, pile the zucchini spaghetti into bowls. Top with meatballs and sauce, fresh basil and shaved parmesan cheese.

Slow-roasted lamb shoulder with fig and pistachio stuffing

Lamb (especially grass fed) is one of the richest sources of conjugated linoleic acid and is high in zinc, making this beautiful dish anti-inflammatory and healing.

SERVES 4-6

1 × 1.2 kg (2 lb 10 oz) boned lamb shoulder

Fig and pistachio stuffing
4 organic, sulphur-free dried figs
2 tablespoons cultured butter (see recipe page 303)
1 tablespoon olive oil, plus extra for drizzling
3 purple shallots, thinly sliced
1 clove garlic, finely chopped
½ teaspoon ground cumin
½ teaspoon ground cinnamon
½ teaspoon chilli powder
¼ teaspoon ground allspice
1 cup (135 g/5 oz) cooked quinoa
⅓ cup (45 g/1½ oz) pistachios, coarsely chopped
finely grated zest of 1 unwaxed lemon
1 large handful flat-leaf (Italian) parsley, finely chopped
Himalayan salt and freshly ground black pepper, to taste

Preheat the oven to 130°C (265°F).

To prepare the stuffing, soak the figs in hot water for 15 minutes, or until softened.

Heat the butter and oil in a medium frying pan over low heat. Cook the shallots and garlic, until softened. Add the cumin, cinnamon, chilli powder and allspice and cook until fragrant. Remove from the heat.

Thinly slice the figs. Add the figs and remaining ingredients to the spiced onion mixture and stir to combine. Season with salt and pepper.

Lay the lamb out, skin-side down, on a clean kitchen bench. Spread the stuffing in the centre of the lamb and then roll up tightly to enclose. Tie with kitchen string to secure.

Preheat a large frying pan over high heat.

Drizzle the lamb with oil and rub to coat. Season with salt and pepper. Sear the lamb in the hot pan, turning frequently, until browned all over.

Place the lamb, seam-side down, in a deep roasting tin. Cook for 3½–4 hours, until very tender.

Transfer the shoulder into a clean roasting tray, cover with foil and rest for 45 minutes before serving.

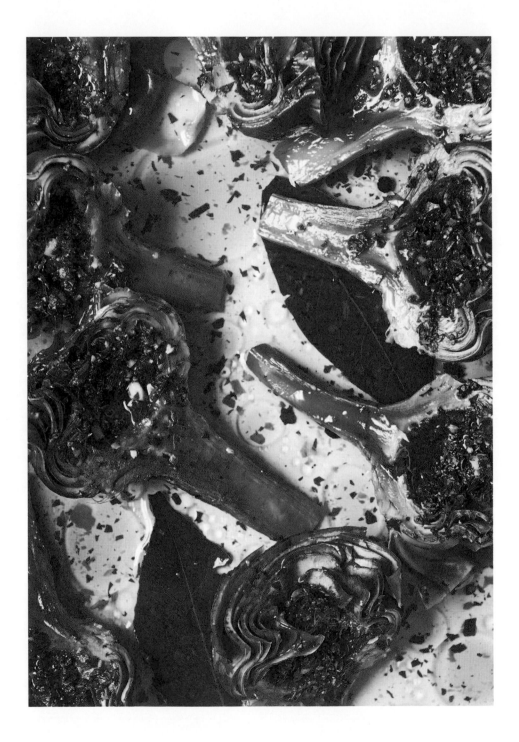

Sides

....

You can't ever underestimate the power of a side dish. It embellishes a simple roast or grilled fish and balances the flavours of the meal. Depending on the ingredients, it may help support the body in digesting meat: salads and veggies help the liver process fats, as well as improve the nutritional prowess of a dish.

Side dishes also help to make the main dish go around. When unexpected guests arrive at the door and you have only made enough of a roast for your family, a couple of sides will ensure everyone at the table is nourished and satisfied. It's also important to have more veggies on your plate than meat – which is a good approach for better health generally.

While traditional sides such as baked veggies and vibrant salads are common in Western cuisines, many cultures have a tradition of adorning meals with delicious and nutritious fermented veggies and condiments (see Basics), such as kimchi in Korea, miso in Japan and sauerkraut in Eastern Europe. You will find on my plate, no matter what time of day, some sort of lacto-fermented food as a side. It makes meals so tasty and also helps you digest your meal.

Roasted Brussels sprouts with baby kale, crisp pancetta and walnuts

SERVES 4

This dish is delicious and if there is one family of foods that will clarify your skin and protect it from cellular damage, it is the cruciferous one, which includes Brussels sprouts and kale. Both are anti-inflammatory and rich in protective compounds including sulphur, vitamins A, C and K, great for skin, bone and heart health.

500 g (1 lb 2 oz) Brussels sprouts
olive oil, for drizzling
Himalayan salt and freshly ground black pepper
100 g (3½ oz) thinly sliced sulphur-free pancetta
½ cup (60 g/2 oz) walnuts
3 large handfuls baby kale, or 3 large leaves, deveined, coarsely chopped

Preheat the oven to 200°C (400°F).

Remove the outer Brussels sprout leaves if very dark and trim the bases. Halve the sprouts lengthways.

Place the sprouts in a roasting dish. Drizzle with olive oil and season with salt and pepper. Roast for 20 minutes, or until golden brown on the outside and tender inside.

Lay the pancetta slices on a small baking tray. Cook in the oven for 10 minutes, or until crisp and the fat has rendered down. Break into bite-sized pieces.

Place the walnuts on a small baking tray (baking sheet) and roast for 3–5 minutes, until golden. Coarsely chop.

Add the kale to the roasted Brussels sprouts and toss to slightly wilt. Transfer into a large bowl or serving plate.

Scatter with pancetta and roasted walnuts.

Heirloom carrots with orange, honey and miso glaze

SERVES 4-6

The importance of eating organic carrots is paramount because, not only are they better for you, but the flavour is far superior. Carrots are full of skin-rejuvenating pro-vitamin A, C and biotin, and this delightful sweet and savoury combination of flavours works well with both fish and meat.

1 kg (2 lb 3 oz) heirloom carrots (approx 2 bunches)
1½ tablespoons raw honey
1 tablespoon coconut oil
½ cup (125 ml/4 fl oz) water
finely grated zest and juice of 1 unwaxed orange
1 tablespoon coarsely grated ginger
1 tablespoon white (Shiro) miso paste
1 teaspoon sesame seeds, lightly toasted

Wash the carrots and trim the tops, leaving approximately 4 cm (1½ in) of green stem attached.

Melt the honey and coconut oil together in a large frying pan with a fitted lid. Add the carrots and toss to coat. Pour in the water and orange juice. Add the orange zest and ginger and bring to a simmer.

Cover and cook over low heat, shaking the pan occasionally to help the carrots cook evenly, for 8 minutes, or until almost tender. Remove the lid and cook, tossing to coat, for 3–4 minutes, until carrots are tender and liquid has reduced to a glaze.

Remove from the heat, stir in the miso paste and toss to coat.

Transfer onto a serving plate and scatter with sesame seeds.

Heirloom carrots with orange, honey and miso glaze

Roasted asparagus, tomato, olive, garlic and lemon

These flavours blend so beautifully, as do the nutrients, with the oil-soluble antioxidants in the tomato and asparagus made more available for the body to use by the olive oil. Garlic contains around 200 health-giving compounds including quercetin and allium, which is antibiotic and antiviral, making it excellent for both problem skin and when you are ailing.

SERVES 4-6

3 bunches asparagus
250 g (9 oz) mini Roma (plum) or cherry tomatoes, halved lengthways
⅓ cup (60 g/2 oz) pitted Kalamata olives, coarsely chopped
2 cloves garlic, thinly sliced
4 anchovy fillets, cut lengthways into thin strips
extra-virgin olive oil, for drizzling
Himalayan salt and freshly ground black pepper
zest of 1 unwaxed lemon

Preheat the oven to 200°C (400°F).

Snap off and discard the woody ends of the asparagus. Lay the asparagus in a large baking tray (baking sheet).

Scatter the tomatoes, olives, garlic and anchovies over the asparagus. Generously drizzle with olive oil. Season with salt and pepper.

Roast for 15–20 minutes, until the asparagus is tender and tomatoes softened.

To serve, transfer onto a large serving plate. Finely grate lemon zest over the top.

Broccoli and peas with hazelnuts, preserved lemon and mint

A regular side on our table, broccoli and peas are good sources of vitamin A and lutein, and hazelnuts are rich in vitamin E – all of which studies show help keep your skin soft and hydrated.

SERVES 4-6

1 large head broccoli
¼ spiced preserved lemon (see recipe page 319)
     or store-bought
1 cup (140 g/5 oz) fresh or frozen peas
extra-virgin olive oil, for drizzling
juice of ½ lemon
⅓ cup (45 g/1½ oz) roasted hazelnuts, coarsely
     chopped
1 long red chilli, halved lengthways, seeds removed,
     thinly sliced
1 large handful mint leaves, roughly torn
Himalayan salt and freshly ground black pepper

Cut the broccoli lengthways into medium-sized wedges. Rinse well and set aside.

Remove and discard the preserved lemon flesh. Thinly slice the skin.

Bring a large saucepan of water to the boil.

Cook the broccoli for 2 minutes, or until just tender. Add the peas and cook for 10–15 seconds, until tender. Drain.

Place the broccoli and peas in a medium bowl. Drizzle generously with oil and squeeze over the lemon juice. Toss to coat. Add the preserved lemon, hazelnuts, chilli and mint. Season with salt and pepper and toss to combine.

Transfer into a serving bowl or plate.

Cauliflower and jalapeño cheese bake
with crunchy quinoa topping

Here is my healthy version of a hearty, cheesy bake, which is nutritious, kind to digestion, and with robust flavours including jalapeños to give it a spark that cuts through the richness.

SERVES 4-6

1 large cauliflower, broken into large florets

Jalapeño cheese sauce
2 cups (500 ml/17 fl oz) unsweetened almond milk
¼ cup (60 g/2 oz) coconut oil
¼ cup (30 g/1 oz) arrowroot
½ cup (25 g/1 oz) savoury yeast flakes*
12 slices jalapeño, or to taste
1 tablespoon Dijon mustard
Himalayan salt and finely ground white pepper

Crunchy quinoa topping
1 cup (135 g/5 oz) cooked quinoa, cooled slightly
1 tablespoon extra-virgin olive oil
1 large handful flat-leaf (Italian) parsley, coarsely
    chopped
2 teaspoons sweet paprika
1 teaspoon onion powder
½ teaspoon garlic powder
Himalayan salt and freshly ground black pepper
100 g (3½ oz) marinated goat's feta, broken into small
    lumps

Preheat the oven to 180°C (350°F).

To prepare the jalapeño cheese sauce, heat the milk in a medium saucepan over medium heat until hot.

In a separate medium saucepan, melt the coconut oil over low–medium heat. Add the arrowroot and cook, stirring constantly, for 3 minutes, or until it begins to fizz. Gradually add the hot milk, a ladle at a time, stirring constantly with a wooden spoon, until all of the milk is incorporated. Continue to stir and simmer for 3-4 minutes, until thickened to coat the back of the spoon.

Remove from the heat. Add the savoury yeast flakes, jalapeños and mustard and stir to combine. Season with salt and pepper. Cover the surface with a piece of baking paper and set aside.

Bring a large saucepan of water to the boil.

Cook the cauliflower for 4 minutes, or until almost tender. Drain and set aside.

To prepare the crunchy quinoa topping, place all of the ingredients, except the goat's cheese, in a medium bowl and toss to combine. Season with salt and pepper. Add the goat's cheese and fold through.

Arrange the cauliflower in a medium-sized ovenproof dish. Cover with jalapeño cheese sauce and crumble over the quinoa topping.

Bake for 30–35 minutes, until the topping is crunchy and golden brown and the cauliflower is tender.

* Available from health food stores.

Baked globe artichokes with citrus and herb salad

Globe artichokes are one of the oldest cultivated veggies and have been used for millennia for their excellent digestive and cleansing properties. They taste lovely steamed by themselves, or with aioli, or salad, as in this delightful recipe, or as a purée served with baked meats.

SERVES 4–6

1 lemon, juiced

12 smallish globe artichokes (the smaller ones are the most tender)

2 bay leaves

½ teaspoon whole black peppercorns

1¼ cups (310 ml/10½ fl oz) verjuice

¾ cup (180 ml/6 fl oz) water

1 large handful mint leaves, finely chopped, plus 1 large handful mint leaves, torn

1 large handful flat-leaf (Italian) parsley, finely chopped

3 cloves garlic, finely chopped

Himalayan salt and freshly ground black pepper, to taste

¾ cup (180 ml/6 fl oz) extra-virgin olive oil, plus extra to serve

1 orange

1 ruby grapefruit

1 lemon

1 baby fennel bulb, trimmed and thinly shaved

1 large handful basil leaves, torn

1 large handful dill sprigs

¼ cup (35 g/1¼ oz) pine nuts, roasted, to serve

Preheat the oven to 150°C (300°F).

Fill a large bowl with water and add the lemon juice.

To prepare the artichokes, working with one artichoke at a time, trim the top third from each artichoke. Using a teaspoon, scoop out the hairy choke. Peel off and discard the thick outer leaves to reveal the bright tender flesh. Trim stems to 3 cm (1¼ in) from the base and peel off the skin. Halve lengthways and place in the prepared acidic water, to prevent discolouration.

Place the bay leaves and peppercorns in the base of a non-reactive baking dish large enough to hold the artichokes snugly in a single layer. Add the verjuice and water and set aside.

Combine chopped mint, parsley and garlic in a bowl and mix to combine. Season with salt and pepper.

Drain the artichokes. Stuff the cavities with a little of the herb mixture. Arrange, cut-side up, in a single layer in the prepared dish. Drizzle with olive oil. Place a sheet of baking paper on top of the artichokes. Cover the dish with aluminum foil. Bake for 1–1½ hours, until tender.

Using a small sharp knife cut off and discard the orange, grapefruit and lemon skin. Cut out the segments and place in a small bowl. Reserve the remaining pulp.

To serve, remove the artichokes from cooking liquid and arrange on a platter. Scatter with citrus segments, shaved fennel, torn mint, remaining herbs and pine nuts. Drizzle with a little additional oil and squeeze over the juice of the reserved citrus pulp, to taste.

Serve warm or at room temperature.

Fig, pomegranate, radicchio, orange and feta salad

This delicious mix of bitter, sweet and savoury flavours always reminds me of one of my favourite chefs, Yotam Ottolenghi, who would probably have put orange blossom water in this recipe (which would be beautiful). Radicchio contains inulin, a prebiotic, which also increases bile production and helps us utilise skin-loving fats.

SERVES 4

2 oranges
3 ripe figs
1 head radicchio
1 pomegranate, seeds removed
150 g (5½ oz) marinated feta, drained and crumbled
¾ cup (80 g/2¾ oz) walnuts, lightly roasted
2 large handfuls mint leaves, torn

Dressing
¼ cup (60 ml/2 fl oz) red wine vinegar
    (unpasteurised)
1½ teaspoons Dijon mustard
1 teaspoon raw honey
⅓ cup (80 ml/2½ fl oz) extra-virgin olive oil
Himalayan salt and freshly ground black pepper

To prepare the dressing, whisk the vinegar, mustard and honey together in a small bowl. Gradually pour in the oil, continuously whisking, until fully incorporated. Season with salt and pepper. Set aside.

Using a small sharp knife cut off and discard the orange skin. Slice the oranges into approximately 1 cm (½ in)-thick rounds.

Roughly tear the figs into quarters.

Roughly tear the radicchio into pieces.

To assemble, arrange the orange, fig and radicchio on a large serving plate. Drizzle with half of the dressing. Scatter with pomegranate seeds, feta, walnuts and mint. Drizzle with the remaining dressing.

Beetroot, kale, green bean and avocado salad with buttermilk and paprika dressing

This assembly of superfoods includes beans, which are high in skin-toning silica, and the kale and avocado pack a punch of good fats and vitamins for serious skin-glowing action.

SERVES 4

½ cup (100 g/3½ oz) quinoa, rinsed
1 cup (250 ml/8½ fl oz) water
200 g (7 oz) green beans, trimmed
1 beetroot (beet)
1 avocado, halved and stone removed
4 large kale leaves, deveined and shredded
150 g (5½ oz) radishes (approx 4–5), thinly sliced
1 large handful mint, leaves and stems,
    coarsely chopped

Buttermilk and paprika dressing
¼ cup (60 ml/2 fl oz) buttermilk
2 tablespoons freshly squeezed lime juice
1½ tablespoons extra-virgin olive oil
1 clove garlic, finely chopped
1 teaspoon smoked sweet paprika
Himalayan salt and freshly ground black pepper,
    to taste

Place the quinoa and water in a small saucepan and bring to the boil. Cover and decrease the heat to low and simmer for 15 minutes, or until almost all of the water has been absorbed and holes appear on the surface. Keep covered and remove from the heat to finish cooking for a further 5 minutes, or until tails have sprouted and all of the water has been absorbed.

Once cooked, spread out onto a tray and fluff with a fork. Season with salt. Set aside to cool.

To prepare the dressing, place the buttermilk, lime juice, oil, garlic and paprika in a glass jar and seal with a lid. Shake vigorously to combine. Season with salt and pepper.

Bring a medium saucepan of water to the boil.

Blanch the beans for 10 seconds. Drain and refresh in a bowl of iced water. Drain. Slice each bean diagonally into three pieces.

Wearing food-handling gloves, cut the skin off the beetroot. Using a mandoline, thinly slice the beetroot. Cut into strips.

Use a large spoon to scoop the avocado out of its skin. Thickly slice crossways.

Place all of the ingredients in a large bowl. Pour over dressing and toss to coat before serving.

Sweet potato wedges with almond and chilli dukkah, goat's cheese and fresh herbs

Sweet potato is low GI, full of fibre and its high vitamin A content helps keep your scalp healthy and skin free from breakouts. It pairs beautifully with the creamy goat's cheese.

SERVES 4

2 sweet potatoes, peeled
extra-virgin olive oil, for drizzling
150 g (5½ oz) marinated goat's cheese, crumbled
1 large handful flat-leaf (Italian) parsley, coarsely chopped
1 large handful mint leaves, coarsely chopped

Almond and chilli dukkah
½ cup (90 g/3 oz) almonds
2 teaspoons sesame seeds
1 teaspoon chilli flakes
1 teaspoon coriander seeds
½ teaspoon cumin seeds
Himalayan salt and freshly ground black pepper

Preheat the oven to 200°C (400°F).

Cut the sweet potatoes lengthways into approximately 2 cm (¾ in)-thick wedges. Arrange on a large baking tray (baking sheet) and drizzle with oil. Bake for 15–20 minutes, until tender and slightly crisp.

Meanwhile to make the dukkah, spread the almonds onto a small baking tray and roast in the oven for 5 minutes, or until golden brown. Dry-fry the sesame seeds, chilli flakes, coriander seeds and cumin seeds in a small frying pan over low heat, until the sesame seeds are lightly toasted and spices fragrant.

Crush the roasted almonds and toasted seeds together, using a small mortar and pestle or spice grinder, until coarsely ground. Season with salt and pepper and set aside.

To serve, transfer the roasted sweet potato onto a large serving plate. Crumble over goat's cheese. Sprinkle with dukkah and scatter with herbs.

Desserts

....

I love to devour a beautiful dessert, but for me it's all about the timing. There is something counterintuitive about the concept of eating a full meal and following it with a rich, heavy dessert and then sleeping on a very full stomach for eight hours. It just doesn't seem right, especially when our metabolism is fundamentally based on energy in and energy out. In any case, how can you really appreciate the flavours and care that is often put into a dessert when you're not actually hungry?

A healthy dessert can be a meal in itself and I enjoy it when I'm hungry, which is usually away from a main meal. When I entertain, or on weekends, I may deviate from this practice!

Including protein in a sweet dessert helps to balance blood sugar levels that may spike from the sweetener. You can also try the recipes without any added sugar, or reduce the levels found in the recipes. My philosophy when it comes to sugar is to use it in as natural and unprocessed a form as possible, found in fruit or dates, or raw honey or maple syrup, which, unlike refined sugars, contain health-giving minerals and antioxidants. I often use stevia as it is a great sugar-free option. As brands of stevia differ, refer to the packet for substitute percentages.

These are some of my all-time favourites: decadent, creamy, chocolatey, fruity, nutty, caramelly and always full of flavour and texture. As with all treat food containing added sweeteners, even those that are natural, everything is best in moderation! If you are following a gut-healing protocol, then it is best to avoid added sugars – your natural health practitioner will guide you.

Fruit smoothie popsicles with bone broth

Matcha and black tahini caramel ice-cream pops

Fruit smoothie popsicles with bone broth

*I take advantage of any opportunity to add bone broth to a recipe and these delightful, fruity
pops are no exception. Bone broth is highly nutritious and one of the best gut-healing foods,
and when straight shots of broth are not welcomed by young palates, these treats are ideal.*

MAKES 8

250 g (9 oz) strawberries, hulled

125 g (4½ oz) raspberries

250 g (9 oz) peeled pineapple, cut into chunks

1 large handful mint leaves

½ cup (125 ml/4 fl oz) chicken bone broth
(see recipe page 300)

1 tablespoon raw honey, or to taste

Place the strawberries, raspberries, pineapple and
mint in a high-speed blender. Blend until smooth.
Add the chicken broth and blend to combine. Add the
honey, to desired sweetness, and blend to combine.

Pour the smoothie mixture into eight ⅓ cup
(80 ml/2½ fl oz)-capacity popsicle moulds. Insert
popsicle sticks. Freeze for 4 hours or overnight, until
completely frozen.

Run moulds under warm water to help release
the popsicles.

NOTE

The popsicles can be stored in the freezer
for up to 3 months.

Matcha and black tahini caramel ice-cream pops

These pops are heavenly; the rich creaminess of the cashews blends beautifully with the tahini caramel and the sweetness is balanced by the green, slightly bitter tannin note of matcha. They are brimming with antioxidants and minerals from the nuts, dates, tahini and green tea.

MAKES 10

1 cup (150 g/5½ oz) raw cashews, soaked in cold water for 4 hours
2 cups (500 ml/17 fl oz) coconut milk
¼ cup (60 ml/2 fl oz) raw honey
3 teaspoons matcha green tea powder
½ teaspoon vanilla bean powder*
pinch of Himalayan salt

Black tahini caramel
4 medjool dates, pitted
¼ cup (60 ml/2 fl oz) coconut milk
1 tablespoon black tahini paste*
1 tablespoon maple syrup
1 teaspoon vanilla bean powder*
pinch of Himalayan salt

To make the black tahini caramel, soak the dates in hot water for 10 minutes, or until softened. Drain.

Combine the softened dates and remaining ingredients in a high-speed blender. Blend until smooth. Transfer to a small bowl and set aside.

Drain and rinse the cashews under cold water.

Place the cashews and ½ cup (125 ml/4 fl oz) of the coconut milk in a high-speed blender. Blend until smooth. Add the remaining ingredients and blend to combine.

Pour the matcha mixture into ten ⅓-cup (80 ml/ 2½ fl oz)-capacity popsicle moulds, to fill 1.5 cm (½ in) from the top.

Drop 2 teaspoons of black tahini caramel into the centre of each of the moulds. Insert a knife and lift up and drag the caramel to create a marble effect. Insert the popsicle sticks. Freeze for 4 hours or overnight, until completely frozen.

Before serving, run the moulds under warm water to help release the popsicles.

NOTE
The popsicles can be stored in the freezer for up to 3 months.

* Available from health food stores.

Chocolate and gingernut ice-cream sandwiches

Created by my clever friend Rachael, these are one of the most exquisite sweets I have ever eaten. Boasting good fats, prebiotics, antioxidants, fibre and minerals, these cold, gingery, chocolatey, nutty, chewy, caramelly triangles of digestive goodness are seriously moreish. It really is hard to stop at one.

MAKES 16

Blondie
1½ cups (150 g/5½ oz) almond meal
1 cup (155 g/5½ oz) macadamias, lightly roasted
    and coarsely chopped
1 cup (90 g/3 oz) desiccated (shredded) coconut
2 teaspoons ground ginger
1 teaspoon vanilla bean powder*
1 teaspoon ground cinnamon
pinch of Himalayan salt
8 medjool dates, pitted
¼ cup (60 g/2 oz) coconut butter
2 tablespoons maple syrup

Ginger caramel ice-cream
1¼ cups (185 g/6½ oz) raw cashews, soaked in
    cold water overnight
1 cup (250 ml/8½ fl oz) full-fat coconut cream
1 very ripe medium banana
8 medjool dates, pitted
2 tablespoons maple syrup
1 tablespoon coconut oil
1 tablespoon ground ginger
½ teaspoon vanilla bean powder*
pinch of Himalayan salt
½ cup (120 g/4½ oz) glacé (candied) ginger, thinly
    sliced

Raw chocolate coating
⅔ cup (50 g/1¾ oz) cacao powder
50 g (1¾ oz) cacao butter, coarsely chopped
1 tablespoon maple syrup
1 tablespoon coconut oil

NOTE
These can be stored in an airtight container
in the freezer for up to 3 months.

* Available from health food stores.

Lightly grease and line a 25 × 16 × 3 cm (10 × 6¼ × 1¼ in) tray with baking paper.

To prepare the blondie, combine the almond meal, roasted macadamias, coconut, ginger, vanilla, cinnamon and salt in a medium bowl.

Place the dates, coconut butter and maple syrup in a high-speed blender. Blend until smooth.

Add the blended date mixture to the dry ingredients and stir well, until it begins to bind together.

Press half of the blondie mixture into the base of the tray. Smooth with the back of a spoon. Set the remaining mixture aside.

To prepare the ice-cream, drain and rinse the cashews. Place the cashews and the remaining ingredients, except the glacé ginger, in a high-speed blender. Blend until smooth. Add the glacé ginger and stir through. Pour over the base. Freeze for 2 hours, or until almost set firm.

Place the remaining blondie mixture onto a large sheet of baking paper. Compress together to make a rectangular shape. Cover with another piece of baking paper and roll out to the same size as the base of the tray. Transfer on the baking paper onto a tray. Refrigerate until firm or required.

Slide the firm, rolled out blondie onto the set ice-cream. Trim as necessary. Press gently to secure. Cover and freeze for a further 4 hours, or until set firm.

Slice the firm ice-cream slice into 16 triangular ice-cream sandwiches. >

To make the chocolate coating, half-fill a small saucepan with water and bring to a simmer. Place all of the ingredients in a heatproof bowl. Take the pan off the heat and set the bowl over the top. Ensure the base of the bowl does not touch the water. Leave for 5 minutes, or until the cacao butter and coconut oil melt. Stir to combine.

Line two medium trays with baking paper.

Dip the ice-cream sandwiches into the raw chocolate. Use a knife to spread and coat half of the sandwich and make a defined line. Place on the prepared trays.

If serving immediately, refrigerate for 10 minutes, or until set. Alternatively freeze until set or required.

Cardamom and almond milk panna cotta with roasted blood plums

Made with gelatin, which is rich in gut-healing amino acids, and warming and digestive-balancing cardamom and plums, this dessert is much loved in our house.

MAKES 4

coconut oil, for greasing
1 tablespoon green cardamom pods
2 cups (500 ml/17 fl oz) almond milk
1½ tablespoons raw honey
2 level teaspoons grass-fed gelatin powder*

Roasted blood plums
4 small blood, or other medium, dark-fleshed, plums
⅓ cup (80 ml/2½ fl oz) water
1 tablespoon raw honey

Lightly grease four ½ cup (125 ml/4 fl oz)-capacity moulds with coconut oil. Place in the refrigerator until required.

Squash the cardamom pods with the back of a wooden spoon, then place in a small saucepan and toast over low heat for 30 seconds, or until fragrant.

Pour 1½ cups (375 ml/12½ fl oz) of the almond milk into the saucepan. Gently heat for 5 minutes. Remove from the heat and stir in the honey. Set aside to infuse for 10 minutes.

Pour the remaining almond milk into a small bowl. Sprinkle the gelatin in a thin layer over the top and set aside for 10 minutes, to dissolve.

Strain the infused milk through a fine-mesh sieve. Return to the saucepan and gently reheat, until warm. Remove from the heat, add the dissolved gelatin mixture and stir to combine. Set aside to cool.

Pour the cooled mixture into the prepared moulds. Refrigerate for 4 hours, or until set.

Preheat the oven to 180°C (350°F).

Meanwhile to prepare the roasted blood plums, cut the plums in half and remove the stones. Arrange the plums, cut-side up, in a small baking dish. Pour the water into the base of the dish and drizzle the plums with honey. Roast for 20 minutes, or until tender and juices have begun to release to form a syrup. Let cool.

To release the panna cottas from their moulds, use your fingertips to gently pull the panna cotta away from the sides of the mould, breaking the seal. Immediately invert onto serving plates. They will hold their shape but have a lovely wobble.

Serve the panna cottas with roasted plum halves and syrup.

NOTE
The panna cottas can be made in advance and stored in the refrigerator for up to 3 days.

* Available from health food stores.

Watermelon, apple and mint granita

In summer, when heat is at its peak, this fresh, fruity granita is a saviour. Watermelon is hydrating and is full of lycopene, a powerful antioxidant that studies show helps protect our skin from UV damage. How clever is nature, designing foods to suit the season?

SERVES 4

500 g (1 lb 2 oz) seedless watermelon, rind removed, flesh coarsely chopped
1 large tart green apple, such as Granny Smith
2 large handfuls mint stems and leaves
1 lime, peeled and coarsely chopped
5 cm (2 in) knob of ginger, peeled and coarsely chopped
coconut water, to top up, if required
edible flowers, to decorate (optional)

Put the watermelon, apple, mint, lime and ginger through a slow-press juicer.

Top up with coconut water, if necessary, to make 3 cups (750 ml/25½ fl oz) of liquid.

Pour into a small shallow tray.

Freeze for 1–2 hours, until frozen around the edges. Remove from the freezer and mix in the frozen edges. Return to the freezer.

Remove the mixture from the freezer every 30 minutes or so and mix it up. Once all of the liquid begins to freeze, use a fork to drag and scrape the mixture and break it up into small ice crystals. Repeat this over 3 hours, or until mixture is fully frozen into delicate ice crystals.

To serve, scoop into serving glasses or bowls. Decorate with edible flowers, if desired.

NOTE

The granita can be stored in an airtight container in the freezer for up to 3 months.

Blueberry, honey and rose geranium jelly

These charming jellies are so pretty and lovely to eat. Rose geranium, in herbal medicine, is used to soothe inflammation, support digestive health and boost immunity. Perfect for when your tummy is feeling unsettled or when you crave a fresh, light dessert.

SERVES 4

coconut oil, for greasing (optional)
3¼ cups (810 ml/27½ fl oz) water
⅓ cup (80 ml/2½ fl oz) raw honey
4 large rose geranium leaves*
2 strips unwaxed lemon zest
¼ cup (60 ml/2 fl oz) rosewater
6 level teaspoons (2 × 11 g/¼ oz sachets) grass-fed
    powdered gelatin**
125 g (4½ oz) fresh blueberries

If using jelly moulds, lightly grease four 1 cup (250 ml/8½ fl oz)-capacity moulds with coconut oil and refrigerate to set. Alternatively set aside four serving glasses.

Combine 3 cups (750 ml/25½ fl oz) of the water, honey, rose geranium leaves and lemon zest in a medium saucepan. Bring to the boil. Remove from the heat and set aside to infuse, until cool.

Strain the cooled liquid through a fine-mesh sieve. Set aside.

Pour the remaining water and rosewater into a small bowl. Sprinkle the gelatin in a thin layer over the top and set aside for 10 minutes, to dissolve.

Place 1 cup (250 ml/8½ fl oz) of the rose geranium liquid into a small saucepan and gently heat, until hot. Add the gelatin mixture and stir to combine. Pour back into the remaining rose geranium liquid and mix well.

Pour one-quarter of the liquid into the prepared moulds, or alternatively serving glasses. Refrigerate for 20 minutes, or until beginning to set. Scatter with one-third of the blueberries. Repeat layers, par-setting and scattering with the remaining blueberries. End with a final layer of liquid. Refrigerate for at least 4 hours, or until completely set.

If using moulds, gently heat the bases in hot water to help turn out the jellies.

NOTE
The jellies can be stored in the refrigerator for up to 5 days.

* Picked from your garden. If rose geranium leaves are
   unavailable, add 2 teaspoons of rosewater, or to taste,
   to flavour cooled liquid after the gelatin has been added.
** Available from health food stores.

Peach Melba and coconut tartlets

A twist on a classic French dessert, this coconut-based version works beautifully with the flavours of peach and raspberry, which come into season together in summer. Both fruits are rich in vitamin C, which helps to keep our skin's connective tissue healthy and our immune system robust.

SERVES 4

coconut oil, for greasing
2 small–medium peaches, halved and stones removed
1½ cups (375 g/13 oz) natural yoghurt
maple syrup, for glazing
toasted coconut flakes, to garnish
edible flowers, to garnish (optional)

Coconut base
1 large egg
2 tablespoons coconut milk
1 tablespoon coconut oil, warmed
2 teaspoons maple syrup
½ teaspoon vanilla bean powder*
¼ cup (30 g/1 oz) coconut flour
½ teaspoon gluten-free baking powder

Raspberry paste
1½ cups (225 g/8 oz) fresh or frozen raspberries
¾ cup (75 g/2¾ oz) almond meal
1½ tablespoons maple syrup
½ teaspoon vanilla bean powder*

Preheat the oven to 180°C (350°F). Lightly grease four individual loose-based 8 cm (3¼ in) tartlet (flan) tins with coconut oil and refrigerate. Line a small baking tray with baking paper.

To prepare the coconut base, whisk the egg, coconut milk, coconut oil, maple syrup and vanilla together in a medium bowl. Add the coconut flour and baking powder and mix together to make a thick batter. Set aside for 10 minutes, for the coconut flour to rehydrate.

Spoon and press the mixture into the prepared tins, covering the bases and sides evenly. Refrigerate for 15 minutes, or until firm.

Bake the bases for 10–15 minutes, until firm and golden brown. Set aside to cool.

Roast the peaches at the same time, placing them cut-side up on the prepared tray. Cook for 10–15 minutes, until tender and beginning to caramelise but still holding their shape. Set aside to cool.

Meanwhile to prepare the raspberry paste, place the raspberries in a small saucepan and gently heat, until they begin to soften and release their juices. Mash with a fork and simmer until all of the liquid has evaporated, leaving a thick purée. Add the almond meal, maple syrup and vanilla and stir to make a thick paste. Transfer into a small bowl and refrigerate.

To assemble, spoon and spread the raspberry paste into the bases. Top with a dollop of yoghurt and a roasted peach half. Glaze with maple syrup and scatter with toasted coconut. Scatter with edible flowers, if desired.

Serve immediately.

* Available from health food stores.

Mango and passionfruit 'cheesecake'

My husband loves cheesecake, but is allergic to dairy, so I made this with him in mind. Macadamias contain thiamine, which increases acid in the gut to aid digestion and boost skin health. Coconut is rich in anti-inflammatory lauric acid and in medium-chain fatty acids that can easily be used by the body for energy.

SERVES 8

coconut oil, for greasing

Base
½ cup (85 g/3 oz) raw macadamias
½ cup (50 g/1¾ oz) desiccated (shredded) coconut
2 medjool dates, pitted
1 tablespoon coconut oil, warmed
¼ teaspoon ground cinnamon
pinch of Himalayan salt

Mango filling
¼ cup (60 ml/2 fl oz) cold water
1 tablespoon grass-fed powdered gelatin*
¾ cup (180 ml/6 fl oz) full-fat coconut cream
1 cup (150 g/5½ oz) raw cashews, soaked in cold
    water overnight
1 medium–large ripe mango, flesh coarsely
    chopped (approx 300 g/10½ oz of flesh)
1 lime, zest finely grated and juiced
2 tablespoons coconut oil, warmed
2 tablespoons maple syrup, or to taste

Passionfruit topping
⅓ cup (80 ml/2½ fl oz) cold water
1½ teaspoons grass-fed powdered gelatin*
6 passionfruit, plus extra to serve

NOTE
For a vegetarian version, omit the gelatin and freeze at each stage to set. Remove from the refrigerator for 10–15 minutes before serving to soften slightly.

The cheesecake can be stored in the refrigerator for up to 1 week.

* Available from health food stores.

Preheat the oven to 180°C (350°F). Lightly grease and line the base and sides of a 16 cm (6¼ in)-diameter round springform tin with baking paper.

To prepare the base, spread the macadamias onto a small tray and roast for 5–10 minutes, until golden. Set aside to cool.

Place the cooled macadamias and the remaining ingredients in a high-speed blender. Blend to combine and coarsely chop the macadamias. The macadamias should still have some texture. Press into the base of the prepared tin. Smooth with the back of a spoon. Refrigerate for 15 minutes, or until firm.

To prepare the mango filling, pour the water into a small bowl and sprinkle the gelatin over the surface in an even layer. Set aside for 10 minutes to soften.

Gently heat the coconut cream in a small saucepan until hot. Add the softened gelatin and stir to combine. Set aside to cool to room temperature, stirring occasionally.

Drain and rinse the cashews. Combine the cashews, cooled gelatin cream and remaining ingredients in a high-speed food processor. Blend until smooth.

Pour the filling into the base. Tap the base firmly on the bench to remove any air bubbles. Refrigerate for 2 hours, or until beginning to set.

To prepare the passionfruit topping, pour the water into a small bowl and sprinkle the gelatin over the surface in an even layer. Set aside for 10 minutes, to soften.

Scoop out the passionfruit pulp and strain through a fine-mesh sieve. You should end up with approximately 100 ml (3½ fl oz) of passionfruit juice. Discard the seeds. >

Gently heat the passionfruit juice in a small saucepan until hot. Add the softened gelatin and stir to combine. Set aside to cool to room temperature, stirring occasionally to prevent from setting.

Once cooled, pour over the cheesecake filling. Refrigerate for a further 2 hours, or until it is completely set.

Serve drizzled with extra passionfruit pulp.

Molten chocolate puddings with passionfruit-lemon curd

This is probably the most coveted dessert in my household: these delicious, decadent (and healthy) puddings ooze with chocolate sauce and pair beautifully with the piquant notes of passionfruit and lemon curd. Made with lots (and lots) of eggs, they are rich in protein to nourish and sustain our skin and body.

SERVES 4

35 g (1¼ oz) cacao powder

35 g (1¼ oz) cacao butter*

⅓ cup (80 ml/2½ fl oz) maple syrup

¼ cup (60 ml/2 fl oz) coconut oil, plus extra
    for greasing moulds

2 large eggs

2 large egg yolks

2 tablespoons almond meal

½ teaspoon vanilla bean powder*

pinch of Himalayan salt

Passionfruit-lemon curd

3 large egg yolks

¼ cup (60 ml/2 fl oz) strained fresh passionfruit pulp

2 tablespoons raw honey

1½ tablespoons freshly squeezed lemon juice

finely grated zest of 2 unwaxed lemons

¼ cup (60 g/2 oz) coconut oil, firm (not melted)

pulp and seeds from 2 passionfruit, to serve

Grease four ½ cup (125 ml/4 fl oz)-capacity ovenproof moulds or ramekins with coconut oil and line the bases with baking paper.

Half-fill a small saucepan with water and bring to a simmer.

Place the cacao powder, cacao butter, maple syrup and coconut oil in a heatproof bowl. Remove the pan from the heat and set the bowl over the top. Ensure the base of the bowl does not touch the water. Leave for 5 minutes, or until the cacao butter and coconut oil melt. Stir to combine. Set aside to cool slightly.

Whisk the eggs and yolks together in a medium bowl. Stir into the cooled chocolate mixture. Add the almond meal, vanilla and salt and stir to combine.

Pour the mixture into the prepared moulds. Refrigerate for 30 minutes.

Meanwhile to prepare the passionfruit-lemon curd, place the egg yolks, passionfruit juice, honey, lemon juice and lemon zest in a medium heatproof bowl. Whisk to combine.

Set the bowl over a saucepan of not quite simmering water, ensuring the base of the bowl doesn't touch the water. Whisk the mixture over the heat for 4–5 minutes, until it begins to thicken.

Add the coconut oil 1 teaspoon at a time, whisking after each addition, until it is all incorporated, to make a thick curd which coats the back of a spoon. Transfer into a clean bowl. Cover the surface with a piece of baking paper and set aside to cool.

Preheat the oven to 220°C (430°F).

Place the chocolate pudding ramekins in a deep baking tray. Pour boiling water into the tray, until it comes halfway up the sides of the ramekins.

Bake for 12 minutes, or until the edges are puffed and cooked but the centre still looks a little wet. Remove the ramekins from a tray of water and set aside for 10 minutes, to cool and set slightly.

Invert the ramekins onto serving plates, tapping firmly to assist the pudding to release. Discard the baking paper.

Serve with a spoonful of passionfruit-lemon curd and extra passionfruit pulp and seeds.

* Available from health food stores.

Cherry and almond clafoutis

While you can make this French classic with a number of fruits, I love to make it with cherries when they are in season. Sweet and succulent, cherries are sublime and promote healthy cells as well as beauty sleep, as they contain melatonin. Lovely.

SERVES 6

coconut oil or ghee, for greasing
350 g (12½ oz) pitted fresh or frozen cherries
1 cup (250 ml/8½ fl oz) coconut milk
4 large eggs
⅓ cup (30 g/1 oz) almond meal
¼ cup (60 ml/2 fl oz) maple syrup
½ teaspoon vanilla bean powder*
2 tablespoons flaked almonds

Preheat the oven to 180°C (350°F). Lightly grease a 23 cm (9 in) ceramic tart (flan) dish with coconut oil or ghee.

Scatter the cherries over the bottom of the dish.

Combine the coconut milk, eggs, almond meal, maple syrup and vanilla in a blender and process, until smooth. Pour over the cherries. Scatter with flaked almonds.

Bake for 35–40 minutes, until golden brown and set.

Let stand at room temperature for 10 minutes before serving.

Serve warm or at room temperature.

* Available from health food stores.

Salted miso caramel crème brûlée

My nanna often made crème caramel when I was young, and since then anything with custard takes me to a happy place. This nourishing salted miso caramel-infused crème brûlée takes an already special dessert to new heights, and it has the added benefit of containing plenty of nutrients.

SERVES 4

400 ml (13½ fl oz) can full-fat coconut milk
½ teaspoon vanilla bean powder*
6 large egg yolks
1 cup (250 ml/8½ fl oz) salted miso caramel sauce
    (see recipe page 335)
¼ cup (35 g/1¼ oz) coconut sugar, for sprinkling
1 teaspoon Himalayan salt
nasturtium flowers, to decorate (optional)

Preheat the oven to 150°C (300°F).

Place the coconut milk and vanilla bean powder in a small saucepan over medium heat until hot. Do not simmer. Remove from the heat.

Whisk the egg yolks and salted miso caramel sauce together in a medium bowl.

Stirring continuously, gradually pour the hot milk into the egg yolk mixture, until combined.

Place four 1 cup (250 ml/8½ fl oz)-capacity ovenproof ramekins into a deep roasting tin. Pour the salted miso caramel custard evenly into the ramekins.

Fill the roasting tin with enough boiling water to come halfway up the sides of the ramekins. Cover the tray loosely with foil, so air can still circulate through.

Bake for 40 minutes, or until set but still slightly wobbly in the middle. Carefully remove ramekins from the hot water and set aside to cool. Cover and refrigerate for 4 hours, overnight or until required, up to 3 days.

Combine the coconut sugar and salt in a small bowl.

To serve, stand the brûlées at room temperature for 20 minutes, to take the chill off the cream. Generously sprinkle the coconut sugar and salt mixture over the surface of the cooked custards to make an even layer. Use a kitchen blowtorch to caramelise the sugar until it is dark brown. Alternatively, you can place under a very hot grill (broiler), close to the heat, for 2–3 minutes, until caramelised.

Serve immediately, decorated with nasturtium flowers if desired.

*   Available from health food stores.

Sweet potato and pecan tart

*This sweet, warming, nourishing and fragrant tart is beautiful for a winter's afternoon tea.
It's important that your pecans are super fresh, not only because they taste so much better,
but so that their vitamin E and fatty acid content is still potent.*

SERVES 6-8

1½ cups (375 g/13 oz) natural yoghurt
edible flowers, to decorate (optional)

Pastry
1½ cups (165 g/6 oz) pecans
1 cup (100 g/3½ oz) almond meal
2 tablespoons arrowroot
1 teaspoon ground cinnamon
1 large egg, lightly beaten
2 tablespoons maple syrup
1 tablespoon macadamia oil, plus extra for greasing

Filling
400 g (14 oz) sweet potato, peeled and cut into
    chunks
½ cup (125 ml/4 fl oz) almond milk
3 large eggs
¼ cup (60 ml/2 fl oz) maple syrup
1 teaspoon ground cinnamon
1 teaspoon ground ginger
½ teaspoon vanilla bean powder*
½ teaspoon ground nutmeg
⅛ teaspoon ground cloves
pinch of Himalayan salt

Glazed salted pecans
¼ cup (60 ml/2 fl oz) maple syrup
¾ cup (100 g/3½ oz) pecans
¼ teaspoon Himalayan salt

NOTE
The finished tart can be covered and stored
in the refrigerator for up to 5 days.

* Available from health food stores.

To make the pastry, blend the pecans in a food
processor or high-speed blender, until finely ground.
Transfer into a medium bowl. Add the almond meal,
arrowroot and cinnamon and stir to combine. Add the
egg, maple syrup and oil and mix until it begins to
bind together.

Press the mixture into a 20 cm (8 in) pie dish lightly
greased with oil, to make an even layer on the base
and sides. Cover and refrigerate for 15 minutes.

Preheat the oven to 180°C (350°F). Cover the base
with a piece of baking paper and fill with baking
weights, dry rice or beans. Bake the base for 10
minutes. Remove the baking weights and paper and
bake for a further 5 minutes, or until golden brown.

To prepare the filling, steam the sweet potato for
10–15 minutes, until tender.

Place the sweet potato and remaining ingredients in
a food processor. Blend until smooth. Pour into the
prepared base and spread to make a smooth surface.

Bake for 35–40 minutes, until set. Cover the pastry
edge with foil if it begins to darken too much. Set
aside to cool.

Meanwhile to make the salted glazed pecans, line
a small baking tray with baking paper. Heat the
maple syrup in a small saucepan over low heat, until
simmering. Add the pecans and salt and toss to coat.
Continue to heat, tossing occasionally, until the
syrup reduces to a thick and sticky coating over the
nuts. Drop the glazed pecans in small clusters on the
prepared tray. Set aside to cool and harden.

Spoon the natural yoghurt in the centre of the cooled
tart and spread out. Decorate with clusters of the
glazed salted pecans, and edible flowers if desired.

Roasted pineapple with tamarind, date and chilli sauce

Pineapple is a formidable beauty food. High in collagen-building manganese and vitamin C,
it also contains bromelain, an enzyme that is anti-inflammatory and aids digestion.
Its intense sweetness marries well with the tart, sticky tamarind, a fruit used medicinally
in Asia for easing stomach discomfort.

SERVES 6

1 small ripe pineapple
1 tablespoon ghee
1 tablespoon maple syrup
coconut cream, to serve

Tamarind, date and chilli sauce
4 medjool dates, pitted
½ cup (125 ml/4 fl oz) boiling water
¼ cup (60 ml/2 fl oz) tamarind purée
2 tablespoons freshly squeezed lime juice
2 tablespoons maple syrup
½ teaspoon chilli flakes
½ teaspoon vanilla bean powder*
¼ teaspoon Himalayan salt

Preheat the oven to 200°C (400°F).

Trim the pineapple and remove all the skin.
Cut lengthways into six wedges. Place in a large
roasting tin.

Melt the ghee and maple syrup together in a small
saucepan. Brush over the pineapple. Roast for
45 minutes, basting every 15 minutes, or until
the pineapple is caramelised and tender.

Meanwhile to make the tamarind, date and chilli
sauce, cover the dates with the boiling water and
set aside for 10 minutes, or until softened.

Place the dates and any remaining soaking liquid
in a food processor or high-speed blender. Add the
remaining ingredients. Blend until smooth. Transfer
into a small bowl.

Serve the roasted pineapple with the tamarind, date
and chilli sauce and coconut cream.

* Available from health food stores.

Dessert tasting platter

This is my absolute favourite way to have dessert and share it with family and friends.
It looks so beautiful, is healthy, and caters to varying tastes and dietary requirements.
It is also a wonderful way to experiment with the very different combinations you can create.

SERVES 4–6

200 g (7 oz) good-quality dark chocolate, cut into
    bite-size chunks
250 g (9 oz) strawberries, hulled and sliced
125 g (4½ oz) blueberries
1 small handful Brazil nuts
1 small handful hazelnuts
1 small handful pecans
2 tablespoons desiccated (shredded) coconut
1 small handful basil leaves, torn
1 small handful fresh edible rose petals*
1 tablespoon edible dried lavender
1 long red chilli, sliced
1 teaspoon sea salt

Arrange the ingredients on a serving platter or chopping board and share with friends.

This is a wonderful way to experiment with the very different combinations you can enjoy with dark chocolate: chocolate and lavender, chocolate with basil and blueberries, chocolate and sea salt.

NOTE
You can add or omit ingredients as desired
to create your own unique tasting platter.

* Pesticide-free.

Baking

....

There is something so wonderful and miraculous about a biscuit (cookie), a cake or a loaf of bread; they are nothing short of works of art. Then there are the enjoyable rituals around these culinary joys, of sitting down with friends and family with a pot of tea and sharing food made with love.

My mum is a great cook, but when I was growing up she rarely baked, which meant that I learned her instinctive knack of throwing savoury dishes together without having to refer to a recipe, but as I got older, I inevitably became very frustrated by the exact science of baking – it was a foreign language to me. However, with practice and patience, I have begun to revel in its mindful, rewarding ritual, as well as learning to accept that not everything always turns out right, such as a cake that fails to rise or that if I don't follow a baking recipe with the utmost respect, it may not work. However, there is creativity within science, and once you understand the mechanisms of baking you can begin to play with flavours and textures.

With gluten intolerance rife in our household, I have created baked goods that support digestive health and cakes that are actually good for you – and they taste scrumptious. In terms of sweeteners, I believe in a broad-spectrum approach. I use different sweeteners, sometimes honey, occasionally maple syrup and then stevia – moderation in all foods.

TIPS

———   You can reduce the amount of sweetener called for in these recipes if you wish, or use alternatives. For those who are focusing on avoiding all added sweeteners as part of a gut-healing protocol, substitute with stevia.

Beetroot and chocolate brownies

Cacao is super high in tryptophan, a precursor to the happiness-inducing chemicals serotonin and dopamine. The beetroot (beet) lends a sweetness and earthiness to the flavour as well as being one of the richest sources of glutamine, a powerful amino acid that helps to heal the lining of the gut. Squares of pure joy!

MAKES 12 PIECES

250 g (9 oz) beetroot (beet)
6 medjool dates, pitted
¾ cup (60 g/2 oz) cacao powder
¼ cup (60 ml/2 fl oz) coconut oil, melted
3 eggs
¼ cup (60 ml/2 fl oz) maple syrup
1 cup (100 g/3½ oz) almond meal
¼ cup (60 ml/2 fl oz) coconut drinking milk (or any nut milk)
1 teaspoon gluten-free baking powder
1 teaspoon vanilla bean powder*
¼ teaspoon bicarbonate of soda (baking soda)
pinch of Himalayan salt

Preheat the oven to 190°C (375°F). Lightly grease and line a 25 × 16 × 3 cm (10 × 6¼ × 1¼ in) tray with baking paper.

Peel the beetroot and cut 150 g (5½ oz) into chunks of approximately 3 cm (1¼ in). Place in a small saucepan, cover with cold water and bring to the boil. Simmer for 20–25 minutes, until tender. Drain.

Soak the dates in enough boiling water to just cover for 10 minutes, or until softened. Drain.

Place the cooked beetroot and softened dates in a high-speed blender and process until smooth. Add the cacao powder, coconut oil, eggs and maple syrup and blend to combine. Add the almond meal, coconut milk, baking powder, vanilla, bicarbonate of soda and salt and blend to combine.

Pour the mixture into the prepared tray.

Using a mandoline or vegetable peeler, thinly slice the remaining beetroot. Arrange and twist beetroot slices into the top of the batter.

Bake for 25–30 minutes, until just firm and a skewer comes out clean when inserted into the centre. Set aside to cool completely.

Cut into 12 even pieces.

NOTE

It is important that the brownie is cooled completely before serving to ensure the texture is not too moist.

The brownies can be stored in an airtight container in the refrigerator for up to 1 week. Alternatively, they can be frozen for up to 3 months.

* Available from health food stores.

Quinoa, orange and cardamom cake

Pistachio and cacao nib biscotti

Quinoa, orange and cardamom cake

This moist, flavourful cake makes any occasion special. Made from quinoa and almond meal, it's high in protein and full of complex carbohydrates, making it slow to digest, helping to stabilise blood sugars and keeping you satiated longer – perfect to get you through to lunch or dinner.

SERVES 8

¾ cup (150 g/5½ oz) quinoa, rinsed

1½ cups (375 ml/12½ fl oz) freshly squeezed orange juice

¾ cup (75 g/2¾ oz) almond meal

3 large eggs

100ml (3½ fl oz) maple syrup

¼ cup (60 ml/2 fl oz) macadamia oil

1 teaspoon ground cardamom

1 teaspoon gluten-free baking powder

½ teaspoon bicarbonate of soda (baking soda)

finely grated zest of 2 unwaxed oranges

pinch of Himalayan salt

edible flowers, to decorate (optional)

yoghurt, to serve (optional)

Orange and cardamom glaze

8 green cardamom pods, bruised

¾ cup (180 ml/6 fl oz) freshly squeezed orange juice

1½ tablespoons maple syrup

2 tablespoons flaked almonds, lightly toasted

Preheat the oven to 180°C (350.°F). Lightly grease a 19 × 10 cm (7½ × 4 in) loaf (bar) tin. Line the base and sides with baking paper, coming up and over the edge to aid in removal of the cake from the tin when cooked.

Place the quinoa and orange juice in a small saucepan and bring to the boil. Cover and decrease the heat to low and gently simmer for 15 minutes, or until almost all of the water has been absorbed and holes appear on the surface. Keep covered and remove from the heat to finish cooking for a further 5 minutes, or until tails have sprouted and all of the juice has been absorbed. Spread the quinoa out onto a tray and set aside to cool.

Combine the cooled quinoa, almond meal and eggs in a high-speed blender and blend to roughly chop the quinoa and make a thick batter. Add the maple syrup, macadamia oil, cardamom, baking powder, bicarbonate of soda, orange zest and salt and blend to combine. Pour into the prepared tin.

Bake for 1 hour or until golden brown and a skewer comes out clean when inserted in the centre.

Meanwhile to prepare the orange and cardamom glaze, lightly toast the cardamom pods in a small saucepan over low–medium heat for 20 seconds, or until fragrant. Add the orange juice and maple syrup and gently simmer for 5–10 minutes, until reduced by half to make a thin syrup. Strain through a fine-mesh sieve. Add the almonds and stir to coat.

Pour the glaze and almonds over the warm cake. Leave the cake in the tin to cool completely.

Using the baking paper overhang as a lever, lift the cake out of the tin. Remove baking paper.

Decorate with edible flowers, if desired. Slice to serve, with yoghurt, if desired.

Pistachio and cacao nib biscotti

There is something quite lovely about dipping biscotti in a cup of tea. 'Biscotti' means twice cooked, and these biscuits are literally cooked twice, so they can be stored for longer. These morsels of nutty, chocolatey goodness are a good source of protein, making them the perfect satiating snack.

MAKES 18

2 large eggs
¼ cup (60 ml/2 fl oz) maple syrup
2 tablespoons coconut oil, warmed,
    plus extra for greasing
finely grated zest of 1 unwaxed lemon
1 cup (100 g/3½ oz) almond meal
½ cup (75 g/2¾ oz) millet flour*
¼ cup (30 g/1 oz) arrowroot
3 teaspoons chia seeds
1 teaspoon gluten-free baking powder
pinch of Himalayan salt
⅓ cup (45 g/1½ oz) pistachios, coarsely chopped
2 tablespoons cacao nibs*

Preheat the oven to 180°C (350°F). Lightly grease and line a large baking tray (cookie sheet) with baking paper.

Beat the eggs, maple syrup, coconut oil and lemon zest together in a medium bowl, until combined.

In a separate bowl place the almond meal, millet flour, arrowroot, chia seeds, baking powder and salt and mix well.

Add the dry ingredients to the wet and mix well to combine. Add the pistachios and cacao nibs and mix to distribute evenly. Set aside for 10 minutes, to allow the chia seeds to hydrate slightly.

Spoon the mixture down the centre of the prepared tray. Using damp hands, shape the dough into a 30 cm (12 in) long × 8 cm (3¼ in) wide, flattish log.

Bake for 35 minutes, or until firm and golden brown. Remove from the oven and set aside until cooled enough to handle, approximately 10–15 minutes.

Decrease the oven temperature to 150°C (300°F).

Using a serrated knife, trim the ends of the log. Cut into 18 × 1.5 cm (7 in × ½ in) thick slices.

Arrange, cut-side down, on the baking tray. Return to the oven and bake for a further 15 minutes on each side, or until crisp, dried out and golden brown. Remove from the oven and set aside to cool completely.

NOTE
These can be stored in an airtight container for up to 2 weeks.

* Available from health food stores.

Coconut jam drop biscuits

This wholesome take on a classic is very popular in our house. Almost macaroon-like in flavour, these yummy treats help ground your blood sugar levels rather than send them skyrocketing. They are rich in coconut fibre, and protein from the almonds, topped with our vibrant and nutritious chia jam recipe.

MAKES 12

coconut oil, for greasing

1 cup (100 g/3½ oz) almond meal

½ cup (50 g/1¾ oz) desiccated (shredded) coconut

½ teaspoon gluten-free baking powder

½ teaspoon vanilla bean powder*

¼ teaspoon Himalayan salt

2 tablespoons maple syrup

2 tablespoons unsalted cultured butter
(see recipe page 303), melted and cooled

¼ cup (80 g/2¾ oz) blackberry and vanilla chia jam
(see recipe page 335)

Preheat the oven to 180°C (350°F). Lightly grease and line a large baking tray (cookie sheet) with baking paper.

Combine the almond meal, coconut, baking powder, vanilla and salt in a medium bowl. Add the maple syrup and melted butter and stir to combine.

Divide the mixture into 12 equal portions. Roll into balls and arrange on the prepared tray. Flatten slightly and press your thumb into the centre of each disc to leave an indent. Reshape the edges as necessary. Fill with jam.

Bake for 15–17 minutes, until golden brown. Leave on the tray for 5 minutes, to cool slightly.

Transfer onto a rack to cool completely.

NOTE

These can be stored in an airtight container for up to 1 week. Alternatively, you can freeze them for up to 3 months.

Vegans, or those particularly sensitive to dairy, can substitute coconut oil for the cultured butter in this recipe.

* Available from health food stores.

Banana buckwheat loaf

You can almost always find some banana bread in our house, either baking or being eaten!
Bananas are a good source of prebiotic fibre which helps to feed our good gut bacteria,
while buckwheat flour and almond meal provide low GI energy release and impart
a subtle nutty flavour to this healthy version of a café staple.

SERVES 8

½ cup (125 ml/4 fl oz) coconut drinking milk

1 teaspoon apple cider vinegar (unpasteurised)

4 overripe medium bananas

2 large eggs, lightly beaten

⅓ cup (80 ml/2½ fl oz) macadamia oil, plus extra for greasing

2 tablespoons maple syrup, plus extra for glazing

1 teaspoon vanilla bean powder*

¾ cup (100 g/3½ oz) buckwheat flour

¾ cup (75 g/2¾ oz) almond meal

2 teaspoons chia seeds

1½ teaspoons gluten-free baking powder

1 teaspoon ground cinnamon

½ teaspoon ground nutmeg

½ teaspoon bicarbonate of soda (baking soda)

pinch of Himalayan salt

Preheat the oven to 180°C (350°F). Lightly grease and line a 19 × 9 cm (7½ × 3½ in) loaf (bar) tin with baking paper.

Combine the milk and vinegar in a small bowl and set aside.

Mash three of the bananas in a medium bowl, to make a thick purée. Add the eggs, macadamia oil, maple syrup and vanilla.

In a separate medium bowl, place the buckwheat flour, almond meal, chia seeds, baking powder, cinnamon, nutmeg, bicarbonate of soda and salt. Mix well to combine.

Add the dry ingredients and the milk mixture to the banana mixture and stir to make a smooth batter. Pour into the prepared tin.

Peel the remaining banana and cut in half lengthways. Lay the slices, cut-side up, on top of the batter.

Bake for 45–50 minutes, until golden brown and a skewer comes out clean when tested. Leave in the tin for 15 minutes, to cool slightly.

Brush the top of the hot cake with a little maple syrup, to glaze.

Turn out onto a rack to cool completely.

Slice to serve.

* Available from health food stores.

Spiced date and almond meal scones

Scones (biscuits) are a timeless favourite, and here is a delicious, gut-friendly version, which is quick and easy to throw together. With a base of almond meal, the natural sweetness of dates and scents of orange and warming spices, these scones are both satisfying and comforting.

MAKES 8

2 cups (200 g/7 oz) almond meal

½ cup (60 g/2 oz) arrowroot

2 teaspoons gluten-free baking powder

1 teaspoon ground cinnamon, plus extra for dusting

1 teaspoon ground ginger

⅛ teaspoon ground cloves

pinch of Himalayan salt

¼ cup (60 g/2 oz) coconut oil, frozen solid, plus extra for greasing

8 medjool dates, pitted and coarsely chopped

¼ cup (60 ml/2 fl oz) coconut drinking milk, plus extra for brushing

2 large eggs, separated

1 tablespoon raw honey

finely grated zest of 1 unwaxed orange

Preheat the oven to 200°C (400°F). Lightly grease and line a large baking tray (cookie sheet) with baking paper.

Combine the almond meal, arrowroot, baking powder, ground spices and salt in a medium bowl and stir to combine. Coarsely grate in the frozen coconut oil. Add the dates and stir to distribute through the dry mixture.

Whisk the coconut milk, egg yolks, honey and orange zest together in a small bowl. Add to the dry mixture and stir to form a lumpy dough.

Whisk the egg whites in a medium bowl, until stiff peaks form.

Stir a large spoonful of egg whites into the dough, to loosen. Gently fold through the remaining whites, to make a thick, sticky dough.

Place the dough in the centre of the prepared tray. Using slightly wet hands shape and press the dough to make a 3 cm (1¼ in)-thick disc.

Using a large wet knife, mark the disc into eight portions, pressing the knife halfway through the dough. Brush the top with coconut milk and dust with cinnamon.

Bake for 20 minutes, or until golden brown. Remove from the oven, cover with a clean tea towel (dish towel) and set aside for 10 minutes to cool slightly.

Remove the tea towel (dish towel) and cut into portions. Serve warm or at room temperature.

NOTE

The scones can be stored in an airtight container for up to 3 days. Alternatively, you can freeze for up to 1 month.

Gingerbread men

For me, gingerbread is synonymous with Christmas, and making this recipe is so satisfying, especially when you know it is going to nourish your young one's tummy with wonderful digestion-boosting spices such as ginger and cinnamon. You can also cut these into rounds to make simple ginger biscuits (cookies).

MAKES 12

6 medjool dates, pitted
⅓ cup (80 ml/2½ fl oz) boiling water
½ cup (125 g/4½ oz) almond butter
2 tablespoons maple syrup
½ teaspoon vanilla bean powder*
1 cup (150 g/5½ oz) buckwheat flour
½ cup (75 g/2¾ oz) millet flour*
¼ cup (30 g/1 oz) arrowroot
2 teaspoons ground ginger
2 teaspoons cacao powder
1 teaspoon ground cinnamon
1 teaspoon gluten-free baking powder
½ teaspoon bicarbonate of soda (baking soda)
½ teaspoon ground nutmeg
pinch of Himalayan salt
coconut oil, for greasing
dried currants, for decorating

Soak the dates in the boiling water in a small bowl for 10 minutes, or until softened.

Place the softened dates and any remaining liquid, the almond butter, maple syrup and vanilla in a food processor or high-speed blender. Blend until smooth.

Sift the buckwheat and millet flours, arrowroot, ginger, cacao powder, cinnamon, baking powder, bicarbonate of soda, nutmeg and salt into a medium bowl. Add the date mixture and stir until it begins to form a dough. Turn out onto a clean kitchen bench and shape into a disc. Wrap in plastic and refrigerate for 20 minutes.

Preheat the oven to 180°C (350°F). Lightly grease and line two large baking trays (cookie sheets) with baking paper.

Roll the dough out between two sheets of baking paper to approximately 3 mm (⅒ in) thick. Using a gingerbread man cookie cutter, press out shapes. Arrange on the prepared baking trays. Re-roll any scraps and cut out further men.

Decorate with currants to make eyes and buttons.

Bake for 8 minutes, or until light golden brown. Leave on the tray to cool slightly. Transfer onto a rack to cool completely.

NOTE
You can store these in an airtight container for up to 1 week.

*Available from health food stores.

Pistachio and lime cakes
with roasted rosewater strawberries

Ground pistachios, almond, honey, lime and rosewater marry beautifully here to create
a Middle Eastern spin on a French classic – friands – to produce delicate, light little cakes.

MAKES 6

⅓ cup (80 ml/2½ fl oz) mild-flavoured raw honey
2 tablespoons coconut oil, melted, plus extra
    for greasing
3 large eggs, separated
finely grated zest of 2 unwaxed limes
½ cup (50 g/1¾ oz) almond meal
½ cup (70 g/2½ oz) ground pistachios
½ teaspoon gluten-free baking powder
1½ cups (375 g/13 oz) natural yoghurt

Roasted rosewater strawberries
6 medium–large strawberries, hulled and halved
freshly squeezed juice of 1 lime
2 tablespoons raw honey
1 teaspoon rosewater

edible flowers to decorate (optional)

Preheat the oven to 160°C (320°F). Lightly grease a
6-hole large muffin tin and line the bases with a piece
of baking paper.

Whisk the honey, coconut oil, egg yolks and lime zest
together in a medium bowl.

Add the almond meal, pistachios and baking powder
and stir to combine.

In a separate medium bowl, whisk the egg whites,
using an electric mixer, until stiff peaks form.

Add a large spoonful of the whites to the pistachio
mixture and stir to combine and loosen. Gently fold
through the remaining whites. Spoon the mixture
into the prepared muffin tin.

Bake for 20–25 minutes, or until the cakes are golden
brown and they spring back when lightly pressed on
top. Leave in the tin for 10 minutes to cool slightly.

While the cakes are cooking, prepare the roasted
rosewater strawberries. Place the strawberries in
a small ovenproof dish. Pour over the lime juice,
honey and rosewater and toss to coat. Roast for
15 minutes, or until very soft. Set aside to cool.

Turn the cakes out. Discard the baking paper.
Place onto a rack and set aside to cool completely.

To decorate, top the cakes with yoghurt, roasted
rosewater strawberries and their syrup and flowers, if
desired. Serve immediately.

Carrot and rosemary cake with labneh and cacao butter frosting

This is my favourite version of my favourite cake! It is jam-packed with good proteins, gut-loving nutrients and soluble fibre and is super-moist and very moreish.

SERVES 12

3¼ cups (400 g/14 oz) peeled and grated carrot

1 cup (125 g/4½ oz) grated red apple

1½ cups (180 g/6½ oz) walnuts, coarsely chopped

8 medjool dates, pitted and coarsely chopped

3 large eggs

⅓ cup (80 ml/2½ fl oz) maple syrup

¼ cup (60 ml/2 fl oz) macadamia oil, plus extra for greasing

2 teaspoons apple cider vinegar (unpasteurised)

1 tablespoon finely chopped rosemary

1½ cups (150 g/5¼ oz) almond meal

½ cup (75 g/2¾ oz) buckwheat flour

⅓ cup (40 g/1½ oz) arrowroot

1½ teaspoons gluten-free baking powder

2 teaspoons ground cinnamon, plus extra for dusting

½ teaspoon bicarbonate of soda (baking soda)

1 teaspoon ground nutmeg

fresh rosemary leaves and flowers, to decorate

Cacao butter frosting

50 g (1¾ oz) cacao butter

2 tablespoons maple syrup

250 g (9 oz) labneh, strained for 2 days (see recipe page 306)

Preheat the oven to 180°C (350°F). Lightly grease and line a 20 × 7.5 cm (8 × 3 in) round cake tin with baking paper.

Combine the carrot, apple and walnuts in a large bowl.

Blend the dates, eggs, maple syrup, macadamia oil and apple cider vinegar together in a food processor, until smooth. Add to the carrot mixture along with the rosemary and stir to combine.

Whisk the almond meal, buckwheat flour, arrowroot, baking powder, cinnamon, bicarbonate of soda and nutmeg together in a medium bowl. Add to the wet carrot mixture and stir to combine. Pour into the prepared tin.

Bake for 1 hour and 15 minutes, or until a skewer comes out clean when inserted into the centre of the cake. Remove from the oven, cover with a clean tea towel (dish towel) and leave in the tin for 10 minutes to cool slightly.

Turn out onto a rack to cool completely.

Once the cake has cooled, prepare the frosting. Place the cacao butter and maple syrup in a medium heatproof bowl and set over a saucepan of just simmering water for 5 minutes, or until melted.

Whisk a large spoonful of the labneh into the cacao butter, the mixture will be very lumpy looking, like half-churned butter, but don't panic! Remove from the heat and continue adding the labneh, whisking until smooth and creamy.

Spoon and spread the frosting over the cake to completely cover the top. Dust with cinnamon and decorate with rosemary sprigs.

Layered chocolate and blackberry cake with cacao and cultured butter frosting

Serve this amazing cake with pride to sceptics and watch them eat their words. It looks and tastes just like a traditional chocolate cake, but nourishes, not depletes.

SERVES 10–12

coconut oil, for greasing
1 cup blackberry and vanilla chia jam
    (see recipe page 335)
edible flowers, to decorate (optional)
fresh blackberries, to decorate (optional)

Chocolate pumpkin cake
450 g (1 lb) peeled pumpkin (winter squash), cut into
    chunks, or 1 cup (250 g/9 oz) purée
6 medjool dates, pitted
½ cup (125 ml/4 fl oz) boiling water
3 large eggs
⅓ cup (80 g/2¾ oz) almond butter
⅓ cup (80 ml/2½ fl oz) maple syrup
¼ cup (60 ml/2 fl oz) macadamia oil, plus extra
    for drizzling
2 teaspoons vanilla bean powder*
1 cup (100 g/3½ oz) almond meal
¼ cup (35 g/1¼ oz) buckwheat flour
1 cup (80 g/2¾ oz) cacao powder
¼ cup (30 g/1 oz) arrowroot
2 teaspoons gluten-free baking powder
½ teaspoon bicarbonate of soda (baking soda)
pinch of Himalayan salt

Cacao and cultured butter frosting
8 medjool dates, pitted
½ cup (125 ml/4 fl oz) boiling water
100 g (3½ oz) unsalted cultured butter, softened
    (see recipe page 303)
¾ cup (60 g/2 oz) cacao powder
1½ teaspoons vanilla bean powder*

NOTE
Refrigerate this cake until required. The frosting will begin to melt off the cake if left out, especially on a warm day.

* Available from health food stores.

Preheat the oven to 180°C (350°F). Lightly grease and line a 20 cm (8 in) springform cake tin with baking paper. Place the pumpkin chunks on a baking tray (baking sheet). Drizzle with macadamia oil. Roast for 20–25 minutes, or until tender and caramelised. Set aside to cool.

Reduce the oven to 170°C (340°F). Soak the dates in the boiling water for 10 minutes, or until softened.

In a high-speed food processor, blend the dates and their liquid, the eggs, almond butter, maple syrup, macadamia oil and vanilla bean powder until smooth. Add the pumpkin and blend to combine. Transfer into a medium bowl.

Place the dry ingredients in a medium bowl and stir to combine. Add to the wet mixture and stir to make a smooth batter. Pour the batter into the prepared tin.

Bake for 50–55 minutes, until a skewer comes out clean when inserted into the centre to test. Leave in the tin for 10 minutes to cool slightly. Turn out onto a rack to cool completely.

Once cooled, slice the cake in half horizontally. Spread the blackberry and vanilla chia jam over the base. Sandwich the other cake half on top.

To prepare the cacao and cultured butter frosting, soak the dates in the boiling water for 10 minutes, or until softened. Cream the butter in a medium bowl using an electric mixer, until pale and creamy.

Remove the skins from the dates and place them, with their liquid, in a high-speed food processor. Add the cacao and vanilla and blend until smooth. Add this mixture to the creamed butter and mix until combined.

Using a spatula, spread the frosting on top and over the cake, to completely cover. Decorate with edible flowers and fresh blackberries, if desired.

Banana and coconut cream pie with coconut toffee

*I was only introduced to banoffee pie a few years ago and it was a sweet revelation.
So delicious and so delightful, that I had to make my own healthier version. Banana, toffee
and cream is a winning combination and this pie will satisfy your sweet tooth.*

SERVES 8

3 ripe bananas, sliced into ½ cm (¼ in)-thick rounds
1½ cups (375 g/13 oz) natural yoghurt
edible flowers, to decorate (optional)

Base
4 medjool dates, pitted
¼ cup (60 ml/2 fl oz) boiling water
1 cup (155 g/5½ oz) macadamias
1½ cups (150 g/5½ oz) almond meal
2 tablespoons arrowroot
½ teaspoon ground cinnamon
pinch of Himalayan salt
2 tablespoons maple syrup
1 tablespoon coconut oil, plus extra for greasing

Filling
15 medjool dates, pitted
½ cup (125 ml/4 fl oz) boiling water
1 cup (150 g/5½ oz) raw cashews, soaked in cold water
    for at least 4 hours, or up to overnight
1 teaspoon vanilla bean powder*
½ teaspoon ground cinnamon
¼ teaspoon Himalayan salt

Coconut toffee
1 cup (60 g/2 oz) flaked coconut
100 ml (3½ fl oz) maple syrup
pinch of Himalayan salt

Preheat the oven to 180°C (350°F). Lightly grease a
34 × 10 cm (13½ × 4 in) loose-based rectangular tart
(flan) tin with coconut oil. Refrigerate.

To prepare the base, soak the dates in the boiling
water for 10 minutes, or until softened. Place the
macadamias, almond meal, arrowroot, cinnamon
and salt in a food processor or high-speed blender.
Process until the macadamias are finely chopped
and mixture combined. Transfer to a bowl.

Combine the dates and any remaining liquid,
maple syrup and coconut oil in the food processor
or blender. Blend until smooth. Add to the dry nut
mixture and stir to combine. Press into the prepared
tin to cover the base and sides in an even layer. Prick
the base several times with a fork. Refrigerate for
15 minutes, then bake for 10–15 minutes, until golden
brown. Set aside to cool.

Meanwhile to prepare the coconut toffee, cook the
coconut in a small frying pan over low–medium heat,
tossing occasionally, until lightly toasted. Add the
maple syrup and salt. Cook, tossing to coat, until the
maple syrup has reduced to a thick sticky caramel.
Pour onto a baking tray lined with baking paper
and let cool.

Meanwhile to prepare the filling, soak the dates in the
boiling water for 10 minutes, or until softened. Drain
and rinse the cashews under cold water. Place the dates
and any remaining water, cashews and remaining
ingredients in a high-speed blender. Blend until
smooth. Spoon and spread the filling into the base.

Arrange slices from two of the bananas over the
filling then top with dollops of natural yoghurt
Arrange the remaining banana slices on top to
decorate. Scatter with coconut toffee and decorate
with edible flowers, if desired.

* Available from health food stores.

Drinks

....

The joy of drinks is reflected in the lovely social rituals around them, a shared morning coffee, a pot of tea with a friend on a weekend afternoon, or a glass of wine in the evening.

Drinks are probably the easiest way to be creative in the kitchen, and it is fun to experiment with flavours and textures. They are also the simplest way to consume and digest nutrients quickly and in turn will give you an instant boost of energy and hydration, satisfy hunger, ease digestion and help the body wind down.

Our bodies are 60 per cent water, and it's important that we keep ourselves adequately hydrated. Water carries oxygen and nutrients to every cell in the body and it is integral to our skin health and wellbeing. It gives cells energy and flushes out toxins. Hunger and thirst signals can often be confusing, so if you are constantly hungry, it may be that you're actually dehydrated. You can liven up your glass of H_2O by infusing it with a variety of herbs, lemon zest or rosewater.

Smoothies should almost be in a category of their own. Somewhere between a drink and a meal, they are a wonderful way to give your body a turbocharge of nutrients, and are perfect for busy lives. However, our digestive systems won't be cheated. Creating calm rituals around food is important for digestive health, as is chewing – always chew your smoothies, so your body produces enzymes to help you digest them.

Raspberry, pear and orange blossom smoothie

Spirulina, coconut and vanilla omega-boost smoothie

Raspberry, pear and orange blossom smoothie

SERVES 2

This nutrient-dense smoothie is a wonderful beauty food. Raspberries, pears, slippery elm, chia and avocado are all great sources of gut-boosting soluble fibre and orange blossom promotes healthy digestion – its beautiful fragrance and flavour make this recipe so special.

2 teaspoons chia seeds, soaked in ½ cup
    (125 ml/4 fl oz) water for 10 minutes
½ cup (125 ml/4 fl oz) water
¾ cup (90 g/3 oz) frozen raspberries
½ frozen medium banana, coarsely chopped
½ medium ripe pear, coarsely chopped
¼ avocado, peeled
⅓ cup (80 ml/2½ fl oz) coconut milk kefir (see recipe
    page 304, or coconut yoghurt or natural yoghurt)
1 tablespoon cashew butter
1 teaspoon slippery elm powder*
1 medjool date, pitted and coarsely chopped
1 tablespoon orange blossom water

Raspberry purée
½ cup (60 g/2 oz) frozen raspberries
squeeze fresh lemon juice
fresh raspberries, to serve

To prepare the raspberry purée, heat the raspberries and lemon juice together in a small saucepan over low heat for 3–4 minutes, until softened. Using a fork, mash to a pulp. Strain through a fine-mesh sieve and set aside.

Place all of the ingredients in a high-speed blender and blend until smooth.

Pour smoothie into glasses and top with raspberry purée and fresh raspberries.

Spirulina, coconut and vanilla omega-boost smoothie

SERVES 1

This lovely creamy smoothie is rich in good fats, including omegas 3, 6, 7 and 9. Consuming spirulina is an easy way to sneak more beauty nutrients into your diet, especially when you have a busy lifestyle. It also contains a very special skin-loving fatty acid – gamma-linolenic acid – which helps reduce skin inflammation and promotes healthy hair as well as detoxifying chlorophyll.

¼ avocado, peeled
¾ cup (180 ml/6 fl oz) coconut drinking milk
1 large handful baby spinach leaves
½ frozen banana, coarsely chopped
2 tablespoons ground LSA*
2 ice cubes
1 medjool date, pitted
1 tablespoon freshly squeezed lime juice
1 teaspoon spirulina powder*
1 teaspoon vanilla bean powder*
pinch of Himalayan salt

Place all of the ingredients in a high-speed blender. Blend until smooth.

* Available from health food stores.

Sweet potato pie and cashew smoothie

*Naturally sweetened, this nourishing, spiced smoothie is like dessert in a glass.
But unlike desserts made with refined sugar, the natural sugars from sweet potato
and banana (both prebiotics) are released slowly into the bloodstream, providing
a balanced source of energy and helping to keep blood sugar spikes at bay.*

SERVES 1

2 tablespoons raw cashews

½ cup (125 ml/4 fl oz) water

1 medjool date, pitted

¼ teaspoon vanilla bean powder*

pinch of Himalayan salt

100 g (3½ oz) sweet potato, peeled, cubed and
steamed

⅓ cup (80 ml/2½ fl oz) almond milk

¼ frozen banana

6 ice cubes

1 teaspoon maple syrup

¾ teaspoon finely grated ginger

¼ teaspoon ground cinnamon, plus extra to serve

⅛ teaspoon ground nutmeg

pinch of ground cloves

coconut cream, to serve (optional)

toasted flaked coconut, to serve (optional)

Soak the cashews in enough cold water to cover for
1 hour, or up to overnight, in the refrigerator.

Drain and rinse the cashews.

Place the cashews and remaining ingredients
in a high-speed blender. Blend together to make
a thick smoothie.

Pour into a tall glass. Drizzle with coconut cream,
if desired, and dust with extra cinnamon to serve.
Top with toasted flaked coconut, if desired.

* Available from health food stores.

Chai-spiced kombucha

Kombucha, a fermented probiotic drink, is said to originate from China, making its way through Asia and Russia before reaching us in the West where it is now attracting a growing number of fans due to its health benefits. It is quite easy and inexpensive to make, just requiring a few ingredients.

MAKES 4 CUPS (1 LITRE/34 FL OZ)

5 cups (1.25 litres/42 fl oz) water

½ cup (110 g/4 oz) organic raw (demerara) sugar

2 organic English breakfast tea bags, or 2 teaspoons organic loose-leaf English breakfast tea

1 organic rooibos tea bag, or 1 teaspoon loose-leaf rooibos tea

1 kombucha scoby with ½ cup (125 ml/4 fl oz) starter liquid, bought online or sourced from a friend

5 cm (2 in) knob of organic ginger, skin on, thinly sliced

1 cinnamon stick

3 green cardamom pods, bruised

2 whole cloves

3 whole black peppercorns

NOTE

Begin by drinking ½ cup (125 ml/4 fl oz) kombucha daily and gradually increase as desired.

Kombucha can be stored in the refrigerator for up to 3 months.

Over time your scoby will grow additional layers and will become quite thick. Once the scoby becomes approximately 1 cm (½ in) thick, the additional layers can be left intact or removed and given to a friend with 1 cup (250 ml/8½ fl oz) of starter liquid to brew their own kombucha. Alternatively remove and use to make extra batches of your own.

The scoby and kombucha starter can be stored in the refrigerator for up to 3 months when it is not in use.

* For sterilising instructions, see page 299.

Bring the water to the boil in a medium saucepan. Remove from the heat. Add the sugar and stir to dissolve. Add the tea bags or loose-leaf tea and steep for 3 minutes.

Remove the tea bags, or if using loose-leaf tea strain through a non-reactive sieve, such as stainless steel or plastic. Pour into a sterilised jar*. Set aside to cool to room temperature.

Once cooled, add the kombucha starter liquid and stir using a wooden spoon. Add the scoby, its smooth, shiny side facing up. Cover the jar with a double layer of muslin (cheesecloth) and secure with a rubber band.

Stand at room temperature, out of direct sunlight in a well-ventilated place. Ferment for 7–10 days, until the mixture becomes effervescent with a pleasant slightly sour taste, similar to that of sparkling apple cider.

To bottle, remove the scoby using wooden spoons and place in a sterilised glass jar with 1 cup (250 ml/8½ fl oz) of the kombucha liquid. Store in the jar in the refrigerator until you are ready to brew your next batch of kombucha.

Add the ginger and spices to the remaining kombucha. Re-cover with muslin and stand at room temperature for a further 1–2 days to infuse.

Strain the kombucha through a sieve lined with muslin cloth into sterilised bottles with swing-top lids. Refrigerate for 1 week to carbonate.

To prepare your next batch of kombucha, repeat as described above, using the reserved scoby and starter liquid to make another 1 litre.

KOMBUCHA

Kombucha is made by feeding a scoby (symbiotic culture of bacteria and yeast), or mother culture, a sugary tea mixture. The scoby eats the sugar, converting it into healthy digestive bacteria while carbon dioxide is produced through the process of fermentation, creating a refreshing, gut-loving, effervescent beverage. The digestive bacteria colonise the intestines aiding digestion and supporting the immune system.

Here, I've used a mixture of black and rooibos tea for my brew, with the addition of chai spices, creating a mellow yet richly spiced tea tonic.

A small amount of alcohol is also produced during the fermentation process and a small amount of sugar also remains after fermentation – how much is dependent on how long you brew it for. I recommend bottling when your brew tastes and smells pleasantly sour, with a slight sweetness remaining.

Iced peach and thyme Jun kombucha

Jun kombucha is a lesser-known variety of kombucha requiring a specific Jun scoby or mother culture. Jun kombucha is made from a green tea and honey brew, resulting in a lighter, more delicate version of the traditional black tea and sugar method.

MAKES 4 CUPS (1 LITRE/34 FL OZ)

5 cups (1.25 litres/42 fl oz) water

⅓ cup (80 ml/2½ fl oz) organic raw honey

3 organic green tea bags, or 3 teaspoons organic loose-leaf green tea

1 Jun kombucha scoby with ½ cup (125 ml/4 fl oz) Jun starter liquid, bought online or sourced from a friend

1 organic peach, sliced

16 sprigs thyme

NOTE

Begin by drinking ½ cup (125 ml/4 fl oz) of kombucha daily and gradually increase as desired.

Kombucha can be stored in the refrigerator for up to 3 months.

Over time your scoby will continue to grow additional layers and will become quite thick. Once the scoby becomes approx 1 cm (½ in) thick the additional layers can be left intact or removed and given to a friend with 1 cup (250 ml/8½ fl oz) of starter liquid to brew their own kombucha. Alternatively, you can remove and use to make extra batches of your own.

The scoby and kombucha starter can be stored in the refrigerator for up to 3 months when it is not in use.

Sterilise an 8 cup (2 litres/68 fl oz) glass jar by washing it in hot soapy water and rinsing thoroughly. Dry out in a cool oven (50°C/120°F). Remove from the oven and leave to cool.

Bring the water to the boil in a medium saucepan. Remove from the heat and let cool. Add the honey and stir to dissolve. Add the tea bags or loose-leaf tea and steep for 5–7 minutes.

Remove the tea bags or if using loose-leaf tea strain through a non-reactive sieve, such as stainless steel or plastic. Pour into the prepared jar. Let cool.

Once cooled, add the Jun starter liquid and stir using a wooden spoon. Add the scoby with the smooth, shiny side facing up. Cover the jar with a double layer of muslin (cheesecloth). Secure with a rubber band.

Stand at room temperature, out of direct sunlight in a well-ventilated place. Ferment for 7–10 days, until the mixture becomes effervescent with a pleasant slightly sour taste, similar to sparkling apple cider.

To bottle, remove the scoby using wooden spoons and place in a sterilised glass jar with 1 cup (250 ml/8½ fl oz) of the kombucha liquid. Refrigerate until you are ready to brew your next batch.

Add the peach slices and thyme to the remaining kombucha. Re-cover with muslin and stand at room temperature for a further 2 days to infuse. Strain the kombucha through a sieve lined with muslin into sterilised bottles with swing-top lids.

Refrigerate for 1 week to carbonate. Serve poured over ice.

To prepare your next batch of kombucha, repeat as described above, using the reserved scoby and starter liquid to make another 4 cups (1 litre/34 fl oz).

Blueberry and lemon verbena water kefir

Kefir grains are a combination of healthy bacteria and yeast that forms small, translucent cauliflower-like watery crystals. They swell and multiply as they feed on a sugary mixture, converting the sugars into beneficial gut bacteria, very much in the way that a kombucha scoby does, but in much less time.

MAKES 4 CUPS (1 LITRE/34 FL OZ)

4 cups (1 litre/34 fl oz) tepid filtered water
2 tablespoons organic raw (demerara) sugar or
    rapadura sugar
⅛ teaspoon Himalayan salt
⅛ teaspoon bicarbonate of soda (baking soda)
2 tablespoons (30 g/1 oz) water kefir grains
    (bought online or sourced from a friend)
2 tablespoons fresh blueberries
6 fresh lemon verbena leaves

NOTE

Water kefir, once opened, can be stored in the refrigerator for up to 2 weeks.

Water kefir produces fewer strains of bacteria and yeast than the milk kefir grains, which feed on milk sugars (lactose), yet still they are much higher in bacteria than cultured dairy products such as yoghurt. When ready, the liquid will turn cloudy and lighten in colour. It will have a pleasant tang and slightly sour taste and aroma. I have flavoured my kefir with blueberry and lemon verbena which adds a slightly sweet, lovely lemony undertone.

* For sterilising instructions, see page 299.

Place the water in a sterilised jar*. Add the sugar, salt and bicarbonate of soda. Stir to dissolve. Add the kefir grains. Cover the jar with a double layer of muslin (cheesecloth) and secure with a rubber band. Place in a warm spot (20°C/70°F), out of direct sunlight and well-ventilated.

Ferment for 2 days, until the kefir reaches the desired pleasant, slightly sour taste.

Strain through a non-reactive sieve, such as stainless steel or plastic, into a sterilised 6 cup (1.5 litre/51 fl oz)-glass bottle. Reserve the grains. Ensure there is a 5 cm (2 in) gap between the liquid and the lid of the bottle to allow space for gases to be released as part of the fermentation process. Bottles with a swing-top lid are best. Use the reserved grains to begin culturing your next batch of water kefir or store in a sterilised glass jar in the refrigerator for up to 2 weeks.

Add the blueberries and lemon verbena.

Seal and stand at room temperature and out of direct sunlight for 18–24 hours to allow pressure to build up and the flavours to infuse. Ensure you open the bottle every 12 hours to release gases (known as burping), to prevent pressure build-up, which could cause the bottles to explode.

Strain through a non-reactive sieve. Discard the blueberries and lemon verbena. Pour the water kefir back into the swing-top bottle and seal. Refrigerate for 1 week to carbonate before use.

WATER KEFIR GRAIN STORAGE

1 day–3 weeks
in a sterilised glass jar covered with 1 cup
(250 ml/8½ fl oz) filtered water mixed with
1 tablespoon organic raw (demerara) or rapadura
sugar. Refrigerated.

3 weeks + up to 6 months
dehydrate at room temperature or using a dehydrator
set at 30°C (85°F). Freeze in a zip-lock bag.

REACTIVATING WATER KEFIR GRAINS

The longer you store kefir grains the longer they take to
regain their original fermenting strength. To give them
a kick-start, place the kefir grains in a sterilised glass
jar, cover with 1 cup (250 ml/8½ fl oz) tepid filtered
water, add 1 tablespoon organic raw (demerara) sugar,
a pinch of Himalayan salt and a pinch of bicarbonate
of soda (baking soda) and stir to combine. Cover with
muslin (cheesecloth) and secure with a rubber band.
Stand at room temperature for 12 hours. Strain and
repeat one to three more times, until the grains begin
to ferment water effectively. The time this takes will
depend on how long the grains have been stored.

Ginger and turmeric beer

Naturally fermented drinks have been consumed as daily tonics for centuries. Somehow over time these medicinal beverages have morphed into the sugar-laden fizzy sodas commercially available today. The good news is that these tonics are quite easy to prepare, requiring just a little patience while the process of fermentation works its magic.

MAKES 7 CUPS (1.75 LITRES/60 FL OZ)

1 cup (250 ml/8½ fl oz) ginger and turmeric bug
    (see recipe page 336)
½ cup (110 g/4 oz) organic raw (demerara) sugar
¼ cup (60 ml/2 fl oz) freshly squeezed lemon juice
1 tablespoon coarsely grated organic ginger, skin on
1 tablespoon coarsely grated organic turmeric,
    skin on
4 cracked black peppercorns
6 cups (1.5 litres/51 fl oz) filtered water
lemon verbena, to garnish (optional)

NOTE

Once opened, the ginger and turmeric beer can be stored in the refrigerator for up to 2 weeks.

This ginger and turmeric beer is full of probiotics and beneficial enzymes, which help to rebalance the digestive system and colonise the intestinal tract with healthy bacteria.

Ginger is renowned for easing nausea and general stomach complaints and is paired here with the highly antioxidant and anti-inflammatory properties of turmeric, which help to ease arthritic pain and gastrointestinal conditions. With the addition of black pepper, turmeric's active ingredient curcumin becomes more bioavailable to the body.

This ale will be the most familiar tasting of the fermented beverages to the novice palate. It can easily be converted to a straight extra-gingery beer, replacing the turmeric for an equal quantity of ginger. This is one of the more carbonated beverages, so be sure to 'burp' your bottles to prevent any mishaps.

Combine the ginger and turmeric bug, sugar, lemon juice, ginger, turmeric and peppercorns in a sterilised 8 cup (2 litre/68 fl oz) glass jar or specialised fermentation jar with an airlock lid. Stir using a wooden spoon, to dissolve the sugar. Add the water and stir to combine.

Cover the jar with a double layer of muslin (cheesecloth) and secure with a rubber band. If using a specialised fermenting jar, secure the lid.

Leave to stand at room temperature for 3–5 days, or until the mixture becomes pleasantly tangy with a little sweetness remaining.

Strain the liquid through a fine-mesh sieve into two sterilised 4 cup (1 litre/34 fl oz) glass bottles, leaving a 5 cm (2 in) gap between the liquid and the lid to allow space for gases to be released as part of the fermentation process. Bottles with a swing-top lid are best.

Let stand at room temperature for 2–3 days, until carbonated. Ensure you open the bottles every 12 hours to release gases (known as burping), to prevent pressure build-up, which could cause bottles to explode.

Refrigerate for 3 days to carbonate before use. Pour into glasses and garnish with a sprig of lemon verbena if desired.

Beetroot and orange kvass

Kvass, a cleansing, fermented beetroot (beet) tonic hailing from Russia, has long been consumed for its health benefits. Its slightly salty, earthy, sour yet subtly sweet taste is an acquired one, but once you're converted it can be quite addictive. I've added orange, lemon and ginger to my kvass for some extra sweetness.

MAKES 5 CUPS (1.25 LITRES/42 FL OZ)

4 medium (500 g/1 lb 2 oz in total) organic beetroot (beets), washed
1 organic orange, cut into 8 wedges
1 organic lemon, cut into 8 wedges
1 tablespoon coarsely grated organic ginger
¼ cup (60 ml/2 fl oz) sauerkraut liquid, kimchi liquid, or ginger and turmeric bug (see pages 314, 315 and 336)
1 tablespoon Himalayan salt
4 cups (1 litre/34 fl oz) filtered water
outer cabbage leaf, for covering

Cut the beetroot into 2 cm (¾ in) cubes.

Combine the beetroot, orange, lemon and ginger in a sterilised 8 cup (2 litre/68 fl oz) glass jar or specialised fermentation jar with an airlock lid.

Add the sauerkraut, kimchi liquid, or ginger and turmeric bug and muddle using a wooden spoon to soften the citrus and release the juice.

Dissolve the salt in 1 cup (250 ml/8½ fl oz) of the water in a small bowl. Add the salt solution and remaining water to the jar. Muddle with a wooden spoon, to combine.

Cover the beetroot mixture with a cabbage leaf and firmly press down to completely submerge in liquid. If using an ordinary jar, weigh down with a smaller jar filled with water. Ensure there is a 5 cm (2 in) gap between the beetroot mixture and the top of the jar to allow for extra liquid released during the fermentation process. Set the jar on a large plate to catch any overflow. Cover the jar with a double layer of muslin (cheesecloth) and secure with a rubber band. If using a specialised fermenting jar, secure the lid.

Stand at room temperature, out of direct sunlight in a well-ventilated place. Ferment for 5–7 days, until the mixture becomes pleasantly tangy. Check daily to ensure the beetroot mixture is completely submerged in liquid, to prevent mould from forming. Press down with a wooden spoon if necessary.

Strain the liquid through a fine-mesh sieve into two sterilised 4 cup (1 litre/34 fl oz) glass bottles, leaving a 5 cm (2 in) gap between the liquid and the lid to allow space for gases to be released as part of the fermentation process. Bottles with a swing-top lid are best.

Let stand at room temperature for 2–3 days, until carbonated. Ensure you open the bottles every 12 hours to release gases (known as burping), to prevent pressure build-up, which could cause the bottles to explode.

Refrigerate for 3 days to carbonate before use. Drink ½ cup (125 ml/4 fl oz) of kvass daily, or as desired.

NOTE

Once opened, the beetroot and orange kvass can be stored in the refrigerator for up to 2 weeks.

You can reserve ½ cup (125 ml/4 fl oz) of the kvass and use it as a kick-starter for your next brew.

The addition of sauerkraut or kimchi juice or ginger and turmeric bug gives this kvass a fermenting kick-start. For a refreshing summer tonic, serve it over ice in a tall glass topped up with some mineral water.

Pineapple, mint and kombucha ice

SERVES 4–6

Pineapple's tropical sweetness and the cooling and calming properties of mint paired with probiotic-rich Jun kombucha make this ice a refreshingly delicious digestive aid. Part drink, part dessert, this ice is perfect as an after-dinner palate cleanser and to ease the effects of a rich or heavy meal.

1 pineapple
3 large handfuls mint leaves
1 cup (250 ml/8½ fl oz) Jun kombucha (see recipe page 272)

Using a sharp knife cut off and discard the pineapple skin. Cut the pineapple flesh, reserving a small amount to garnish, into a size suitable for your slow-press juicer.

Pass the pineapple and mint through your juicer, catching the juice in a jug underneath. Add the Jun kombucha and stir to combine.

Pour into a small shallow tray.

Freeze for 1–2 hours, until frozen around the edges. Remove from the freezer and mix in the frozen edges. Return to the freezer.

Remove the mixture from the freezer every 30 minutes or so and mix it up. Once all of the liquid begins to freeze use a fork to drag and scrape the mixture and break it up into small ice crystals. Repeat this over 3 hours, or until the mixture is fully frozen into delicate ice crystals.

Serve in chilled glasses, topped with diced pineapple.

NOTE
The pineapple, mint and kombucha ice can be stored in an airtight container in the freezer for up to 3 months.

Kimchi Virgin Mary

SERVES 1

This is such a fabulous way to use up excess kimchi juice. It has all the tomato spiciness that you love in a Virgin Mary, but with added probiotics to populate your intestinal tract. Tomatoes are a good source of skin-protective lycopene, collagen and immune-boosting vitamin C.

¾ cup (180 ml/6 fl oz) chilled organic tomato juice
½ cup (125 ml/4 fl oz) chilled kimchi juice
    (see recipe page 315)
juice of ½ lime
3 ice cubes
½ teaspoon Korean chilli powder
    (kochukaru/gochugaru)*, plus extra to serve
Himalayan salt and freshly ground black pepper,
    to taste
inner stick celery, to serve (optional)
lime wedge, to serve (optional)

Combine the tomato juice, kimchi juice, lime juice, ice and Korean chilli powder in a cocktail shaker or jug. Shake or mix to combine and chill. Season with salt and pepper.

Pour into a serving glass. Sprinkle with Korean chilli powder. Garnish with a celery stick and a lime wedge, if desired.

Serve immediately.

* Available from Asian grocers.

Pineapple, mint and kombucha ice

Cold-pressed green juice with herbs

Cold-pressed almond milk with turmeric

Cold-pressed green juice with herbs

SERVES 1

This light and zingy, nutrient-packed juice is super hydrating, alkalising and anti-inflammatory. Chlorophyll from the greens and coriander (cilantro) helps to remove heavy metals and toxins from the body. Add a little flax seed (linseed) oil to assist with the absorption of vitamins A and K from the greens.

1 green apple, cored
½ Lebanese (short) cucumber
2 large kale leaves
2 large handfuls mint leaves
1 large handful flat-leaf (Italian) parsley
1 large handful coriander (cilantro)
½ lemon, peeled and coarsely chopped
½ lime, peeled and coarsely chopped
2 cm (¾ in) knob of ginger

Coarsely chop the apple, cucumber and kale into a size suitable for your cold (slow) press juicer.

Pass all of the ingredients through your juicer, catching the juice in a jug underneath.

Pour into a tall glass.

Drink immediately.

NOTE
Cold-pressed juice can be stored in an airtight container in the refrigerator for up to 2 days.

Cold-pressed almond milk with turmeric

SERVES 1

Warm and creamy, this bright yellow, lightly spiced milk is sweet and nurturing. Turmeric's active ingredient curcumin has powerful anti-inflammatory and antioxidant properties, helping to protect our cells from disease and premature ageing. It is paired here with black pepper to increase its bioavailability and absorption by the body.

¼ cup (45 g/1½ oz) raw blanched almonds
1 cup (250 ml/8½ fl oz) water
1½ teaspoons raw honey, or to taste
½ teaspoon ground turmeric
¼ teaspoon ground cinnamon
¼ teaspoon ground ginger
⅛ teaspoon finely ground black pepper
pinch of Himalayan salt

Soak the almonds in enough cold water to cover for at least 4 hours or up to overnight in the refrigerator.

Strain and rinse the almonds.

Pass the almonds and the water through a cold (slow) press juicer, catching the milk in a jug underneath. Pour the almond milk into a small saucepan and gently heat, until warm–hot.

Combine the honey, turmeric, cinnamon, ginger, black pepper and salt in your favourite mug. Pour in a little hot almond milk and stir to make a thick paste.

Gradually pour in the remaining milk, stirring to combine.

Mulled rosehip iced berry cooler

MAKES 6 CUPS (1.5 LITRES/51 FL OZ)

Packed with immune-boosting vitamin C, hibiscus imparts a gorgeous red hue and subtle natural sourness to this summer quencher. Paired with a warming blend of mulled spices and sweetened with a little honey it's the perfect balance of flavours and an ideal alcohol-free drink.

2 cinnamon sticks
3 star anise
6 whole cloves
7 whole black peppercorns
3 cups (750 ml/25½ fl oz) water
3 rosehip and hibiscus tea bags
¼ cup (60 ml/2 fl oz) raw honey
crushed ice, to serve
250 g (9 oz) strawberries, hulled and quartered
125 g (4½ oz) blueberries
125 g (4½ oz) raspberries
3 cups (750 ml/25½ fl oz) sparkling mineral water

Dry-roast the spices in a medium saucepan over low–medium heat for 1 minute, or until fragrant.

Pour in the water and bring to the boil. Decrease the heat and simmer for 5 minutes.

Remove from the heat. Add the tea bags and steep for 5 minutes.

Remove and discard the tea bags. Add the honey and stir to combine. Set aside to cool.

Refrigerate to chill.

When ready to serve, quarter-fill a large serving jug or individual serving glasses with crushed ice and top with the berries. Pour over the chilled spiced tea mixture and top up with mineral water.

Roasted dandelion and chicory frappé

SERVES 1

The roasted dandelion and chicory root in this recipe produce a bitter coffee-like flavour, making it a perfect base for this iced coffee style frappé. Dandelion acts as a gentle diuretic, helping the liver to flush out toxins, reduce fluid retention and aid digestion.

½ cup (125 ml/4 fl oz) water
1 tablespoon roasted dandelion and chicory root*
12 ice cubes
½ cup (125 ml/4 fl oz) coconut milk, plus extra
    to serve
2 teaspoons raw honey, or to taste
½ teaspoon vanilla bean powder*
½ teaspoon ground cinnamon,
    plus extra to serve (optional)
¼ teaspoon ground allspice,
    plus extra to serve (optional)

Combine the water and roasted dandelion and chicory root in a small saucepan and bring to a simmer over low heat. Simmer for 5 minutes, or until reduced by half. Set aside to cool and infuse.

Strain infused liquid through a fine-mesh sieve.

Place the cooled liquid and remaining ingredients in a high-speed blender. Blend for 20 seconds, or until ice is crushed. Taste and sweeten further, as desired.

Pour into a tall glass to serve. Top with additional coconut milk and sprinkle with spices, if desired.

NOTE
The dandelion and chicory base can be made in advance and stored in an airtight container in the refrigerator for up to 5 days.

* Available from health food stores.

Mulled rosehip iced berry cooler

Roasted dandelion and chicory frappé

Rose, vanilla and marshmallow root chai

Rose, vanilla and marshmallow root chai

SERVES 1

A rosy twist on much-loved Indian chai spices, this fragrant chai, with the addition of gut-soothing marshmallow root, is wonderful for those moments when you just need to stop and relax. It's the perfect body–mind medicine. Let the spiced rose aroma waft over you and just be.

½ cup (125 ml/4 fl oz) water
½ cinnamon stick, crumbled
2 green cardamom pods, bruised
2 whole cloves
2 whole black peppercorns
½ teaspoon vanilla bean powder*, plus extra for sprinkling
1 cup (250 ml/8½ fl oz) almond milk
2 teaspoons marshmallow root powder*
2 teaspoons edible dried rose petals, plus extra to garnish (optional)**
1½ teaspoons raw honey, or to taste
1 teaspoon rosewater

Combine the water, cinnamon, cardamom, cloves, peppercorns and vanilla in a small saucepan and gently simmer for 5 minutes, or until reduced by half. Add the almond milk, marshmallow root powder and rose petals and simmer for a further 3 minutes, or until flavours are infused. Remove from the heat. Stir in the honey and rosewater.

Strain the chai through a tea strainer into your favourite cup.

Sprinkle with vanilla and scatter with edible rose petals to serve, if desired.

*   Available from health food stores.
** Available from specialty grocers.

Peppermint, liquorice, ginger and fennel tea

MAKES 20 SERVES

This tea blend is great when a cleansing, digestive aid is called for. An ideal post-meal tea, especially if you've got an upset tummy. Ginger, fennel and peppermint increase the production of digestive enzymes. Liquorice adds a natural sweetness and acts to reduce inflammation, soothe and restore the protective intestinal lining.

2 teaspoons fennel seeds
½ cup (10 g/¼ oz) dried peppermint leaves*
1 tablespoon (9 g/¼ oz) dried ginger root*
1 tablespoon (4 g/¼ oz) dried shredded liquorice root**
lime, thinly sliced into rounds, to serve

Toast the fennel seeds in a small dry frying pan over low–medium heat for 30 seconds, or until fragrant. Set aside to cool.

Combine the toasted fennel seeds, dried peppermint leaves, ginger root and liquorice root in a jar. Seal with a lid and shake to combine.

To prepare the tea, place a heaped teaspoon of dried tea mixture per serve in a teapot or tea infuser ball in a cup. Cover with a cup (250 ml/8½ fl oz) of boiling water per serve. Set aside to steep for 3–5 minutes.

To serve, strain through a tea strainer into cups and top with a slice of fresh lime.

*   Available from health food stores.
** Available from Asian grocers.

Chipotle and hazelnut hot chocolate

This Mexican-inspired hot chocolate, spiced with vanilla, cinnamon and chipotle chilli, and featuring magnesium-rich cacao, dates and healthy coconut oil, is energising and comforting. Coconut oil is a wonderful addition as it contains medium-chain fatty acids that are used by the body quickly for energy.

MAKES 1 MUG OR 2 SMALL CUPS

¼ cup (40 g/1½ oz) raw hazelnuts
1 cup (250 ml/8½ fl oz) water
2 medjool dates, pitted
1 tablespoon cacao powder
½ teaspoon vanilla bean powder*
½ teaspoon ground cinnamon
¼ teaspoon chipotle powder**
pinch of Himalayan salt
1 teaspoon coconut oil

Soak the hazelnuts in enough cold water to cover for at least 4 hours, or overnight in the refrigerator.

Drain and rinse the hazelnuts.

Combine the hazelnuts and the water in a high-speed blender. Blend to finely grind the nuts, making nut milk.

Strain the milk through a nut bag or double layer of muslin (cheesecloth), set over a jug or bowl to catch the milk. Squeeze the pulp to ensure all the liquid is extracted. Keep the hazelnut pulp for another use, such as adding to smoothies, muesli (granola) or in baking.

Return the milk to the blender, add the dates, cacao, vanilla, cinnamon, chipotle and salt. Blend to combine.

Pour into a small saucepan. Add the coconut oil and gently heat, until very warm–hot and the coconut oil has melted.

Serve in your favourite mug or share with a friend, dividing the hot chocolate into two smaller cups.

NOTE

The fresh hazelnut milk makes the hot chocolate extra creamy. However, if you're short on time substitute your favourite store-bought nut milk.

Substitute ⅛ teaspoon chilli powder for the chipotle powder if unavailable. Alternatively the chilli can be left out for an equally delicious, but a little less spicy drink.

* Available from health food stores.
** Available from specialty grocers.

Peppermint, liquorice, ginger and fennel tea

Chipotle and hazelnut hot chocolate

Matcha latte

Matcha, a Japanese green tea powder, has a subtle sweet grassy flavour.
High in antioxidants, teamed here with creamy cashew milk it makes a great alternative
to coffee, as its phytonutrients help slow the body's absorption of caffeine, which gives you
a consistent energy throughout the morning.

SERVES 1

¼ cup (35 g/1¼ oz) raw cashews
1 cup (250 ml/8½ fl oz) water
1 medjool date, pitted
¼ teaspoon vanilla bean powder*
pinch of Himalayan salt
1 teaspoon matcha (green tea powder),
    plus extra for sprinkling
1 tablespoon boiling water
raw honey, to sweeten further (optional)

Soak the cashews in cold water for at least 1 hour
or up to overnight in the refrigerator.

Drain and rinse the cashews.

Combine the cashews and water in a high-speed
blender. Blend to finely grind the nuts, making
nut milk.

Strain the milk through a nut bag or double layer of
muslin (cheesecloth), set over a jug or bowl to catch
the milk. Squeeze the pulp to ensure all the liquid is
extracted. Keep the cashew pulp for another use, such
as adding to smoothies, muesli (granola) or in baking.

Return the milk to the blender, add the date, vanilla
and salt and blend to make a slightly sweet milk.

Gently heat the cashew milk in a small saucepan
over low heat, until hot.

Blend the matcha powder with the boiling water in
a small bowl, to make a smooth paste. Stir in a little
of the hot milk. Pour the matcha mixture into the pan
with the remaining hot milk and stir to combine.

Return the hot milk to the high-speed blender and
blend until frothy.

Pour into your favourite cup and sprinkle with a little
extra matcha powder. Sweeten with a little honey,
if desired.

NOTE

Alternatively, you can use a milk frother to heat the
milk and simply blend the matcha and boiling water
in your mug and pour the milk over the top.

The fresh cashew milk makes the matcha latte extra
creamy. However, if you're short on time substitute
your favourite store-bought nut milk.

* Available from health food stores.

Basics

....

The basics we use every day, from stock to seasoning to sauces, can have an accumulative impact on our health and skin. We tend to season, sauce and adorn each meal and, while packet sauces are convenient, there really is no short cut when it comes to looking after your health. Making your own basics means that you know what is going into them, that they are rich in nutrients with no additives. As well as being healthful, they taste so much better.

I like to set time aside every week to make basics that I can use for almost every meal, that can be used to add zing, herbaceousness, creaminess or enhance other foods' health-giving benefits. Cultured butter on toast, kimchi on a poached egg, stocks as the base for stews, soups and sauces, coconut miso caramel on some yoghurt, poached pears on your porridge, chutney or salsa verde on grilled fish or meat, preserved lemon in a stew, gravlax on a wrap for lunch ... having a few delicious basics on hand makes cooking so much easier and more interesting.

Herbs are also an easy way to add flavour and nutrients to dishes and drinks. They are high in protective plant chemicals and dress up a dish with lovely aromatic, fresh flavours: marinate your meat in rosemary and thyme, infuse lavender and other herbs into teas, dress tomato with basil, and so on. If you have your own herb garden, then it's easy to snip a few as you need them.

Fermentation

Fermented foods have existed in traditional cultures for centuries. However, the introduction of modern refrigeration, canning, pasteurisation and mass food production have replaced a lot of traditional food preparation and preservation methods, causing a severe decline in these wonderfully nutritious, probiotic-rich foods as part of a daily diet. With thanks to the Slow Food movement and a growing awareness of the importance of gut health there's been a resurgence of interest in making things from scratch using traditional methods, helping to put these delicious sour, tangy fermented foods back on the menu.

WHAT IS FERMENTATION?

Fermentation is a metabolic process in which beneficial bacteria, yeasts and moulds feed on carbohydrates such as sugars and starches, converting them into lactic acid or ethanol. They are sourced from the skin or leaves of organic fruit and vegetables, attracted wild from the air or introduced in the form of various starters. They break down and transform raw ingredients into much-loved fermented vegetables, breads, drinks (alcoholic and non-alcoholic), cured meats and dairy products. The byproduct of this process is carbon dioxide, its bubbles the tell-tale sign of an active ferment. These gases can be released or allowed to build to create naturally carbonated beverages.

BENEFITS

1   Fermenting neutralises enzyme inhibitors present in nuts, grains and legumes, making them much easier for the gut to digest and absorb nutrients.

2   Food is broken down making it easier to digest and nutrients more bioavailable.

3   They populate the intestinal tract with beneficial bacteria, helping to bring microflora into balance, strengthening immune and digestive systems.

4   Fermented vegetables are high in antioxidants and higher in minerals than non-fermented foods.

5   Fermenting helps to lower 'bad' gut bacteria, which cause inflammation in the digestive system and which can compromise health.

6   A diverse population of gut bacteria helps to maintain a healthy weight.

7   Boosts nutrition of vegetables, elevating levels of vitamins B and C when already present.

8   Preserves seasonal produce when at its freshest and cheapest.

TYPES OF FERMENTATION

There are two main types of fermentation:

• *Acid fermentation* – sugars or starches are converted into lactic acid (known as lacto-fermentation) or acetic acids (known as acetic-fermentation).

• *Alcohol fermentation* – sugars are converted into ethyl alcohol.

The method of fermentation featured in recipes in this book is acid fermentation.

ACID FERMENTATION

• *Lacto-fermentation* – despite its name it doesn't necessarily require dairy for fermentation. Lacto refers to the *Lactobacillus* bacteria, which is found on the skin and leaves of organic fruits and vegetables. *Lactobacillus* converts sugar (or starch) from carbohydrates, such as vegetables, into lactic acid, inhibiting the growth of harmful bacteria and acts as a natural preservative. *Lactobacillus* also feeds on lactose (milk sugars), breaking them down quickly and making them more easily digestible for those with lactose intolerances.

Creating an anaerobic environment

Lacto-fermentation requires an anaerobic (oxygen free) environment to take place. This can be created using a few different methods. All are effective, however, using a specialised fermenting jar with airlock lid is a guaranteed way of maintaining an anaerobic environment.

• *Water seal* – vegetables or fruits are submerged in brine, creating a water-sealed anaerobic environment. The jar is then covered with muslin cloth (cheesecloth) or a loose-fitting lid to help prevent contamination as well as allow the release of carbon dioxide.

• *Sealed mason or preserving jar* – a lid creates an anaerobic environment, keeping the oxygen out, however, it prevents the release of carbon dioxide. Hence if using this method the lid will need to be opened slightly (a process known as burping), to release built-up carbon dioxide and the consequent pressure, preventing a possible explosion. Initially, burping is required every 12–24 hours after the first 24 hours, for the first 3–4 days of fermentation. As the production of carbon dioxide decreases over time, longer ferments will only require burping every 5–7 days thereafter.

• *Specialised fermenting jar with airlock lid* – one-way valve on top of the lid allows excess gases to be released while keeping oxygen out.

Common ingredients

• Vegetables or fruit – fresh and organic is best. *Lactobacillus* required for lacto-fermentation is found on the skin and leaves of veggies and fruit grown close to the ground. Conventionally farmed produce may contain chemicals, which will inhibit good bacteria growth.

• Salt is important as it helps to kill unwanted bacteria, while allowing beneficial bacteria to grow. *Lactobacillus* are relatively salt-tolerant and will continue to

propagate. I prefer to use Himalayan salt, which adds valuable trace minerals. Unrefined sea salt also works well. Do not use iodised salt, as the iodine inhibits the growth of beneficial bacteria. Also avoid salt with anti-caking agents.

Using straight salt is the traditional and my preferred method of preparing lacto-vegetables. However, a combination of salt and fresh whey, strained from yoghurt (in which case the salt quantity needs to be reduced), or adding a starter culture, can be used.

• Cultures, such as water kefir and milk kefir grains, yoghurt and probiotic powder are used instead of salt to start the fermentation process in kefir, cultured butter and cultured nut 'cheese'.

• Water must be non-chlorinated. Chlorine is a steriliser and inhibits the growth of, if not destroys, good bacteria. Filtered or bottled is best. Alternatively, you can measure out your required amount of water and leave it in a bowl open to the air overnight; the chlorine will evaporate.

Lacto-fermented recipes in this book:

1. Cultured butter
2. Coconut milk kefir
3. Cultured nut 'cheese'
4. Fermented beetroot (beet) and onion with caraway and parsley
5. Fermented spiced pear, date and walnut chutney
6. Sauerkraut with apple, fennel and kale
7. Kimchi with daikon (white radish), cabbage and carrot
8. Sweet and sour fermented vegetables
9. Spiced preserved lemons
10. Fermented tomato and coriander (cilantro) salsa
11. Blueberry and lemon verbena water kefir
12. Ginger and turmeric beer
13. Beetroot (beet) and orange kvass

ACETIC FERMENTATION

Starches, sugars and alcohols are converted into acetic acid aerobically (with oxygen). This highly acidic environment inhibits the growth of harmful bacteria while allowing acid-tolerant bacteria *Acetobacter* to flourish. Starter (mother) cultures are used for this type of fermentation.

• *Vinegars* – *Acetobacter* bacteria consumes the ethanol (ethyl alcohol) in wine, beer and apple cider, converting it into acetic acid and familiar kitchen staples of red and white wine, malt and apple cider vinegars. Commercially made vinegars have been pasteurised, destroying all beneficial bacteria.

• *Kombucha* – a scoby (symbiotic culture of bacteria and yeast) is used, introduced to a sweet tea mixture. Yeasts feed on the sugars converting them into alcohol and carbon dioxide. This process happens aerobically (with air). *Acetobacter* bacteria consumes the ethanol (ethyl alcohol) and converts it into acetic acid.

The water used must be unchlorinated – refer to information on lacto-fermenting (see page 297).

Fermentation does not eliminate the caffeine, therefore levels will remain the same as the tea base used, also a small amount of alcohol (.05–1%) will remain.

Acetic-fermented recipes in this book:

1   Chai-spiced kombucha
2   Iced peach and thyme Jun kombucha

Lacto-ferment and kombucha hints and tips

The ideal temperature for lacto-fermenting and acetic-fermenting is room temperature, 18–24°C (65–75°F). Too cold and fermentation will be sluggish or potentially won't start. Too hot and fermentation will happen too quickly and could potentially destroy the bacteria.

Successful ferment

Signs that your lacto-ferment or kombucha is ready to be bottled, sealed and refrigerated to stop further fermentation:

• Carbon dioxide bubbles can be seen on the surface, attached to vegetables or scoby, or throughout a sauce or liquid. There is a pleasant, sour, slightly vinegary smell. It has a pleasantly tangy, slightly sour taste.

Unsuccessful ferment

Signs that your lacto-ferment has gone bad and it's time to throw it out, wash and sterilise your jars and start again:

• Smell of rotting vegetables; slimy; mould – many sources, including fermenting guru Sandor Katz, say a thin white film is safe to scrape off and discard without damaging the ferment or causing any harmful effects. In the presence of all other mould – green, black, thick white – throw it out and start again.

Signs that your kombucha has gone bad

• If there is any sign of mould, green, black or thick white, discard and begin again with cleaned equipment, fresh mother and starter liquid.

• A thick, pale white film will form on top of the mother scoby; this is just a baby scoby forming and perfectly safe. Wait until it thickens and strengthens, peel it off and give it to a friend to start their own kombucha. Alternatively leave it attached.

If you are new to consuming fermented foods, slowly introduce them into your diet, giving your gut time to adapt to the change in microflora. Adverse effects of too much too soon, or just too much may include bloating, gas, diarrhoea/constipation, headaches and skin conditions.

ALCOHOL FERMENTATION

Although not featured in this book, in this process yeasts convert sugars into ethyl alcohol (ethanol) and carbon dioxide anaerobically (without oxygen). Both carbonated and non-carbonated alcoholic beverages such as wine and beer are a result of this process.

SOURDOUGH

Sourdough bread also uses this yeast process aerobically, the alcohol being destroyed when baked. Carbon dioxide produced from this method is what causes the bread to rise.

STERILISING JARS AND BOTTLES

—— Line a tray with a clean tea towel (dish towel).

—— Wash jars and lids in hot soapy water. Rinse.

—— Place jars, bottles and lids in a large deep saucepan. Pour in enough cold water to completely submerge. Cover with a lid and bring to the boil. Gently boil for 10 minutes. Wearing kitchen gloves and using metal tongs carefully remove the jars and lids, emptying out the water as you go.

—— Arrange the jars, right-side up, on the prepared tray.

—— Fill immediately if filling with hot mixture. Leave jars to cool, covered with a clean tea towel (dish towel), if filling with cold mixture.

—— If using funnels to fill jars or bottles, wash and rinse as per jars. Set in a saucepan of boiled water for 1 minute. Stand to dry.

Chicken bone broth

Chicken soup is probably the simplest and most restorative beauty tonic,
as well as being great for the flu, issues with leaky gut, joint health, skin health and allergies.
It is rich in anti-inflammatory and detoxifying amino acids, including glycine and proline,
which make up our skin's collagen.

MAKES APPROXIMATELY 8 CUPS (2 LITRES/68 FL OZ)

1.5 kg (3 lb 5 oz) chicken bones, carcass, necks and
    wings (a carcass from a roast works well)
1 medium onion, skin on, quartered
1 medium carrot, unpeeled, coarsely chopped
1 small leek, coarsely chopped
1 stick celery, plus leaves, coarsely chopped
1 tablespoon apple cider vinegar (unpasteurised)
5 stalks parsley
4 sprigs thyme
1 clove garlic, unpeeled
5 whole black peppercorns
2 bay leaves
12 cups (3 litres/101 fl oz) cold water

Rinse the chicken pieces under cold water.

Place the chicken and the remaining ingredients in
a large heavy-based saucepan.

Pour in the water. Bring to the boil over high heat.
Decrease the heat and simmer undisturbed for
2 hours. Skim the fat and impurities off the surface
occasionally; this will help to give you a clearer broth.

Line a large sieve or colander with a double layer of
muslin (cheesecloth). Strain the broth and discard
the bones and remaining solids. Set aside to cool,
cover and refrigerate overnight. Remove and discard
the layer of fat that forms on top of the broth. Use
as required.

NOTE

If you prefer a darker broth, the bones and vegetables
can be roasted for around 45 minutes in a 200°C
(400°F) oven, before boiling.

Bone broth can also be made in a slow cooker.
Add all the ingredients to the slow cooker, cover
with water and cook on low for 12–24 hours.

Bone broth can be stored in the refrigerator for
5–7 days, or frozen in batches for up to 4 months.

Beef bone broth

*Beef broth is a highly gelatinous, richly flavoured gut, joint and beauty tonic.
Your broths can be popped into your sauces, used as soup bases or simply enjoyed
in a cup as a nourishing, remedying warm drink.*

MAKES APPROXIMATELY 8 CUPS (2 LITRES/68 FL OZ)

2 kg (4 lb 6 oz) grass-fed beef soup bones
1 leek, coarsely chopped
1 large onion, skin on, quartered
1 carrot, unpeeled, coarsely chopped
1 tomato, quartered
2 sticks celery, plus leaves, coarsely chopped
1 tablespoon apple cider vinegar (unpasteurised)
5 sprigs flat-leaf (Italian) parsley
4 sprigs thyme
2 cloves garlic, unpeeled
5 whole black peppercorns
2 bay leaves

Preheat the oven to 200°C (400°F). Place the bones, leek, onion, carrot and tomato in a large roasting tin and roast for 45 minutes, or until well browned and slightly blackened.

Transfer the roasted bones and vegetables into a large heavy-based saucepan. Pour off any fat in the tray.

Pour 1 cup (250 ml/8½ fl oz) of water into the baking tray and stir, scraping the base to remove any stuck pieces and the cooking juices. Pour into the saucepan.

Add the remaining ingredients to the bones. Pour in enough cold water to generously cover the bones.

Bring to the boil over high heat. Decrease the heat and gently simmer for at least 6–8 hours, and up to 36 hours, topping up with water as required to keep the bones submerged. Skim the fat and impurities off the surface occasionally; this will help to give you a clearer broth.

Use tongs to remove the bones from the broth. Line a large sieve or colander with a double layer of muslin (cheesecloth). Strain the broth, discarding the remaining solids. Set aside to cool, then cover and refrigerate overnight. Remove and discard the set layer of fat that forms on top of the broth. Use as required.

NOTE

Bone broth can be stored in the refrigerator for 5–7 days or frozen in batches for up to 4 months.

Simmering times for beef broth can vary between 8 and 24 hours, even up to 3 days! I recommend using a slow cooker for longer simmering times. The longer you simmer the more minerals will be released from the bones.

Vegetable broth

Made from prebiotics (onion, leek and garlic) and anti-inflammatory spices,
the addition of mushroom offers a boost of vitamin D, which helps support the immune
system, increase calcium absorption and adds a lovely depth of flavour.

MAKES APPROXIMATELY 8 CUPS (2 LITRES/68 FL OZ)

1 large leek, coarsely chopped
3 sticks celery, plus leaves, coarsely chopped
1 large onion, skin on, quartered
1 large carrot, unpeeled, coarsely chopped
125 g (4½ oz) button mushrooms
1 tomato
1 small bulb garlic, broken apart but unpeeled
10 cm (4 in) knob of turmeric, coarsely chopped
5 cm (2 in) knob of ginger, coarsely chopped
olive oil, for drizzling
1 tablespoon apple cider vinegar (unpasteurised)
6 sprigs flat-leaf (Italian) parsley
5 sprigs thyme
5 whole black peppercorns
2 bay leaves
10 cups (2.5 litres/85 fl oz) cold water

Preheat the oven to 200°C (400°F).

Place the leek, celery, onion, carrot, mushrooms, tomato, garlic, turmeric and ginger in a roasting tin. Drizzle generously with oil. Roast for 30 minutes, or until browned and slightly blackened.

Transfer the roasted vegetable mixture into a large saucepan. Add the remaining ingredients.

Bring to the boil over high heat. Decrease the heat and simmer undisturbed for 2 hours.

Line a large sieve or colander with a double layer of muslin (cheesecloth). Strain the broth and discard the solids.

Use as required.

NOTE
Broth can be stored in the refrigerator for 5–7 days or frozen in batches for up to 3 months.

Cultured butter

*By culturing butter you eliminate the lactose and reduce the casein, and are left
with a health-giving spread, rich in beauty-boosting fats, vitamins A, D and E and selenium,
all of which promote cellular rejuvenation and protect our cells from oxidative damage.*

MAKES 275 G (9½ OZ)

2 cups (500 ml/17 fl oz) organic full-fat (double/
   heavy) cream
2 tablespoons organic full-fat natural yoghurt,
   no stabilisers or additives
iced water
½ teaspoon Himalayan salt

NOTE

Cultured butter can be stored in the refrigerator
for up to 1 month, or frozen for up to 3 months.

Buttermilk can be stored in an airtight container
for up to 5 days in the refrigerator.

For an added twist, try making flavoured butter:
garlic, herb, porcini mushroom, paprika and chilli
work well. One of my favourite additions is miso;
it is so lovely with baked fish or on steamed green
veggies. Simply add the additional flavourings
when you add the salt.

Whisk the cream and yoghurt together in a medium
glass or ceramic bowl. Cover with plastic wrap.
Alternatively, shake together in a large glass jar,
sealed with a lid. Wrap the bowl or jar in a clean hand
towel. Stand in a warm place (around 21–23°C/70°F)
for 12–24 hours, until thickened, slightly bubbly and
beginning to smell sour.

Refrigerate for 1 hour, or until it reads 15°C (60°F) when
tested with a food thermometer. The cream mixture
can be left in the refrigerator for longer at this stage,
up to 2 days, just stand it out at room temperature to
bring it back up to 15°C (60°F) before proceeding with
the next step.

Whip the cream using an electric mixer for 2 minutes,
or until the cream turns lumpy and the buttermilk
begins to separate from the fat. Pour the buttermilk out
into a container and reserve for a future use. Whip the
cream for a further 1–2 minutes to remove more of the
buttermilk and then pour off again as it separates.

Add 1 cup (250 ml/8½ fl oz) of iced water to the
butterfat. Using a spatula, wash the butter, folding
it over itself. The water will become cloudy as the
remaining buttermilk is released. Drain and refresh
the water three more times (discarding the cloudy
water), or until the water remains clear and the butter
begins to harden. It is important to remove all the
buttermilk as this will extend the life of your butter.
Buttermilk will encourage the butter to go rancid
more quickly.

Drain and pat the butter dry with a clean kitchen cloth.

Using a spatula, fold and knead the salt into the
butter, until smooth. Shape the butter into a ball,
cylinder or rectangle. Wrap in baking paper and foil.
Refrigerate until required.

Coconut milk kefir

Traditionally made from cow's milk, milk kefir grains can also be used to transform coconut milk into a tangy, probiotic drink, making it a great alternative for those with lactose sensitivities. Drink a small glass each morning, or add to smoothies as a simple way to supercharge your gut.

MAKES 2 CUPS (500 ML/17 FL OZ)

2 cups (500 ml/17 fl oz) organic coconut milk
1 teaspoon coconut sugar
10 g milk kefir grains (can be purchased online or
    sourced from a friend)

Pour the coconut milk into a sterilised 4 cup (1 litre/34 fl oz) glass jar*. Add the coconut sugar and grains and stir with a wooden or ceramic spoon.

Cover the jar with muslin (cheesecloth) and secure with a rubber band. Stand at room temperature, out of direct sunlight and in a well-ventilated place for 12–24 hours, until the coconut milk develops a pleasant sour taste.

Strain through a non-reactive strainer, such as stainless steel or plastic. Reserve the grains. Use the grains to begin culturing your next batch of coconut milk kefir or store in a sterilised glass jar in the refrigerator for up to 1 month. (See below and right for care and storage instructions.)

Seal the jar and refrigerate for a second ferment of 1–2 days, until thickened to the consistency of drinking yoghurt.

Store the coconut milk kefir in a 2 cup (500 ml/ 17 fl oz)-capacity sterilised glass jar or bottle in the refrigerator for up to 2 weeks.

NOTE
Milk kefir grains – miniature cauliflower-looking clumps with a cottage cheese-like texture – are a combination of healthy bacteria and yeast which feed on lactose, the sugars found in milk. As coconut milk does not contain lactose it is important that the kefir grains are rested in milk every 1 or 2 batches in order to maintain their strength, health and structure. Although kefir grains used to make coconut kefir work effectively as a culture, they will generally not be strong enough to multiply. To get your grains up to reproducing strength feed on the lactose in dairy milk, using the same culturing method as for making coconut kefir for 2–3 weeks, or until desired.

For those particularly sensitive to lactose, grains can be rinsed under cold water when transferring from dairy milk to coconut.

CARING FOR COCONUT MILK KEFIR GRAINS
Coconut milk kefir grains require lactose to remain healthy and reproducing. After fermenting every second batch of coconut kefir it is best to feed your grains to aid optimum health. Simply place the grains in a sterilised glass jar and cover with organic cow's milk. Cover with a muslin (cheesecloth) and secure with a rubber band. Stand out at room temperature for 12–24 hours. Strain. If avoiding dairy, rinse the grains under cold filtered water.

* For sterilising instructions see page 299.

COCONUT MILK KEFIR GRAIN STORAGE

1–7 days
In a sterilised glass jar covered with organic cow's milk. Refrigerate.

7–14 days
in a sterilised glass jar with no liquid. Refrigerate.

14 + days up to 6 months
dehydrate at room temperature or using a dehydrator set at 30°C (85°F). Freeze in a zip-lock bag.

REACTIVATING COCONUT MILK KEFIR GRAINS

The longer you store kefir grains the longer they take to regain their original fermenting strength. To give them a kick-start, place the kefir grains in a sterilised glass jar, cover with organic cow's milk, add ½ teaspoon of organic raw (demerara) sugar and stir to combine. Cover with muslin (cheesecloth) and secure with a rubber band. Let stand at room temperature for 12 hours. Strain and repeat one to three more times, depending on how long they have been stored. If avoiding dairy, rinse the grains under cold filtered water.

Labneh

Originating in the Middle East, labneh, a fresh yoghurt cheese, is essentially strained yoghurt. The process of straining drains the whey from the curd, resulting in a thick, spreadable, cream cheese–like consistency.

MAKES 2 CUPS (500 G/1 LB 2 OZ)

4 cups (1 kg/2 lb 3 oz) natural yoghurt
½ teaspoon Himalayan salt

Line a large sieve with a triple layer of muslin (cheesecloth). Set over a large bowl.

Place the yoghurt and salt in a medium bowl and stir to combine. Spoon the yoghurt into the muslin. Bring the edges of the cloth together and tie in a knot to enclose. Refrigerate to strain for 24–36 hours, until the whey has drained from the curd, resulting in a labneh the consistency of cream cheese.

Store in an airtight container for up to 1 week.

NOTE

Labneh can be spread onto crackers for a quick snack, used as a creamy addition to a salad or served as a dip with crudités. To use as a dip, spread labneh into a shallow bowl and scatter with assorted chopped nuts and herbs or sprinkle with za'atar.

The longer the yoghurt is strained the thicker the consistency becomes and the stronger, more cheese-like the flavour. After a few days it will be thick enough to roll into small cheese balls and marinated in oil for storage. Balls can be rolled in dried herbs or herbs and spices can be added to the oil to infuse.

Cultured nut 'cheese'

A wonderful 'cheesy' cheese alternative. Ranging in texture from cream cheese to sliceable cheddar, depending on how long you leave it to 'cure'. A great alternative for cheese-loving vegans looking for ways to add the cultured goodness of probiotics into their diet.

MAKES 375 G (13 OZ)

2 cups (300 g/10½ oz) raw cashews, soaked in water
    for 12 hours or overnight
½ cup (125 ml/4 fl oz) lukewarm water
½ teaspoon (5 capsules) probiotic powder
1½ tablespoons savoury yeast flakes*
2 teaspoons freshly squeezed lemon juice
1 teaspoon onion powder
1 teaspoon Himalayan salt
½ teaspoon ground turmeric (optional)

Coating or wrapping options
2 tablespoons herbs de Provence or your choice
    of spice mix
fresh vine leaves

Drain and rinse the cashews. Place the cashews, lukewarm water and probiotic powder in a high-speed blender. Blend until smooth. Transfer to a glass or ceramic bowl. Cover with a piece of muslin (cheesecloth) and secure. Stand at room temperature in a warm place (on top of the fridge is a good spot) for 1–2 days, until thickened with a pleasant sour taste.

Add the yeast flakes, lemon juice, onion powder, salt and turmeric, if using, and stir to combine.

Spoon the mixture onto a double-layered square of muslin cloth (cheesecloth). Bundle up into a ball, tie and hang off a spoon suspended over a bowl. Stand at room temperature for 4 hours, or until the 'cheese' reaches your desired firmness.

'Cheese' can be served plain, wrapped in vine leaves or coated in spices. If serving plain, press into a plastic wrap–lined mould or shape and wrap in clean muslin or baking paper. Serve immediately if you prefer a softer, spreadable texture. Alternatively refrigerate for 2 hours or up to 3 days, to firm your cheese up further, until the desired consistency is reached.

If wrapping the 'cheese' in vine leaves, place a large spoonful of the 'cheese' into the centre of a large vine leaf. A softer, spreadable consistency is best for wrapping. Fold the edges in to enclose and form a parcel. Serve immediately or refrigerate until desired.

To coat, shape the 'cheese' into desired shape – a log or rectangle works well. Wrap in muslin cloth (cheesecloth) or baking paper and refrigerate for 2 hours, to firm up slightly. Roll in herbs de Provence or your choice of spice mix. Serve immediately or rewrap and refrigerate until required, up to 5 days.

Serve with crackers or crudités or as part of a meal.

NOTE
Store the 'cheese' wrapped in plastic wrap or baking paper in the refrigerator for up to 5 days.

* Available from health food stores.

Fermented beetroot and onion with caraway and parsley

This deliciously tangy condiment makes a great addition to salads, wraps or cooked breakfasts, adding a burst of flavour and vibrant colour. I love this with gravlax, buckwheat pancakes or the rainbow chard, tomato and goat's cheese tart on page 82.

MAKES 2½ CUPS (750 G/1 LB 11 OZ)

½ teaspoon caraway seeds, toasted

4 whole cloves

3 whole black peppercorns

2 beetroot (beets), washed and coarsely grated

½ red onion, thinly sliced

2 large handfuls flat-leaf (Italian) parsley, coarsely chopped

3 teaspoons Himalayan salt

filtered water

outer cabbage leaf, for covering

Dry-roast the spices in a small frying pan over low heat for 30 seconds, or until fragrant.

Combine the spices, beetroot, onion and parsley in a medium glass or ceramic bowl. Add the salt. Wearing food-handling gloves, massage in the salt, until the beetroot and onion soften and liquid is released.

Tightly pack the beetroot mixture and liquid into a sterilised 4 cup (1 litre/34 fl oz)-capacity glass jar* or specialised fermentation jar with an airlock lid. Pour in a little filtered water, to just cover the beetroot, if required. Firmly press down the vegetables to submerge in liquid. Cover the beetroot with a piece of cabbage leaf.

If using an ordinary jar, weigh down with a specialised ceramic weight or smaller jar filled with water. Ensure there is a 5 cm (2 in) gap between the vegetables and the top of the jar to allow for extra liquid released during the fermentation process. Cover with a double layer of muslin (cheesecloth) and secure with a rubber band. If using a Mason, preserving or specialised fermenting jar, secure the lid.

Leave to stand at room temperature, out of direct sunlight and in a well-ventilated place for 5–7 days**, or until the mixture becomes pleasantly tangy. Check daily to ensure the beetroot mixture is completely submerged, to prevent mould from forming. Press down with a wooden spoon if necessary. If using a Mason or preserving jar, open every day to release gases (known as burping) to prevent pressure build-up, which could result in an explosion.

Once fermented, tightly pack the beetroot mixture into sterilised glass jars and seal with a lid. Fermented beetroot can be used immediately or stored in the refrigerator for a week or so to age before use.

NOTE

This can be stored in the refrigerator for up to 3 months. The flavours will continue to develop over time.

For best results when fermenting, use organic produce, as it contains more beneficial bacteria on its skin.

* For sterilising instructions see page 299.

** The length of time will vary according to the temperature of your kitchen.

Fermented spiced pear, date and walnut chutney

The mellow sweetness of pears, warming spices, dates and walnuts meld deliciously with the subtle sour-salty taste of fermentation. Pear is a good source of cellulose, an insoluble fibre that feeds and helps to promote good gut microbes.

MAKES 4 CUPS (1 KG/2 LB 3 OZ)

1 cinnamon stick, broken in half

1 dried red chilli

8 whole cloves

½ teaspoon coriander seeds

6 whole black peppercorns

3 medium (500 g/1lb 2 oz in total) firm pears, cored and cut into 2 cm (¾ in) dice, skin on

8 medjool dates, pitted and coarsely chopped

½ cup (60 g/2 oz) walnuts, coarsely chopped

2 purple shallots, finely diced

2 cm (¾ in) knob of ginger, peeled and finely chopped

1 teaspoon Himalayan salt

finely grated zest and juice of 1 unwaxed organic lemon

filtered water, as required

outer cabbage leaf, for covering

Toast the spices in a dry frying pan over low heat, for 30 seconds, or until fragrant.

Place the spices and remaining ingredients except the water in a large glass or ceramic bowl. Wearing food-handling gloves, massage the ingredients together, to coat and soften slightly. Cover with a muslin cloth (cheesecloth) or a clean tea towel (dish towel) and set aside for 1 hour.

Tightly pack the pear mixture into a sterilised 4 cup (1 litre/34 fl oz)-capacity glass jar*, so that the juice rises to cover the fruit. Pour in a little filtered water to cover completely, if required. Cover the fruit with a cabbage leaf. If using an ordinary jar, weigh down with a specialised ceramic weight or smaller jar filled with water. Cover with a double layer of muslin and secure with a rubber band. If using a Mason, preserving or specialised fermenting jar, secure the lid.

Let stand at room temperature, out of direct sunlight and in a well-ventilated place for 2–4 days**, or until the mixture becomes pleasantly tangy. Check daily to ensure the chutney is completely submerged in brine, to prevent mould from forming. Press down with a wooden spoon if necessary. If using a Mason or preserving jar, open ever so slightly every day to release gases (known as burping) to prevent pressure build-up, which could result in an explosion.

Transfer into smaller sterilised jars, if desired, packing tightly to submerge in brine and seal with a lid.

NOTE

You can store the chutney in the refrigerator for up to 1 month. The flavours will continue to develop.

Flavours can be adapted according to the season, try substituting peaches for the pear in summer for a slightly sweeter outcome. If you like a bit of heat, throw in another dried chilli for a little extra kick. Try it on a sandwich with some leftover slow-roasted lamb shoulder (see recipe page 188).

* For sterilising instructions see page 299.

** The length of time required will vary according to the temperature of your kitchen.

Fermented beetroot and onion with caraway and parsley | Fermented spiced pear, date and walnut chutney

Sauerkraut with apple, fennel and kale | Kimchi with daikon, cabbage and carrot

Sauerkraut with apple, fennel and kale

A popular condiment in Eastern Europe, translated as 'sour cabbage', sauerkraut is traditionally served with fatty foods (think bratwurst) to aid digestion and balance out richness from fatty meat. It's delicious with osso bucco (see recipe page 184).

MAKES 4 CUPS (1 KG/2 LB 3 OZ)

1 small–medium (approx 1 kg/2 lb 3 oz) green cabbage
2 tablespoons Himalayan salt
1 large fennel bulb, trimmed, halved and cored, fronds reserved
2 large tart green apples, such as Granny Smith, quartered and cored
3 stems kale, deveined and finely shredded
1 large handful dill leaves, coarsely chopped

Remove and reserve the outer leaves of the cabbage. Cut the cabbage in half, remove and discard the core. Thinly shred the cabbage. Wash thoroughly and drain. Place the shredded cabbage in a large glass or ceramic bowl. Massage the salt into the cabbage for 2–3 minutes, until it softens and releases liquid to make a brine.

Using a mandoline or sharp knife, thinly slice the fennel and apple. Coarsely chop the fennel fronds. Add the fennel and fennel fronds, apple, kale and dill to the cabbage. Toss to combine.

Tightly pack the vegetable mixture into a sterilised 6 cup (1.5 litre/51 fl oz) glass or ceramic jar* or specialised fermentation jar with an airlock lid. Pour the brine over the top. Firmly press down the vegetables to submerge in liquid. Cover with the reserved cabbage leaves. If using an ordinary jar, weigh down with a specialised ceramic weight or smaller jar filled with water. Ensure there is a 5 cm (2 in) gap between the cabbage leaves and the top of the jar to allow for extra liquid released during the fermentation process. Cover with a double layer of muslin (cheesecloth) and secure with a rubber band. If using a Mason, preserving or specialised fermenting jar, secure the lid.

Let stand at room temperature, out of direct sunlight and in a well-ventilated place for 1–2 weeks**. During this time, if using a jar covered with muslin, check daily to ensure the vegetables are completely submerged in brine. If using a Mason or preserving jar, open ever so slightly every day to release gases (known as burping) to prevent pressure build-up which could result in an explosion. If desired, transfer into smaller sterilised jars, packing tightly to submerge in brine and seal with a lid. Sauerkraut can be used immediately or stored in the refrigerator for a week or so to age before use, and up to 3 months.

NOTE
Store in the refrigerator for up to 3 months.
The flavours will continue to develop over time.

* For sterilising instructions see page 299.
** The length of time will vary according to the temperature of your kitchen.

Kimchi with daikon, cabbage and carrot

This much-loved Korean side dish traditionally accompanies most meals in Korea.
Kimchi has a complex flavour: pungent and tangy with a chilli kick, and it is so good for you.
I love it with eggs and fish and chicken – actually on everything – it's delicious!

MAKES 4 CUPS (1 KG/2 LB 3 OZ)

1 Chinese cabbage (Napa cabbage/wombok)
1 daikon (white radish) peeled
1 carrot, peeled
4 cups (1 litre/34 fl oz) water
¼ cup (70 g/2½ oz) Himalayan salt
4 spring onions (scallions), trimmed
¼ cup (25 g/1 oz) Korean chilli powder
    (kochukaru/gochugaru)*
¼ cup (60 ml/2 fl oz) tamari
2 tablespoons fish sauce (optional)
5 cloves garlic, finely chopped
7 cm (2¾ in) knob of ginger, peeled and finely grated

Reserve the outer leaves of the cabbage then trim the base. Cut through the cabbage horizontally to make approximately 4 cm (1½ in)-thick pieces. Wash thoroughly.

Slice the daikon and carrot into approximately 3 mm (⅒ in)-thick rounds. Combine with the cabbage in a large ceramic or glass bowl. Stir the water and salt together then pour over the vegetables.

Using food-handling gloves or with clean hands, massage the brine into the vegetables for 1–2 minutes, or until the vegetables soften. Cover with the reserved cabbage leaves. Weigh down with a plate, so the vegetables are submerged in brine. Cover with muslin (cheesecloth) and secure in place with a rubber band. Set aside at room temperature, out of direct sunlight and in a well-ventilated place for 8 hours.

Drain the vegetables, reserving 1 cup (250 ml/8½ fl oz) of the brine. Cut the green part of the spring onion into 3 cm (1¼ in) lengths. Finely chop the white part. Place in a medium bowl. Add the Korean chilli powder, tamari, fish sauce, if using, garlic and ginger and stir to make a thick paste.

Combine the drained vegetables and chilli paste in a large bowl. Wearing food-handling gloves, massage the paste into the vegetables, until they begin to soften and release liquid to form a brine.

Tightly pack the mixture into a sterilised 6 cup (1.5 litre/51 fl oz)-capacity glass or ceramic jar** or fermentation jar with an airlock lid. Firmly press down the vegetables to submerge in liquid. Add the reserved brine to top up, if required. Cover with the reserved cabbage leaves. If using an ordinary jar, weigh down with a smaller jar filled with water. Ensure there is a 5 cm (2 in) gap between the cabbage leaves and the top of the jar to allow for extra liquid released during the fermentation process. Reserve any extra liquid for Kimchi Virgin Mary (see recipe page 279) or as a starter for kvass (see recipe page 278).

Set the jar on a large plate to catch any overflow. Cover with a double layer of muslin (cheesecloth) and secure with a rubber band. If using a Mason, preserving or specialised fermenting jar, secure the lid.

Let stand at room temperature, out of direct sunlight and in a well-ventilated place for 5–7 days***, or until the mixture becomes pleasantly tangy. Check daily to ensure the vegetables are completely submerged in brine, to prevent mould from forming. Press down and weight as required.

If desired, transfer into smaller sterilised glass jars, packing tightly to submerge in brine and seal with a lid. Kimchi can be used immediately or stored in the refrigerator for a week or so to age before use, and up to 3 months.

*   Available from Asian grocers.
** For sterilising instructions see page 299.
*** The length of time will vary according to the temperature of your kitchen.

Sweet and sour fermented vegetables

Fermented vegetables are perfect on a mezze platter or added to a salad, whole or thinly sliced and tossed through. This recipe will work for any root vegetable, so if you have a favourite one or two you can alter quantities accordingly for your next batch.

MAKES 6 CUPS (1.5 KG/3 LB 5 OZ)

1 teaspoon mustard seeds
½ cauliflower, broken into small florets
1 carrot, washed and cut into sticks
8 radishes, washed and halved, quartered or sliced
    (depending on size)
6 cloves garlic, peeled
3 bay leaves
2 cups (500 ml/17 fl oz) filtered water
½ cup (125 ml/4 fl oz) apple cider vinegar
    (unpasteurised)
2 tablespoons Himalayan salt
1 tablespoon raw honey
outer cabbage leaf

NOTE

You can store this pickle in the refrigerator for up to 3 months. The flavours will continue to develop over time.

If you've got some fresh vine leaves on hand add one to your vegetables – the tannins released will help to achieve a crunchier outcome. Fermented garlic can discolour to a green/blue colour but it is still perfectly safe to eat. To help prevent this, ensure you use chlorine-free water and non-iodised salt.

* For sterilising instructions see page 299.
** The length of time will vary according to the temperature of your kitchen.

Dry-roast the mustard seeds in a small frying pan over low heat for 30 seconds, or until they begin to pop. Tightly pack the vegetables, mustard seeds and bay leaves into a sterilised 6 cup (1.5 litre/51 fl oz)-capacity glass jar* or specialised fermentation jar with an airlock lid.

Combine the water, vinegar, salt and honey in a jug and stir to dissolve the salt. Pour the liquid over the vegetables, to just cover. Pour in a little filtered water to cover completely, if required. Firmly press down the vegetables to submerge in liquid. Cover the vegetables with a piece of cabbage leaf. If using an ordinary jar, weigh down with a specialised ceramic weight or smaller jar filled with water. Ensure there is a 5 cm (2 in) gap between the vegetables and the top of the jar to allow for extra liquid released during the fermentation process. Set the jar on a large plate to catch any overflow. Cover the jar with a double layer of muslin (cheesecloth) and secure with a rubber band. If using a Mason, preserving or specialised fermenting jar, secure the lid.

Let stand at room temperature, out of direct sunlight and in a well-ventilated place for 5–7 days**, or until the mixture becomes pleasantly tangy. During this time, if using a jar covered with muslin cloth, check daily to ensure the vegetables are completely submerged in brine, to prevent mould from forming. Press down with a wooden spoon if necessary.
If using a Mason or preserving jar, open ever so slightly every day to release gases (known as burping) to prevent pressure build-up which could result in an explosion. Once fermented, seal with a lid. Fermented vegetables can be used immediately or stored in the refrigerator for a week or so to age before use, and up to 3 months.

Spiced preserved lemons

Used extensively in North African cooking, preserved lemons have a salty, mildly tart lemony taste, which traditionally adds flavour to tagines. A great staple to have on hand, they are quite versatile and can also add a lovely lemon punch to salads, braises, bakes, sauces and soups.

MAKES ONE 8 CUP (2 LITRE/68 FL OZ) JAR

1 kg (2 lb 3 oz) organic unwaxed lemons, plus
    1–2 extra lemons for juicing
1 tablespoon coriander seeds
1 tablespoon cumin seeds
1 tablespoon fennel seeds
2 teaspoons whole black peppercorns
1 teaspoon chilli flakes
½ cup (150 g/5½ oz) coarse Himalayan salt
6 bay leaves

Sterilise an 8 cup (2 litre/68 fl oz) capacity Mason jar with a screw-top lid or preserving jar with rubber seal and metal clip.

Keeping the bases intact, cut the lemons in quarters lengthways.

Roast the spices in a dry frying pan over low heat, until fragrant.

Combine the salt and spices in a small bowl.

Stuff some of the spiced salt mix into the centre of each lemon. Pack the lemons, cut-side up, in the prepared jar, packing them in very tightly together. Scatter with any remaining salt mix as you go.

Using a pestle or handle of a wooden spoon, pound the lemons in the jar to release some of their juice. Insert bay leaves around the sides of the jar. Seal and set aside in a cool place overnight to allow the juice to release.

The following morning, pound the lemons down again and top up with additional lemon juice to completely cover the lemons.

Stand at room temperature for 6–8 weeks, until the rind is very tender. Every few days, invert the jars once or twice, to distribute the spices and juice evenly.

NOTE

Store preserved lemons in a cool, dark place or in the refrigerator for up to 1 year.

Lemons can be cut into quarters and packed into smaller jars as desired.

Any lemons can be used – thick-skinned Eureka and Lisbon lemons, abundant in acidic juice and readily available, fruiting throughout the year, make big fleshy preserves. Meyer lemons, a hybrid between a lemon and orange on the other hand, have a shorter season, from winter to early spring and are much smaller with thinner skin and a milder slightly sweet juice. They are both delicious; here I've used Eureka.

The process of fermentation softens and removes the bitterness from the most commonly used part, the peel. The pulp can also be used, although with care, as it absorbs a lot more of the salt.

Fermented tomato and coriander salsa

MAKES 4 CUPS (1 KG/2 LB 3 OZ)

This salsa is a great introduction to fermented foods for the unseasoned palate.

1 kg (2 lb 3 oz) organic tomatoes, diced
1 medium red onion, diced
3 large handful, coriander (cilantro) leaves and stems, coarsely chopped
2 jalapeño chillies or 2 long red chillies, thinly sliced
juice of 1 lemon
juice of 2 limes
2 tablespoons Himalayan salt
1 clove garlic, finely chopped
1 teaspoon ground cumin
½ teaspoon freshly ground black pepper
outer cabbage leaf, for covering

In a large glass bowl, mix the tomatoes, onion, coriander, chilli, lemon and lime juice, salt, garlic, cumin and pepper. Cover with muslin (cheesecloth) or a clean tea towel (dish towel) and set aside for 1 hour.

Tightly pack the salsa mixture into a sterilised 4 cup (1 litre/34 fl oz)-capacity Mason, preserving or glass jar*. Firmly press down to submerge. Cover with cabbage leaves. If using an ordinary jar, weigh down with specialised ceramic weight or a smaller jar filled with water. Ensure there is a 5 cm (2 in) gap between the cabbage leaves and the top of the jar. Cover with a double layer of muslin and secure with a rubber band. If using a Mason, preserving or specialised fermenting jar, secure the lid.

Leave to stand at room temperature, out of direct sunlight in a well-ventilated place for 2–4 days**. Check daily to ensure the salsa is completely submerged in brine. Press down and weight as required. Transfer into smaller sterilised jars, if desired, ensuring the salsa is covered in liquid.

Chilli sauce

MAKES 1½ CUPS (375 G/13 OZ)

Tangy, with a wonderful burst of heat, this chilli sauce can be drizzled on just about anything, if you're that way inclined. I love it over eggs, fritters and it's oh-so-good on chicken congee (see recipe page 50)!

500 g (1 lb 2 oz) long red chillies
½ red capsicum (bell pepper), seeded and coarsely chopped
1 large purple shallot, finely chopped
3 cloves garlic
⅓ cup (80 ml/2½ fl oz) apple cider vinegar (unpasteurised)
1 teaspoon Himalayan salt

Trim the stalks of the chillies and chop coarsely. If you prefer a mild sauce, remove the membrane and seeds from one-third of the chillies and discard. Place the chilli and remaining ingredients in a high-speed blender. Blend to purée.

Transfer into a sterilised* Mason, preserving or glass jar. If using an ordinary jar, cover with a double layer of muslin (cheesecloth) and secure with a rubber band. If using a Mason, preserving or specialised fermenting jar, secure the lid.

Let stand at room temperature, out of direct sunlight and in a well-ventilated place for 3–5 days**, until the mixture becomes foamy. During this time, if using a Mason or preserving jar, open ever so slightly every day to release gases (known as burping) to prevent pressure build-up which could result in an explosion. Pour the sauce into a sterilised glass bottle* or airtight container.

* For sterilising instructions see page 299.
** The length of time depends on the temperature of your kitchen.

It's important to introduce probiotics slowly into your diet to allow your gut time to adapt, helping to prevent any digestive discomfort.

The sauce and the salsa can be stored in the refrigerator for up to 3 months.

Salmon gravlax

A Swedish classic, gravlax came about before refrigeration out of necessity to store freshly caught fish. Salmon or herring were placed in a shallow grave (the origin of name gravlax), covered with salt, buried and left to ferment. I prefer to use the fridge.

MAKES 1 SIDE SALMON

1.2–1.5 kg (2 lb 10 oz–3 lb 5 oz) side salmon, skin on
extra-virgin olive oil, for brushing
1 large handful dill fronds, coarsely chopped
micro herbs, to garnish (optional)

Cure mix
3 cups (420 g/15 oz) Maldon, or other, salt flakes
1½ cups (210 g/7½ oz) coconut sugar
2 unwaxed lemons, zest finely grated and juiced
1½ teaspoons white peppercorns, coarsely cracked
1½ teaspoons coriander seeds, coarsely cracked

Using a pair of kitchen tweezers, remove the pin bones from the salmon. You can also ask your fishmonger to do this for you.

To prepare the cure mix, combine all of the ingredients in a medium bowl. Mix well.

Line a deep tray, large enough to fit the salmon, with baking paper.

Spread approximately one-quarter of the cure mix to make a thin layer onto the baking paper to the length of the salmon. Lay the salmon, skin-side down, on top of the cure mix. Spread the remaining cure mix over the salmon in an even layer. Do not rub in.

Place a sheet of baking paper directly over the salmon. Cover with plastic wrap. Place a tray on top and weigh it down to flatten the salmon slightly. Refrigerate for 24 hours.

After 24 hours, brush the cure mix off the salmon. Rinse the salmon under cold water then pat dry with kitchen paper.

Brush the salmon with olive oil. Coat with the dill. Wrap tightly in plastic wrap and refrigerate for 2 hours, or until required, up to 2 weeks.

To serve, use a sharp knife to thinly slice the salmon off the skin. Garnish with micro herbs, if desired.

NOTE
You can use the gravlax as a filling for wraps, a protein addition for breakfast or lunch, on crackers or as a starter with pickled vegetables.

Salmon can be cured for up to 3–4 days, the fish becoming firmer in texture over time. The recipe quantities can be reduced to cure a smaller piece of salmon.

Salsa verde

This is a delicious, rustic Italian herb sauce that is bursting with flavour as well as healthy fats from olive oil. The saltiness from the capers and anchovies make this a lovely balanced sauce that can be drizzled on salads, cooked fish and meat.

MAKES 1 CUP (250 G/9 OZ)

2 teaspoons capers, finely chopped
1 clove garlic, finely chopped
4 anchovy fillets, finely chopped
finely grated zest of 1 unwaxed lemon
¼ cup (60 ml/2 fl oz) red wine vinegar
    (unpasteurised)
1 teaspoon Dijon mustard
2 large handfuls basil leaves, finely chopped
2 large handfuls flat-leaf (Italian) parsley, finely
    chopped
1 large handful mint leaves, finely chopped
100 ml (3½ fl oz) extra-virgin olive oil
Himalayan salt and freshly ground black pepper,
    to taste

Place the capers, garlic, anchovy and lemon zest in a medium bowl. Add the vinegar and mustard and stir to combine. Add the herbs.

Gradually pour in the oil, stirring to combine. Season with salt and pepper.

Store in an airtight container in the refrigerator for up to 1 week.

NOTE
Vegetarians can omit the anchovies and add an extra teaspoon of capers for an equally delicious herbed oil.

Millet and flax seed and spinach wraps

Soft and pliable, these wraps are a saviour when it comes to portable lunches.
They can be made in advance, and keep well in the fridge for up to a week,
or the freezer for longer periods.

EACH VARIATION MAKES 8 WRAPS

Base ingredients
4 large eggs
1 cup (250 ml/8½ fl oz) almond milk
½ cup (75 g/2¾ oz) millet flour*
⅓ cup (40 g/1½ oz) arrowroot
2 teaspoons psyllium husk*
2 teaspoons apple cider vinegar (unpasteurised)
1 teaspoon gluten-free baking powder
1 teaspoon ground cumin
¼ teaspoon Himalayan salt

Millet spinach
60 g (2 oz) baby spinach leaves (approx 2 large
   handfuls)
2 tablespoons arrowroot

Millet and flax seed
¼ cup (60 ml/2 fl oz) almond milk
2 tablespoons ground flax seeds (linseeds)

To prepare the spinach wraps, place the base ingredients, the spinach and extra arrowroot in a high-speed blender. Blend to make a smooth batter. Transfer into a bowl. Cover and refrigerate for 30 minutes.

To prepare the millet and flax seed wraps, place the base ingredients and the extra almond milk in a high-speed blender. Blend to make a smooth batter. Transfer into a bowl. Stir in the ground flax seeds. Cover and refrigerate for 30 minutes.

To cook both variations, preheat a 20 cm (8 in) non-stick frying pan over medium heat.

Pour ¼ cup (60 ml/2 fl oz) of the batter into the centre of the pan. Quickly tilt and rotate the pan to swirl the batter over the base in a thin, even layer.

Cook for 30 seconds, or until the surface is dry and the base lightly coloured. Turn and cook for a further 30 seconds or until lightly coloured in patches. Stack the wraps onto a plate, cover with a clean tea towel (dish towel) and set aside to cool.

NOTE
The wraps can be made in advance and stored in an airtight container in the refrigerator for up to 1 week. Alternatively, stack, layering with baking paper between each wrap, seal well in plastic wrap and freeze for up to 3 months.

* Available from health food stores.

Granola with nuts and spices

*This fragrant and moreish granola is a fantastic staple and I make it weekly,
as it really doesn't last long in our house. It's delicious by itself with some yoghurt or
can be used as a topping for smoothie bowls, desserts or in little containers for snacks.*

MAKES 1½ CUPS (375 G/13 OZ)

¼ cup (35 g/1¼ oz) coarsely chopped Brazil nuts
¼ cup (35 g/1¼ oz) coarsely chopped macadamias
¼ cup (35 g/1¼ oz) coarsely chopped cashews
¼ cup (20 g/¾ oz) flaked almonds
¼ cup (35 g/1¼ oz) coarsely chopped walnuts
¼ cup (50 g/1¾ oz) buckwheat groats*
1½ tablespoons pumpkin seeds (pepitas)
1½ tablespoons sunflower seeds
½ cup (30 g/1 oz) flaked coconut
½ teaspoon ground cinnamon
1 tablespoon coconut oil, warmed
1 tablespoon maple syrup

Preheat the oven to 180°C (350°F).

To prepare the granola, place all of the ingredients
in a medium bowl and toss to combine. Spread out
onto a baking tray lined with baking paper, clumping
together to form clusters. Bake, stirring frequently
for 10 minutes, or until crisp and golden brown.

Remove from the oven and set aside to cool.

NOTE
You can store this in an airtight container
for up to 1 month.

* Available from health food stores.

Buckwheat and seeded bread

Despite its name buckwheat is not a wheat, or even a grain, it's a seed!
This delicious and dense bread is packed with seeds, making it a complete protein food,
rich in skin-hydrating omega-3 fats and collagen-boosting minerals.

MAKES 1 LOAF

2 cups (400 g/14 oz) buckwheat groats*, soaked in cold water for 1 hour, drained and rinsed

1 cup (250 ml/8½ fl oz) water

¼ cup (60 ml/2 fl oz) extra-virgin olive oil, plus extra for greasing

2 tablespoons chia seeds

2 tablespoons ground flax seeds (linseeds)

1 tablespoon raw honey

2 teaspoons apple cider vinegar (unpasteurised)

1 teaspoon bicarbonate of soda (baking soda)

1 teaspoon Himalayan salt

⅓ cup (65 g/2¼ oz) amaranth, soaked in cold water for 1 hour, drained and rinsed

⅓ cup (65 g/2¼ oz) quinoa, rinsed

⅓ cup (50 g/1¾ oz) pumpkin seeds (pepitas), soaked in cold water for 1 hour, drained and rinsed

⅓ cup (50 g/1¾ oz) sunflower seeds, soaked in cold water for 1 hour, drained and rinsed

Preheat the oven to 160°C (320°F). Lightly grease a 23 × 10 cm (9 × 4 in) loaf (bar) tin with olive oil.

Blend the soaked buckwheat in batches in a high-speed food processor, to finely grind to a porridge-like consistency. Transfer into a large bowl. Add the water, olive oil, chia seeds, ground flax seeds, honey, apple cider vinegar, bicarbonate of soda and salt. Mix well to combine. Set aside for 10 minutes, for the chia and ground linseed to hydrate, to make a thick batter.

Combine the amaranth, quinoa, pumpkin and sunflower seeds in a medium bowl. Set aside ½ cup of the seed mixture. Add the remaining mixture to the buckwheat batter and stir to combine. Pour the batter into the prepared tin. Scatter the reserved seeds over the top.

Bake for 2 hours, until golden brown and the loaf sounds hollow when tapped on the base. Leave in the tin for 15 minutes, to cool slightly.

Turn out onto a rack to cool completely.

Slice to serve.

NOTE

The bread can be wrapped in plastic wrap and stored in the refrigerator for 3 days. Alternatively freeze for up to 1 month.

* Available from health food stores.

Paleo bread

A lighter bread, this works really well for sandwiches. The high level of protein from the almonds and seeds means that you will feel fuller for longer and it will boost your body's basal metabolic rate – which you can't say for most sandwich breads!

MAKES 1 LOAF

2 cups (200 g/7 oz) almond meal

½ cup (60 g/2 oz) arrowroot

¼ cup (30 g/1 oz) golden flax seed (linseed) meal

1 tablespoon white chia seeds

1 teaspoon bicarbonate of soda (baking soda)

½ teaspoon Himalayan salt

5 large eggs

¼ cup (60 ml/2 fl oz) macadamia oil

1 tablespoon apple cider vinegar (unpasteurised)

2 teaspoons raw honey

Preheat the oven to 180°C (350°F). Lightly grease and line an 18 × 8 cm (7 × 3¼ in) loaf (bar) tin with baking paper.

Place the almond meal, arrowroot, flax seed meal, chia seeds, bicarbonate of soda and salt in a medium bowl and stir to combine.

Beat the eggs, macadamia oil, vinegar and honey together in a separate bowl.

Add the egg mixture to the dry ingredients and stir to combine. Spoon into the prepared tin and smooth out to create a flat surface.

Bake for 30–35 minutes, until golden brown and a skewer comes out clean when inserted into the centre to test. Turn out onto a rack and leave to cool completely.

Slice as required.

NOTE

This Paleo bread can be wrapped and stored in the refrigerator for up to 5 days. Alternatively freeze for up to 3 months.

Blackberry and vanilla chia jam

Salted miso caramel sauce

Blackberry and vanilla chia jam

MAKES 2 CUPS (500 G/1 LB 2 OZ)

A far cry from traditional sugar-laden jams, this is a healthy alternative that is rich in soluble fibre, omega-3s, antioxidants and vitamin C. Use as a spread on bread, cakes, biscuits or add a spoonful to some yoghurt for a quick snack or light dessert.

500 g (1lb 2 oz) fresh or frozen blackberries
2 tablespoons freshly squeezed lemon juice
3 teaspoons vanilla bean powder*
3 tablespoons chia seeds
⅓–½ cup (80–125 ml/2½–4 fl oz) raw honey,
   depending on sweetness of berries

Place the blackberries, lemon juice and vanilla in a medium saucepan.

Simmer over low heat for 5–10 minutes, until the berries have softened and liquid is released.

Remove from the heat. Stir through the chia seeds. Let cool, then add the honey and stir to combine.

Spoon the jam into a sterilised glass jam jar**. Cover with a lid and invert to make a seal. Leave to cool.

NOTE
Store in the refrigerator for up to 1 month.

Spread on toast or almond meal English muffins (see recipe page 48) or use in baking.

Your favourite berry, such as raspberry, blueberry or strawberry can be substituted for blackberries.

* Available from health food stores.
** For sterilising instructions see page 299.

Salted miso caramel sauce

MAKES 1 CUP (250 G/9 OZ)

This decadent sauce can be incorporated into crème brûlées (see recipe page 232), or drizzled over a healthy banana split, topped with yoghurt, chopped nuts and cacao nibs. Or add it to your favourite nut milk and give it a quick blitz in your blender. Yum.

8 medjool dates, pitted
⅓ cup (80 ml/2½ fl oz) boiling water
100 ml (3½ fl oz) maple syrup
¼ cup (60 ml/2 fl oz) coconut cream
3 teaspoons white (Shiro) miso paste
1½ teaspoons vanilla bean powder*
½ teaspoon Himalayan salt

Soak the dates in the boiling water for 10 minutes, or until softened.

Place the softened dates and any remaining water together with the remaining ingredients in a high-speed food processor or blender. Blend until smooth.

Store in an airtight container in the refrigerator for up to 5 days.

Ginger and turmeric bug

It's important to use organic ginger and turmeric in this recipe as the naturally occurring bacteria found in the skin is what kick-starts the fermentation process. Non-organic and imported ginger and turmeric are irradiated, which kills the necessary bacteria for fermenting.

MAKES 3 CUPS (750 ML/25½ FL OZ)

3 cups (750 ml/25½ fl oz) filtered water
1 tablespoon coarsely grated organic ginger, skin on
1 tablespoon coarsely grated organic turmeric, skin on
1 tablespoon organic raw (demerara) sugar

To feed bug
4½–7½ tablespoons coarsely grated
    organic ginger, skin on
3–5 tablespoons organic raw (demerara) sugar
1½–2½ tablespoons coarsely grated organic
    turmeric, skin on

NOTE

Filtered or non-chlorinated water is important too as chlorine kills bacteria. If you don't have a filter, measure out the required amount of tap water into a vessel and leave uncovered for several hours, the chlorine will evaporate into the air.

The fermenting ginger, turmeric and sugar mixture attracts wild yeasts and bacteria present in the air, which come to also feed on the sugar. In this process, known as yeast fermentation, yeast converts sugar into carbon dioxide resulting in a bubbling active bug. This powerful bug is then ready to use as a starter for homemade naturally carbonated fizzy drinks. Try our ginger and turmeric beer (see recipe page 276).

* For sterilising instructions see page 299.
** The length of fermentation depends on the temperature of the kitchen.

Combine the water, ginger, turmeric and sugar in a sterilised 4 cup (1 litre/34 fl oz)-capacity glass jar*. Stir to dissolve the sugar. Cover with a double layer of muslin (cheesecloth) and secure with a rubber band. Alternatively use a specialised fermentation jar with an airlock lid.

Let stand at room temperature, out of direct sunlight in a well-ventilated place for 24 hours.

Feed the bug 1½ tablespoons ginger, 1 tablespoon sugar and 2 teaspoons turmeric every 24 hours. Stir with a wooden spoon to dissolve the sugar. Re-cover with muslin. If using a specialised fermenting jar, secure the airlock lid.

Feed for 3–5 days**, until the mixture becomes quite fizzy. Small bubbles should begin to appear on the surface after a couple of days.

Use as required.

STORING BUG

Ginger and turmeric bug can be stored in the refrigerator at this stage without feeding for up to 1 week in a sealed jar. For long-term fridge storage, feed 1½ tablespoons ginger, 1 tablespoon sugar and 2 teaspoons turmeric once a week.

Before use, remove the bug from the refrigerator and feed the starter with ginger, sugar and turmeric as previously. Cover with a double layer of muslin (cheesecloth) and secure with a rubber band. Wrap the sides and base of the jar with a hand towel. Let stand in a warm place, around 23–29°C (75–85°F), feeding daily, for 1–2 days, until bubbles appear indicating the starter is active again. Use as required.

Published in 2017 by Hardie Grant Books,
an imprint of Hardie Grant Publishing, and
The Beauty Chef

First published in 2016 by The Beauty Chef

Hardie Grant Books (Melbourne)
Building 1, 658 Church Street
Richmond, Victoria 3121

Hardie Grant Books (London)
5th & 6th Floors
52–54 Southwark Street
London SE1 1UN

hardiegrantbooks.com

The Beauty Chef
Suite 11/402 New South Head Road,
Double Bay, 2028
Sydney, Australia

A catalogue record for this
book is available from the
National Library of Australia

The Beauty Chef
ISBN 9781743793046

Printed in China by Leo Paper Products LTD.

Thank you to everyone
involved in the making of
the book and for the love
and creativity poured into it:
my creative team, the Beauty
Chef family and my family.
Thanks to Michelle Margherita
and special thanks to Rachael
Lane for her collaboration
and dedication to the recipe
development. Thank you.

OUR CREATIVE TEAM

Creative director: Carla Oates
Designer: Evi O / OetomoNew
Editor: Kayte Nunn
Recipe development: Rachael Lane
Food stylist: Lee Blaylock
Food photographer: Rochelle Seator
Lifestyle photographers: Justine Kerrigan
& Luke Schuetrumpf
Lifestyle stylists: Dani Butchart & Brenda Burcul
Make up artist: Emmily Banks
Hair stylist: Victoria Maude